Kevin Ray

The First Christian Centuries
Perspectives on the Early Church

PAUL MCKECHNIE

InterVarsity Press
Downers Grove, Illinois

InterVarsity Press
P.O. Box 1400, Downers Grove, IL 60515-1426
World Wide Web: www.ivpress.com
E-mail: mail@ivpress.com

InterVarsity Press® is the book-publishing division of InterVarsity Christian Fellowship/USA®, a
student movement active on campus at hundreds of universities, colleges and schools of nursing in the
United States of America, and a member movement of the International Fellowship of Evangelical
Students. For information about local and regional activities, write Public Relations Dept., InterVarsity
Christian Fellowship/USA, 6400 Schroeder Rd., P.O. Box 7895, Madison, WI 53707-7895, or visit the
IVCF website at <www.ivcf.org>.

ISBN 0-8308-2677-7

Printed in the United States of America ∞

Library of Congress Cataloging-in-Publication Data
McKechnie, Paul, 1957-
    The first Christian centuries: perspectives on the early church / Paul McKechnie.
      p. cm.
    Includes bibliographical references and index.
    ISBN 0-8308-2677-7 (alk. paper)
      1. Church history—Primitive and early church, ca. 30-600. 2. Christianity and other
    religions—Roman. 3. Rome—Religion. I. Title.
    BR162.3 .M39 2002
    270.1—dc21
                                                                                    2001051564

P	18	17	16	15	14	13	12	11	10	9	8	7	6	5	4	3	2	1
Y	16	15	14	13	12	11	10	09	08	07	06	05	04	03	02			

Contents

Preface

In 1994 Calum Gilmour invited me to Northland to introduce church history to his students destined for the church's ministry. Preparing and delivering these classes convinced me that if ever I wrote a book on the early church, what I would say would not be like anything I had ever read. Dr Gilmour supported me in making the classes into a booklet which was published by the Diocese of Auckland in 1997. This book is a distant descendant of that booklet.

It is for history students, theology students, clergy, students of religion in the ancient or modern world, people in (or outside) churches, and anyone who wants to know how (after Jesus) the Christian church got going. I hope it is well enough put together to seem sensible to experts in church history, and I hope they will understand why it takes the directions it does; above all, I hope they will excuse its inevitable limitations. It is not a book of theology. At points where it touches on 'the question of god' (as Tom Wright calls it), 'I have uttered what I did not understand, things too wonderful for me, which I did not know ... therefore I despise myself, and repent in dust and ashes' (Job 42:3, 6).

Those of us who work in supportive environments, but know what the other kind is like, realize the difference they make. I wish to thank the University of Auckland for giving me research and study leave to work on this book in 1999, and the Department of Ancient History at Macquarie University, Sydney, the Faculty of Classics in the University of Cambridge, and Westcott House, Cambridge, for their hospitality. In addition, I wish to thank the following for help with the book: Prof.

10 *The first Christian centuries*

J. A. Crook, the Rev. Prof. W. H. C. Frend, Prof. Samuel N. C. Lieu, Mrs Doreen McKechnie, the Rev. John McKechnie, Mr Jonathan Markley, Prof. Brent D. Shaw, the Rev. Terry Wall, and colleagues and students in the Department of Classics in the University of Auckland. Dr Mark Smith and Dr Philip Duce of IVP have borne with my failings from proposal to published book. Jenny McKechnie and our excellent children, James, Emily and Benjamin, have supported me. None of the people named here is responsible for any errors I have made.

Auckland   Paul McKechnie
December 2000

Introduction
Christians from a distant perspective

This is an introductory (but not always elementary) book about people in (mostly) the Roman world, living as Christians and building Christianity in the Christian church's first three centuries. The narrative does not advance year by year from cover to cover: instead there is a thematic structure. Readers who want the view decade by decade would do best to go to W. H. C. Frend's *The Rise of Christianity* (1984, a much longer book than this), or (at intermediate size) Robin Lane Fox's *Pagans and Christians* (1987).

Now is an interesting moment for a new historical summary of the early church. The Coptic manuscript discoveries from Nag Hammadi appeared in English translation in 1977, and have received a couple of decades' discussion; feminist insights have advanced beyond an initial stage; and new thinking in the sociology of religion has contributed to understanding how religious communities grow and live in society. Important recent books offer distinct views about the early church. Rodney Stark's *The Rise of Christianity* (1996) analyses mainly by considering social factors which enabled Christianity to grow, above all in the urban context, in the Roman empire. Justin J. Meggitt's *Paul, Poverty and Survival* (1998) challenges the ideas of Gerd Theissen, Wayne A. Meeks and others – the 'New Consensus' – about the role of the 'not many ... wise by human standards, not many ... powerful, not many ... of noble birth' among members of the early churches, especially the Pauline churches:[1] Meggitt reasserts the view that the

---
[1] See Theissen 1982 and Meeks 1983.

first Christians belonged unambiguously and substantially among the poor. John Dominic Crossan's *The Birth of Christianity* (1998) adopts a 'thick description' approach, using New Testament and other written sources to get a picture of Christianity in the earliest years after Jesus – a picture which differs considerably from either Stark's social analysis or Meggitt's economic calculation. Theissen's *The Religion of the Earliest churches* (1999) traces the growth of Christianity towards autonomy and distinctiveness as a cultural sign-system. Marianne Sawicki's study of the archaeology of Galilee and its implications in *Crossing Galilee: Architectures of Contact in the Occupied Land of Jesus* (2000) bears on similar questions to those Crossan chooses, but comes at them with a different methodology. Gerd Lüdemann's *Heretics* (1996) argues for the intellectual and religious legitimacy of theological conclusions drawn by first-century and second-century heretics from the legacy of Jesus and Paul. Ute E. Eisen's *Women Officeholders in Early Christianity* (2000) takes a new step towards codifying how women participated in church leadership.

What I want to offer, therefore, is a composite introduction both to the early church and to the debate about it. The story I will tell is (consciously) a human one, which grounds itself more in what Christians did than in how the early theologians developed and defended Christian doctrine. I am in sympathy with Meggitt when he says that 'New Testament scholarship should recognise afresh its place in the broader discipline of history' (Meggitt 1998: 1), and when in this book I use the things Christians wrote (in the New Testament and outside it), or the things others wrote about Christians, the aim will be to get down to what they show about ordinary Christian and Roman life.

All the same, much as I admire Meggitt's focus on economic conditions, and Stark's analysis of social interactions (and want to give them the right weight), the issues of doctrine and theology – of what Christianity as a religion amounted to, for its first teachers and adherents – cannot be kept altogether in the background. From its first generation, Christianity had roots in not one but two literate cultures, the Jewish and the Greek. Both valued learning and teaching, and both had at their hearts evolving systems of thought about God/the gods, how to worship, and how to live. The Greeks had Socrates, Plato, Aristotle, Zeno and the Stoics, Epicurus and the Epicureans; the Jews from a similar period onward had Ezra, Ecclesiastes/*Qoheleth*, Sirach and the writer of the *Wisdom of Solomon*. Ideas in both cultures had been contestable and subject to development – and so were they to be in Christianity. Thus the history of the church has to be (in part) the history of the development of Christian teaching.

For all their cultural centrality, however, the ideas of people in the past have limitations as tools for historians. It is dangerously easy to assume that where there is physical evidence for the past existence of a theory, there must have been people – let us say, a sect – who followed that theory. People are inferred from ideas. At that point, a weak assumption turns into a fallacy. Then a second assumption may be derived: that where there is written evidence for two (or more) competing ideas, those ideas must have attracted comparable degrees of support, or numbers of adherents. Fallacy follows on fallacy. On the contrary, the simple existence of an ancient text does not prove that its content was widely valued. This is true even when that content is (on a modern view) worthy of esteem. Conversely, a thin or non-existent written record does not prove that an idea has died out. The gap between the history of ideas and the history of people can be wide.

Theology and history

For these reasons, there are real difficulties about writing a history of Christianity by starting from the way Christian thinking grew. Not that the attempt has not been made. In one version of the project, the author starts by combining an account which retells events in the New Testament with an 'inner' narrative following the steps taken in the Gospels and Epistles to expound Jesus' message, and then goes on to say how the church survived (even thrived on) persecution and martyrdom, to arrive at a (perhaps equivocal) triumph when Christianity was legalized and made official under Constantine. In the telling of this story there may be a wish to demonstrate how a doctrinally preferable Christianity dealt with challenges to itself from heretics, or how it came to have a predominant place.

In the opposite version of the project, the author may begin by noting that Christians competed with each other to have their voices heard. He or she will trace New Testament denunciations of false teachers, then sidelining of Gnostics or other heretics (the really vigorous element, in the view for example of Lüdemann [1996: 215], who says that 'Marcion and his church are the great motive power in second-century church history'), and growing institutional inflexibility in the third century. So the story will be of a shift to authoritarian

and exclusive orthodoxy, which made itself into the perfect organization for the government to co-opt as a partner in repression. Or cri-
tique can be still more direct: an author may compare Christianity
unfavourably with other religious options in the Roman world; this is
the essence, for example, of Keith Hopkins' *A World Full of Gods*
(1999).

None of these stories does justice to the complex growth of Christianity. It is not enough only to record the advance of 'those of the
majority', the 'Great Church' (as the anti-Christian writer Celsus
called them in the late second century[2] – I shall usually use this
phrase), as if theirs was the only game in town. Not enough, because
limiting the focus that way cramps explanation. Christianity grew and
succeeded, and its vigour lay in diversity as well as in uniformity. The
impulse to do and say something new was important. Yet the con-
verse claim, that a repressive mainstream destroyed the creative potential of diverse Christianities, misunderstands the early church's
situation still more radically: far from having the power to repress,
the majority was itself an illegal minority in society – and a small
one, until the third century; and at the moment of being legalized by
Constantine, Christianity was as divided and prone to fragmentation
as ever.

Who was, or was not, Christian?

So this book will discuss the development of the Christian movement
in the widest sense through (approximately) its first three centuries,
down to the Edict of Milan. The definition of 'the Christian movement in its widest sense' will be that a Christian is someone of whom
there is reason to believe that he/she regarded Jesus as Messiah or
Saviour, or in some comparably strong role within a religious system
with Jewish derivation or connections.

I imagine that hardly any theologian will be satisfied with this: as
experts on divine revelation and human response to it, they are used to
going far beyond an approach so near to 'if it looks like a duck, it's a
duck'. Historians, too, may look askance: Marta Sordi (1986: 5–6, 72–
73) speaks of late second-century Montanism being 'confused with
Christianity' by polytheists who disapproved of (Montanist) enthusiasm for martyrdom. But I think Montanists and other Christians

[2] Origen, *Against Celsus* 5.61, 59.

behaved so similarly that it is not surprising if outsiders failed to understand a technical difference between them.

The definition I propose casts the net wide, and includes many whose beliefs were not acceptable to churches whose principal sacred texts were the Old and New Testaments; but the inclusions and exclusions seem sensible to me. As well as Great Church Christians, most Gnostics are covered, as are Marcionites, Montanists and Manichaeans; but the Emperor Severus Alexander (222–35) is not, even though he had images of Abraham and Christ in his private chapel,[3] because his idea was to add Christ to the pantheon of Greco-Roman polytheism; and his mother Julia Mamaea is also (presumptively) out, because although she asked Origen to explain Christianity to her,[4] there is no reason to think that she adopted it for herself.

Why such an inclusive view? Because drawing any other line obscures more than it reveals. The existence of people in the Christian movement whom others did not consider real Christians is observable early; but to an outside observer the disputes they had were hard to comprehend – often the (divided) Christians had more in common with each other than either side did with the polytheistic world.

Differences appeared most easily between Christian *teachers*. Speaking at Miletus to elders of the Ephesian church, Paul (Acts 20:29–30) says, 'I know that after I have gone, savage wolves will come in among you, not sparing the flock. Some even from your own group will come distorting the truth in order to entice the disciples to follow them.'

If this sort of discussion of what counted as Christianity and Christian teaching (not merely discussion – conflict over inclusion and exclusion) had been occasional or peripheral, it might be economical to ignore it; but in fact the conflict goes where Christianity goes, throughout the early centuries and beyond.

Ways of understanding differences between Christians

So, faced with contested development in a movement which came out of Judaism (itself a system in which varied teachings coexisted), how should judgments be made (now) on what was (then) becoming normal and normative? In recent literature on Christianity in the first and second centuries, and even the third, it has become usual for

---

[3] *Scriptores Historiae Augustae, Alexander* 29.2.
[4] Eusebius, *Ecclesiastical History* 6.21.3–4.

authors to spell out that there was no such thing as orthodoxy. How should this observation be fleshed out, and what were its consequences in the lives of Christians? A key historical juncture for the diversity/ orthodoxy debate comes in the second century, when generations of Christians for whom the apostles were before living memory had to work out in practice where the interface between replication and innovation in Christianity ought to lie.

Historians in the last couple of decades have held very different opinions about that crucial moment. Consider first Frend's *The Rise of Christianity* (1984), a conservative narrative, which copes with co-existent strands through the second century by giving three separate chapters, covering (three times) the vital years through the middle of it, when the Christian movement was clearly larger than before 100. He deals first with what he calls 'opposition cult' (1984: 162–192), relating the work of Christian apologists to conditions in the Roman empire, and detailing debate between Christians and non-Christians; next he writes on 'acute Hellenization' (1984: 194–228), saying that 'the middle years of the second century belong to the Gnostics' (1984: 195), and expounding the growth and success of Gnostic theories; and third, he traces 'the emergence of orthodoxy' (1984: 230–266), observing that the church's 'developing organization favoured the guardian of tradition rather than the speculative thinker' (1984: 230). For depth and detail, Frend can hardly be faulted, but the conceptual problem which his arrangement partially elides is real: the three stories he tells all went on at the same time, and to participants they must have appeared inextricably interwoven.

Elaine Pagels writes from another angle, bringing non-normative Christianities to the centre, and expounding them in terms drawn from feminist analysis. In the introduction to her *Gnostic Gospels* (1982), she gives a snapshot which is perhaps truer to moment-to-moment reality than Frend's neatly demarcated streams of events, saying:

> ... the canon of Scripture, the creed, and the institutional structure emerged in [their] present form only towards the end of the second century. Before that time, as Irenaeus and the others attest, numerous gospels circulated among various Christian groups, ranging from those of the New Testament ... to such writings as the *Gospel of Thomas*, the *Gospel of Philip*, and the *Gospel of Truth*, as well as many other secret teachings, myths,

and poems attributed to Jesus or his disciples ... Those who identified themselves as Christians entertained many – and radically differing – religious beliefs and practices. And the communities scattered throughout the known world organized themselves in ways that differed widely from one group to another. Yet by AD 200 the situation had changed. Christianity had become an institution headed by a three-rank hierarchy of bishops, priests and deacons, who understood themselves to be the guardians of the only 'true faith'. The majority of churches, among which the church of Rome took a leading role, rejected all other viewpoints as heresy.'

Anything was on, then, until things tightened up soon before 200.[5] There are difficulties for Pagels' argument: the books she refers to were written and circulated, yes, but how many people read them? Were they influential, just because they existed?

Even so, the 'no orthodoxy' viewpoint thrives, and is taken further than Pagels took it. The degree to which this historical approach reflects on up-to-date theological concerns becomes clear in the work of a radicalizing historian like Denise Kimber Buell; she, discussing Clement of Alexandria, projects on to modern writers the impulse to make the orthodox/non-orthodox distinction:

... orthodoxy and heresy are the flexible by-products of the rhetoric of kinship and procreation, not the reverse. Scholars who do not recognise this will continue to reinscribe selectively the categories of heretical and orthodox despite any concessions that these categories are polemical as well as anachronistic for the second century ... The issue is not who can call whom heretical, but rather, whether the recognition of the pervasiveness of this boundary-drawing gesture exposes as contentless and thus untenable historical reconstructions of Christianity that employ 'heretical' and 'orthodox', or even their masked analogues 'gnostic' and 'catholic' (1999: 80).

Loyalties *in the here and now* are at issue. Buell's way of understanding the differences between Christians is individualistic: Clement,

[5] Except that a few pages earlier, Pagels (1982: 17) argued that 'the Nag Hammadi texts, and others like them ... were denounced as heresy by orthodox Christians in the middle of the second century'. 200, or 150, or when?

she notes, was a teacher who claimed to have got Christianity right (and deployed many devices to carry conviction for his claim), but (on the Buell view) his competitors were struggling for influence on a level playing field. Only in retrospect could those whose writings were accepted come to seem more important voices in Christianity than those who lost out.

The Buell argument against selecting which early Christians ought to have their views of themselves echoed has something to commend it. At any rate the ploy of name-calling could be used on any side: second-century Valentinians and Marcionites might have preferred to be known as Christians (and so, in the New Testament period, might the Nicolaitans).[6] Not that it was always a matter of the majority naming and shaming minorities. As Pagels points out, Hippolytus, splitting from the majority church in Rome in the early third century, called his antagonists 'Callistians' after their bishop.[7] Similarly at Edessa in northern Syria, where the first version of Christianity introduced, about 150, had been Marcionite, the adherents of (later) orthodoxy could be called Palûtians, after Palût, the first (about 200) to bring non-Marcionite Christianity to town (W. Bauer 1971: 21–29). The Palûtians did not want to be distinguished from 'Christians', as a hymn by Ephraim of Edessa shows: 'They again call us "Palûtians", and this we quite decisively reject and disown. Cursed be those who let themselves be called by the name Palût instead of the name Christ! . . . Even Palût would not wish that people call themselves by his name.'[8]

But Buell goes too far in attacking *all* terminology: 'heretical'/ 'orthodox'; 'gnostic'/'catholic'. She may be right to be wary of Eusebius' evidence that Clement had official support from the bishop in Alexandria,[9] but cases of other second-century teachers, Valentinus and Marcion, should induce caution. Valentinus started out as a Christian teacher in Rome during the episcopate of Hyginus (138–41),[10] and Marcion was of the same generation, but (Irenaeus says) 'on account of their ever restless curiosity, with which they even infected the brethren, they were more than once expelled' – and in the end permanently excluded from the church of Rome.[11] Teachers (in Rome) could be

---

[6] Clement of Alexandria, *Miscellanies* 7.108.1–2, comments on how heresies get named after founders, or geographical locations, or doctrines/practices (cf. Buell 1999: 89 n. 31).

[7] Hippolytus, *Refutation of all Heresies* 9.12.26; cf. Pagels 1982: 120.

[8] Ephraim of Edessa, *56 Hymns against the Heresies* 22.5–6.

[9] Eusebius, *Ecclesiastical History* 6.6.1; cf. Buell 1999: 12.

[10] Irenaeus, *Against Heresies* 3.4.3; cf. Eusebius, *Ecclesiastical History* 4.11.1.

[11] Tertullian, *Ruling out of Court of the Heretics* 30.

officially *banned*. The situation in Alexandria may not have been the same: Winrich A. Löhr (1996: 333) considers a list of heretical teachers who may have worked in Alexandria (Basilides, Isidore, Julius Cassianus, Carpocrates) and concludes that it is 'in no way certain whether they were regarded as heretical or Gnostic in their own time'. *Perhaps* in Alexandria, unlike in Rome, teachers could teach a wide range of ideas and remain in good standing with the other Christians.

A story of both centre and periphery

Frend, Pagels and Buell, then, all make useful observations, but none expounds an integrated perspective on Christians and Christianity in the phase of second-century advance on the first-century beginnings. 'Orthodox' may be a word to avoid, but some sort of terminology has to be applied. There never was a Garden of Eden for Christian theologians, in which no envious opponent would challenge one's right to hold any speculative theory while remaining Christian, nor any bishop exclude the disciples of teachers with minority views. At the same time it is right to be wary of too many distinctions: Christians were part of a small minority movement, still in 200 and all the more in 100. At the temporal distance from which we look at early Christians, the similarities between them are more important than the differences.

Therefore, while people's allegiance to Christ was expressed in a variety of theoretical frameworks, modern discussion ought to give the right weight to the distinction drawn by Celsus in the late second century between the 'Great Church', and minority sects. An outsider could see (and attack) Christianity's internal disputes (Christians, Celsus says, 'are divided and rent asunder and each one wants to have his own party'),[12] while realizing that there was an organizationally distinct majority. Celsus' technical impartiality in the disputes he refers to is helpful – he had no interest in making the Christians seem better or more numerous than they were (exactly the reverse), so he has a good claim to be believed. The Christianity he saw resembled a bush (the 'Great Church') which had not been pruned recently, with offshoots ('each one wants to have his own party') in all directions.

What this book aims to do, then, is first to tell the story of the bush – recognizing that the heart of it makes more difference than the edges – and then also to treat the offshoots as part of the whole thing. In the

[12] Origen, *Against Celsus* 3.10–12.

narrative, it will be taken for granted that the reader has some knowledge of Christian beliefs and outlooks: not much space will be given to Great Church theology. The offshoots, on the other hand, may sometimes be given more explanation than strict balance would seem to justify. It is important not to forget that there were Christians who thought the offshoots were not part of the bush, or not part of the bush as it should be.

1
First-century Christianity: the source debate

A portfolio of sources

Almost everything known about the first century of the Christian church comes from what was written about it: virtually no direct physical evidence survives, although Sawicki's *Crossing Galilee* demonstrates that much can be learnt about Jesus, his followers and their aims from the first-century archaeology of the Holy Land. The earliest Christians did not use distinctive buildings which can be identified now as having belonged to them. The house church at Dura-Europos on the river Euphrates, destroyed in a fortification programme in the 240s, is the earliest archaeologically investigated building known to have been adapted for Christian worship. Before the end of the second century catacombs were being used by Christians in Rome for burial of the dead, but until around 200 no-one used a gravestone to identify the deceased as Christian – and even after 200 few burials were marked as Christian until the time of Constantine. Grave goods, in some contexts useful in giving clues about the deceased, are no help, since Christians were normally buried without grave goods – a feature which makes it hard to distinguish between a Christian burial and a (non-Christian) poor burial.

In Egypt, where dry sand preserves ancient writing materials, Christian papyri come from the second century at the earliest: more come from the third and fourth. Philip W. Comfort and David P. Barrett have collected the fragments, with commentary, in a single volume (1999). The oldest surviving New Testament papyrus is P.Rylands

457, kept at the John Rylands Library in the University of Manchester: recent editors date it between 100 and 125. Carsten Peter Thiede and Matthew d'Ancona (1996) argue for a much earlier date for a pair of fragments of Mark, but there is no reason either to think they must be as early as Thiede and d'Ancona say, or to identify Dead Sea Scrolls Qumran fragment 7Q5, as they do, with Mark 6:52–53. Papyri with Greek Old Testament fragments can come from the first century AD or earlier, but any given Old Testament papyrus is more likely (on a probability calculation) to have been used by Jews than by Christians.

The sources for first-century Christianity accessible today are therefore in written texts copied for continued use after they were first produced, which reached the modern world through the medieval manuscript tradition. These fall into three categories: first, the New Testament books; second, non-New Testament contemporary sources (Christian and non-Christian); and third, later texts. There are only a few non-Christian literary references to first-century Christianity, and they will be introduced in the proper places, but I will deal first with what Christians themselves said about Christianity.

The central issue is how the New Testament should be treated: dated, read, and related to other writings. Some other Christian writings are uncontroversial, and clearly follow on the New Testament – like Clement of Rome's letter to Corinth, which echoes Hebrews and the Pauline epistles, and was probably written in the 90s. Others, like the *Didache*, may be early – perhaps early enough to have been written before the latest of the New Testament books – and show a type of Christian teaching similar to strands present in the New Testament. More controversy has come from attempts to identify other strands of Christian teaching in early books.

So, while no-one doubts that the New Testament is important as a source for first-century Christianity, everything else is disputed, including how important it is relative to other Christian documents. R. Alistair Campbell (1994: 236) summed up New Testament studies by saying that

> ... there is no such thing as a consensus view to be found on any subject within New Testament scholarship. In the first place, there is hardly ever a position so discredited that it completely lacks defenders; no finding of scholarship so self-evidently true that it lasts for long without assailants. In the second place, every consensus contains within itself a spectrum

of views, the agreement of consenting scholars being confined to broad outlines for the most part.

The New Testament

The New Testament is a collection of works by participants in early Christianity. Its key feature is that it includes the books which Christians in different places thought worth keeping. It does not pre-serve in full the works of its main writers: Paul at Colossians 4:16 asks his readers to read his letter to the Laodiceans and to give them Colossians to read in exchange (but Paul's Laodiceans is lost); and at 2 Corinthians 1:13 and 2:3–4 he refers to at least one previous letter to Corinth other than 1 Corinthians. Writers are not always identified, as in Hebrews; and neither are recipients of epistles always precisely defined.

Some of the actions which made the New Testament the exact col-lection it now is took place after the period this book covers. In the fourth century, churches began collecting biblical books together in one codex (a codex being a book with a spine and covers, not a scroll), and hand in hand with that move went a concern to define which early Christian books should be in or out: differing lists resulted (see Hahneman 1992: 134–135). But this fourth-century movement was not asking a new question: discussion on what counted as sacred texts (and how to read them) began much earlier.[1] A vital part of the New Testament canon, the fourfold Gospel (Matthew, Mark, Luke, John) was standard early: as soon as the second half of the second century, Christians who met another book called *The Gospel of X* (or *Y*) would usually not have recognized it as authoritative (McKechnie 1996: 416–417).

But an energetic and long-lasting modern dispute centres on how important were ideas *not* expressed in the list of texts-later-canonized, in Christianity as it actually existed in the first century. Granted that later generations were selective, did that selectivity suppress important strands in the Jesus tradition? Were they ideas with a big following in Christianity's earliest years? Since more is known about minority Christian groups in the second century than in the first, can their antecedents be traced back into types of first-century Christianity not, or poorly, reflected in the New Testament?

---

[1] As at 2 Pet. 3:15–16, on misinterpretations of Paul.

Two things have to be done to reach a fair decision on this great dispute: first, understand and date the New Testament we have, book by book, and second, quantify the merits of the case for what I will call the 'shadow New Testament' – the early traditions posited by scholars who think the canonical New Testament collection is unrepresentative because it resulted from selection based on the requirements of the majority churches in the third and fourth centuries (see e.g. Pagels 1982: 32). The dispute conditions how everything in Christianity should be understood, up to the time when the canon was fixed. This makes it a debate which this book cannot bypass.

Fragmented discussion

The parties to it are prone to talk past each other. The 'intracanonists', as I will call the more conservative scholars, build their picture of earliest Christianity from the New Testament (with later corroborating evidence), and minimize the attention they pay to the difference a 'shadow New Testament' might make. To take some examples: Meeks in his *The First Urban Christians* (1983) keeps to the Pauline communities (as the plan of his book requires, 216 n. 36) and has little to say of Pagels and her then recent (and widely read) *The Gnostic Gospels* (first published 1980); Meggitt, in *Paul, Poverty and Survival* (1998), sticks to locating (only) the Pauline churches in relation to their place in Roman society; Stark, in his *The Rise of Christianity* (1996: 140–143), deals with the impact of Gnosticism as part of or related to Christianity in three pages; and Hopkins, in his 1998 article on numbers of Christians, writes much as if Gnostic teachers and their sects did not exist within the horizon of his subject.[2] Ekkehard W. Stegemann and Wolfgang Stegemann adopt a similar outlook in *The Jesus Movement: A Social History of its First Century* (1999).

On the opposite side of the divide it is less easy for those whom I will call the 'extracanonists' to write *only* about minority first-century Christianities, or *only* about Gnosticism (at least historically – discussions of the intellectual content of Gnostic texts are another matter); but the danger of producing a slanted view seems almost equal.

---

[2] Hopkins' attitude to Christian diversity shows little but puzzlement: in 1998: 199 n. 29 he cites *Didache* 11–12, saying, 'the notion of false prophets haunts the dispersed early Christian groups. How can they tell?' But *they* thought there were ways of telling.

Crossan, for instance, in his *Birth of Christianity* (1998), has written a book 'on birth not growth, on those years before and especially after Jesus' crucifixion, on those who were with him beforehand and continued within him afterward. It is about the years before Paul; in other words, it concerns what there was for Paul to persecute' (1998: xxi). This aim Crossan does not interpret as excluding consideration of written sources much later than Paul – but his plan authorizes a project which writes around Paul, and centres on the relationship between canonical and non-canonical (i.e. Gnostic) Gospel texts.

By arguing for a Christianity in the 30s and 40s whose nature can be (inferentially) defined by selecting between (often) the *antecedents* of texts which actually exist, Crossan takes directions offered in Pagels' *The Gnostic Gospels* (1980) and Helmut Koester's *Ancient Christian Gospels* (1990), and follows them backwards. The argument of Pagels' book is cast in terms of the orthodox/Gnostic distinction and the struggle it led to over time. As she says, 'For nearly 2,000 years, Christian tradition has preserved and revered orthodox writings that denounce the gnostics, while suppressing – and virtually destroying – the gnostic writings themselves. Now, for the first time, certain texts discovered at Nag Hammadi reveal the other side of the coin: how the gnostics denounced the orthodox' (Pagels 1982: 115).

Crossan's study, however (1998: 108–120), integrates canonical and non-canonical texts, or the predecessors reflected in them, to get back to a formative stage. Although in Crossan's work a straightforward model of opposition between orthodoxy and Gnosticism (as in Pagels) has been left behind, the tendency for the sides in the wider debate about early Christianity to have little they can agree on, remains observable – even though Crossan will usually discuss other authors' views, rather than pass over them in silence.

The gulf in method between intracanonists and extracanonists is deep. Accordingly I will examine both sides, focusing first on the dating and background of the canonical books, then discussing the 'shadow New Testament' hypothesis.

The intracanonists' dispute resolved

The road to dating New Testament books starts from internal clues: all the books were written well before the dates of the earliest surviving papyrus fragments. In a number of places in New Testament books, independently datable events are referred to. Mostly they yield only dates *after* which particular books must have been composed – as with the mention of the famine which happened under the Emperor Claudius (41–54), made at Acts 11:28, which must therefore have been written at least after the early forties, and probably after Claudius died in 54. Sometimes, however, there can be dates before which a book must have been written – as at Romans 1:9–10, where Paul says, 'God ... is my witness that without ceasing I always remember you in my prayers, asking that by God's will I may somehow at last succeed in coming to you.'

Few doubt that this puts Romans before Paul's appeal to Caesar and his journey to Rome about 59 (described at Acts 27–28). But there is a difficulty about dating books this way: it can never be certain that a book is earlier than some event merely because it does not mention it. Therefore if dating by external circumstances is taken too far, it can skew datings late, because the earliest *other* mention of something slips into being treated as the earliest time a book could have been written. As a result, scholars who think they are being conservative by requiring corroboration can end up systematically making books later than they really are.

Conversely, dating from internal evidence can produce subjective results and be difficult to check. A sobering illustration comes from Jude, a letter not much more than a page long. Unless it is assumed that the letter was written by the Jude (= Judas) referred to as Jesus' brother in Matthew 13:55 (alive in the 20s and probably at most ten to twenty years younger than Jesus),[3] there are no clear limiting factors for its date. The letter cautions against people who have 'wormed their way in' to the Christian community, but are irreligious and are 'disowning Jesus Christ, our only Master and Lord' (verse 4). A hostile (but not detailed) description of their teachings follows. It seems the people readers are being warned against are Gnostics:[4] they distinguish between psychics (= ordinary Christians) and pneumatics. 'These people who make the distinction', Jude 19 says, 'are themselves psychics, as they do not have the Spirit.'[5]

It follows that the letter should be dated to a period associated with

---

[3] Bauckham (1990: 174 n. 262) lists scholars since 1880 who have expressed a view on whether Jude is by the named author or pseudepigraphical: forty-six are for authenticity, thirty-five against.

[4] There is something like consensus (but not unanimity) among scholars on Jude's opponents being Gnostic: see Bauckham 1990: 162–167.

[5] My translation of *Houtoi eisin hoi apodiorizontes, psychikoi, pneuma mē echontes.*

tension in a Christian community over Gnostic teachers who call themselves Christian. This gives plenty of scope. Some scholars have thought it safest to place Jude well into the second century, when there is independent non-New Testament evidence for developed forms of Gnostic teaching, and conflict over it. Richard J. Bauckham (1990: 168–169 n. 237) illustrates the broad variety of datings this has allowed by listing them down a page (ranging across more than a hundred years from 54 to 160) and putting beside them the names of scholars since 1869 who have argued for each. There is a striking lack of convergence, even though Bauckham observes a tendency in recent decades not to go later than about 120. This disagreement over a very short New Testament book shows in microcosm the challenge to anyone who wants to make inferences from the New Testament about how Christianity developed in its first century.

The challenge must be faced. There is no chance of telling the story of the early church in the right order, except by applying a consistent and credible idea of what in the New Testament was written when. There is not space in this book to re-examine every possibility – so this section is largely a matter of putting my assumptions out in the open, sometimes with explanation. In the first place, I am not inclined to believe in a long gap between when Jesus' followers started practising Christianity and when they began to write about it. Jesus was literate, and read Isaiah aloud in the synagogue (Luke 4:16–20). He, therefore, knew biblical Hebrew as well as the Aramaic which was the spoken language of Judea. He was a Bible scholar, who taught his disciples using Hillel's rules of biblical interpretation (Ellis 1999: 31 and n. 104), and who sent out his own disciples to teach (Mark 6:30). Viewing him as (e.g.) a 'peasant artisan' (which for Crossan in his *The Birth of Christianity* is 'but a euphemism for a dispossessed peasant ... a landless labourer', Crossan 1998: 350) ceases to be useful if that view is assumed – as it is by Crossan (1998: 235) – to exclude access to literacy and education in the Torah. I would go a step further: I think even to assume that Jesus did not know Greek may misunderstand his background. Greek was fairly widely used in Galilee and Judea (see Schürer 1979: 2:74–80), and Aramaic/Greek bilingualism cannot have been unusual.

Jesus' own education, however, is not as important a question for the route taken by Christianity as the aims and methods of his followers. Some wrote, some did not – and accordingly, large parts of the New Testament were written by people who were not with Jesus during his life. Luke 1:1–4 draws a line (if a fuzzy one) between writing and having witnessed what happened:

> Since many have undertaken to set down an orderly account of the events that have been fulfilled among us, just as they were handed on to us by those who from the beginning were eye-witnesses and servants of the word, I too decided, after investigating everything carefully from the very first, to write an orderly account for you, most excellent Theophilus, so that you may know the truth concerning the things about which you have been instructed.

This introduction has been analysed and commented on – but not quite to death, and it is still worth noting how Luke sees the situation. 'Many have undertaken to set down an ... account', he says, showing that there was a range of written stories of Jesus before Luke began to write – 'many' may perhaps be an exaggeration (J. A. T. Robinson 1976: 100), but in view of the proliferation of writing by Christians at all later dates, there is no reason to exclude the possibility that in Christianity's earliest years a hundred (literary) flowers bloomed. All the same, the *spoken* word mattered – Luke adds that Theophilus can use his written account as a confirmation of what he has heard: 'so that you may know the truth concerning the things about which you have been instructed'. From the beginning, then, written material circulated side by side with oral Christian teaching, and people in the churches used both.

If writing about Christianity was not an afterthought, there are consequences. In particular, if we do not posit decades of hesitation about writing a word, the often argued case that some or all of the Gospels were finalized after the fall of Jerusalem and the destruction of the temple in 70 ceases to be compelling. There might in one respect be more need for a written story of Jesus at that remove (since his first followers were getting old); but people who see the point of communicating in writing are just as likely to write in youth as in old age.

The strongest argument for not placing the synoptic Gospels after 70 (as John A. T. Robinson said, following many others, in *Redating the New Testament* [1976]) is their failure to mention the fall of Jerusalem – that is, to mention it as an accomplished fact: it is mentioned in the form of a prophetic prediction by Jesus at Mark 13:1. 'The silence', Robinson says, 'is ... as significant as the silence for

Sherlock Holmes of the dog that did not bark' (1976: 13). Some argue that the prophetic prediction proves that Mark was written after Jerusalem fell (on the demythologizing ground that no-one knew in advance); but prophets habitually prophesied that sort of thing – for instance, at Jesus' time, the Qumran sect was preparing for a final battle (whether spiritual or physical) against the forces of darkness and/ or the Romans.[6] Discussion of the overthrow of this or that was topical: there is no reason to think, Robinson argues, that Jesus would not have joined in. He goes on to argue for a dating for Mark, and indeed all of the New Testament, before 70.

In his update of Stephen Neill's *The Interpretation of the New Testament* (1988: 361), N. T. Wright describes Robinson's set of early datings of New Testament books as 'a startling thesis' – but concedes that 'few *arguments* have been put up to contest it'. The axioms that Paul is the only Christian writer whose work survives from the 50s, and that much of the New Testament as it exists was written during the second Christian generation, not the first, are not persuasive *a priori*, and as E. Earle Ellis's *The Making of the New Testament Documents* (1999) shows, Robinson's argument must be treated seriously.

The main lines of it go like this. Acts ends with Paul spending two years in Rome waiting for his appeal to Caesar to be heard (these years are identified as 60–62; J. A. T. Robinson 1976: 52–53), and does not say what happened next. The natural inference (Robinson cites von Harnack 1911: 96) is that Acts was written and circulated before Paul's trial took place – hence in or soon after 62 (1976: 89–91). But since Acts 1:1 refers to Luke as 'the first book', Luke (which points back to other accounts) was written before that date. This leaves Matthew and Mark, as Luke's predecessors, in the 50s, though the arguments applying to John (which Robinson places in or after 65, 1976: 307) are different.

Robinson's conclusions on the date and relation of the Gospels fit, broadly, with Irenaeus' late second-century statement of their history:

Matthew among the Hebrews issued a written version of the Gospel in their own tongue, while Peter and Paul were preaching the Gospel at Rome and founding the church. After their decease Mark, the disciple and interpreter of Peter, also handed down to us in writing what Peter had preached. Luke also, the

[6] See *The War of the Sons of Darkness and the Sons of Light* in Vermes 1995.

follower of Paul, recorded in a book the Gospel as it was preached by him. Finally John, the disciple of the Lord, who had also lain on his breast, himself published the Gospel, while he was residing at Ephesus in Asia (*Against Heresies* 3.1.1).

The Pauline letters, all of which Robinson ascribes to Paul, would have been written in that same decade, none as late as Paul's actual time of residence in Rome.[7] James he places no later than 48 (1976: 138), Jude and 2 Peter in 61–2 (with 1 Peter before) (1976: 195–198), 2, 3 and 1 John between 60 and 65 (1976: 307), Hebrews before 68 (1976: 220), and Revelation in 68 or 70 (1976: 252).

There is reason to doubt Robinson on some books, particularly Revelation, which Irenaeus believed to have been written at the end of the reign of Domitian (81–96);[8] and arguments for treating some of the Pauline epistles as compositions by followers of Paul in the generation after his death deserve consideration, even though Anthony Kenny's stylometric study of the New Testament led him to conclude that it was not possible to separate one group of Pauline epistles from the rest on grounds of literary or grammatical style (Kenny 1986: 98): only Titus, Kenny argues, 'is shown as deserving the suspicion cast on the Pastorals' (1986: 100).[9]

Most authors do not attribute all the Pauline letters to Paul. F. C. Baur (1873: 1:246–249; 1875: 2:106–111) argued that only Romans, 1 and 2 Corinthians and Galatians were by him. Of recent writers, Meeks (1983: 7–8) uses a narrow Pauline canon, ascribing Colossians, Ephesians and 2 Thessalonians as well as the Pastoral Epistles (1 and 2 Timothy and Titus) to deutero-Pauline writers, but Meggitt (1998: 8), following Kümmel (1975: 250), adds Colossians and 2 Thessalonians to the list Meeks accepts. Campbell (1994: 97 n. 2) leans towards

[7] J. A. T. Robinson's schedule (1976: 84), given with the reservation that the datings could be a year or so out either way, is: 50 (early), 1 Thessalonians; 50 (or early 51), 2 Thessalonians; 55 (spring), 1 Corinthians; 55 (autumn), 1 Timothy; 56 (early), 2 Corinthians; 56 (late), Galatians; 57 (early), Romans; 57 (late spring), Titus; 58 (spring), Philippians; 58 (summer), Philemon, Colossians and Ephesians; 58 (autumn), 2 Timothy.

[8] Irenaeus, *Against Heresies* 5.30.3: followed by Eusebius, *Ecclesiastical History* 3.18.2–3 and 5.8.6. Cf. J. A. T. Robinson 1976: 221–253.

[9] Berding (1999) notes that in Polycarp, *Philippians* (written in the first half of the second century), the author clusters Pauline citations and allusions in the three passages where Paul's name is mentioned: phrases from 1 Timothy occur in the first cluster, and a phrase from 2 Timothy in the second. Berding concludes that Polycarp 'consciously or unconsciously' considered these references Pauline. Titus, perhaps interestingly in view of Kenny's observation, is not quoted in Polycarp's letter.

bringing Ephesians in too.[10] Lüdemann's assertion (1996: 106) that there is a 'broad consensus of scholars' that seven letters are by Paul and six pseudepigraphical is incorrect (cf. Neill & Wright 1988: 362): almost any variant on the Pauline canon can be found, and there is no common set of criteria for distinguishing between Paul and other 'Pauline' authors.

Robinson's approach and conclusions are at their most convincing in the places where he argues against entrenched assumptions about lateness: that in the first Christian decades no-one (or no-one but Paul) was writing finished literary texts ('in the beginning was the list', as Crossan [1998: 240] puts it); that pseudepigraphical author-ascription is pervasive rather than sporadic; that dates should be assigned on the basis of a theory of theological development over time. His model accounts well for the relations between New Testament books and the world in which they were produced, and, with some adaptations, it seems to me to represent the best balanced approach on offer.

Ellis in his book treats matters which Robinson left aside. Robinson's arguments from external historical evidence impressed him, he says, 'but they left largely unaddressed the issues of literary criticism on which the currently dominant dating of New Testament documents is mainly based' (Ellis 1999: xv). Arguing that the work of Jesus' disciples in preaching the gospel was carried on in four missions (centred around Paul, James, Peter, John) (1999: 252–307), with a fifth ('opposition') Judaizing and Gnosticizing mission which split off from the Jerusalem church (1999: 315–316), Ellis analyses the books of the New Testament in terms of their use of shared traditions and the interaction between the missions which this use implies.[11] The set of datings to which his argument leads is similar but not identical to Robinson's.[12]

The direction in which I think the intracanonists' dispute must be resolved derives, then, from an adapted Robinson/Ellis dating of the New Testament: much of it early, meaning before 70, but Revelation

[10] The effect is to exclude the Pastorals and include everything else – the position Marcion reached in the 130s (see ch. 8 below).

[11] Theissen 1999 embodies a similar project, without a Robinson-style redating programme.

[12] Ellis 1999: 319 offers: 49, Galatians; 51–2, 1 and 2 Thessalonians; 55–8 (proto-)Mark; 55–65, Jude; 56, 1 Corinthians; 57, 2 Corinthians; 58, Romans; 58–60, Ephesians, Colossians and Philemon; c. 60, James; 60–2, Matthew and 2 Peter; 62–3, Philippians; 63–4, 1 Peter, Luke and Acts; 64, 1 Timothy and Titus; 67, 2 Timothy; 68–70, Revelation and Hebrews; 75–90, 1, 2 and 3 John; 85–95, John.

in the 90s and no final judgment made on whether everything ascribed to Paul was written by him. The synoptic Gospels in particular I shall treat as early, while not being certain about John; and I see no reason to doubt the existence of an Aramaic or Hebrew Matthew written prior to the Greek version (cf. Ellis 1999: 393–394). A distinctive feature of our New Testament is that it is a *Greek* New Testament – but it is certainly not probable that Greek was the only language in which the first Christians wrote. The Hebrew/Aramaic Matthew was not only referred to by Irenaeus, but also known to Papias of Hierapolis, writing perhaps in the 130s.[13] Papias' view is known only via Eusebius, but there is nothing improbable *a priori* about his evidence. Material could disappear: Ecclesiasticus, first written in Hebrew, was known only in Greek until Hebrew manuscript discoveries were made at Qumran, Masada and in the Cairo Genizah (Skehan & di Lella 1986: 51–62); and if there is one thing Nag Hammadi shows with particular clarity, it is that material could get translated (there, into Coptic from Greek) and the original be lost. I will argue below that the spread of Christianity in Aramaic-speaking areas outside Judea in the first century was limited, and that Hadrian's genocide in Judea in the mid-130s did great damage to the Jewish and Aramaic-speaking church. There were perhaps not many copies left afterwards, although I will argue in chapter 8 that the Ebionites may have had some.

The extracanonists' case delineated

The situation in which letters by Paul to Laodicea and Corinth, and a Gospel of Matthew in Hebrew or Aramaic, could (from our viewpoint) 'go missing' is one in which careful examination of tradition and transmission is needed. Some in our times view what the early Christians did in reproducing (only) books which were of use to them as discriminatory: Koester (1990: xxx), for instance, describes his excitement at a reprint and an English translation of Bauer's *Orthodoxy and Heresy*:

It seemed as if almost two millennia of discrimination against those whom the Fathers of the church had labelled as 'heretics' would come to an end. If these 'heresies' were not simply secondary deviations from an already established orthodoxy, but

[13] Quoted in Eusebius, *Ecclesiastical History* 3.39.16.

resulted from developments in the Christian communities that occurred as early as the time of Paul's mission to the Gentiles, also their gospels could claim to be genuine continuations of the earliest stages of the formation of the traditions about Jesus of Nazareth ... Only dogmatic prejudice can assert that the canonical writings have an exclusive claim to apostolic origin and thus to historical priority.

Notice this argument's implications: 'heresies' which *result from* developments of Pauline date are genuine continuations of the earliest stages of the Jesus traditions – so, in Koester's version of source criticism, there is no necessary requirement for a *text* which is as early as Paul; just an *idea* which came from that time. The source critic decides first on theology, then on history: if (some) non-canonical writings have apostolic *origin* (as judged by source criticism), they have historical *priority*.

Matters are confused by the fact that Christian legend, and fiction, began to be written early. From the second century, at least (and before, if one believes in widespread pseudepigraphic attribution in the New Testament), Christians – prolific writers of important and unimportant books – were keen to link their ideas and stories with heroic figures in the stories of Jesus and the apostles. Some parts of the second-century (and later) overlay are easily identified. The *Protevangelium of James* fills in things readers wanted to know about Mary; infancy gospels tell stories of Jesus' miraculous childhood. They are legend rather than fiction (if that distinction can be made), and Eusebius – who in the fourth century tried to record the *facts* in his history of the church – does not use them. But there were novelists as well as tellers of legends. The *Acts of Paul and Thecla*, written by a presbyter in Asia perhaps about the 140s, is a fictional story modelled on Greek novels. In it, Thecla, a young convert, decides, instead of acquiescing in a forced marriage, that she will go away preaching the gospel with Paul. Tertullian (*On Baptism* 17) says that the author, when asked why he wrote the story, said he did it out of love for Paul. It apparently had not occurred to him that he would cause confusion with his novel – which, as it turned out, was later taken as history by some readers (Brown 1988: 5–7, 153–159, 328–329; cf. also ch. 9 below).

Paul and Thecla is dated, at least approximately, and is comparatively early. It is a warning that early date is no guarantee that a Christian text is factual. Story-telling easily built bridges between pious imagination and supposed fact. As Christianity spread, people in churches wrote and read stories of how their areas of the world first heard the gospel – and they often had little to go on. Most of these foundation-legends are evidence not for the very early churches, but for what Christians in the second, third and fourth centuries said about their churches' origins.

Other Christian texts, however, require more serious consideration than the legendary material – even though in many cases they are harder to date than *Paul and Thecla*. The *Didache*, for instance, a valuable but brief treatise (nine pages in the Penguin *Early Christian Writings*) first published by Philotheos Bryennios, Patriarch of Nicomedia, in 1883, still attracts discussion over when it was written. It is more probably from the first than from the second century. J. A. T. Robinson (1976: 352–353) puts it between 40 and 60, but his case for putting it so early is not compelling. *1 Clement*, the *Epistle of Barnabas* and Hermas' *Shepherd* are also early, Clement writing in the last decade of the first century, and Hermas possibly between 100 and 110.

The extracanonists' case disproved

The extracanonists argue that a line should be drawn between second-century written material of the legendary story-telling sort (like *Paul and Thecla*) or the partisan sort (like the *Gospel of Philip*, an exposition of Christian mysteries from a Valentinian perspective), and material (mostly) from Nag Hammadi whose contents (they argue) should be traced back to the formative period. Koester's choice of texts from this second category which 'seemed to have contributed to this first phase of the history of gospel literature' (1990: xxxi) includes the Synoptic Sayings Source (Q), the *Gospel of Thomas*, the *Dialogue of the Saviour*, P.Egerton 2, the *Apocryphon of James* and the *Gospel of Peter*.

I am a sceptic about Q, as a written document; but Q is the least problematic element in Koester's choice of writings, since the text of Q (in modern scholarship) is inferred backwards from sayings in Luke and Matthew (see Kloppenborg 1988). The other texts which Koester puts centre stage are almost all clearly late, and belief in their relevance to the development of Christianity in the first century calls either for inferences about sources, or for arguments about what in the texts was or was not adapted from the canonical New Testament.

The *Dialogue of the Saviour*, for instance, is described by Koester and Pagels in their introduction to it in James M. Robinson's *Nag*

Hammadi Library as 'a compilation of various generations of Christianity and composed in its extant form, originally in Greek, some time during the second century' (J. M. Robinson 1988: 244). In a fragmentary text, just ten pages long, how can a judgment be made about what comes from where? Koester and Pagels argue that 'parallels to the author's understanding of baptism in deutero-Pauline epistles suggest a date close to the turn of the first century' – but on the same page they say:

> ... traditional sayings of Jesus used in [the] questions and answers have parallels in the Gospels of Matthew, Luke and John, and particularly in the *Gospel of Thomas*. However, a literary dependence upon any of these writings appears unlikely. Rather, the sayings tradition used here appears to be an independent parallel to the one used in the *Gospel of Thomas* and the Gospel of John.

Their problem is that no differentiating criterion is (or can be) enunciated: all they offer is the (apparently intuitive) 'dependence ... appears unlikely'. So they say that the model of baptism referred to in the *Dialogue of the Saviour* came from the tradition reflected in deutero-Pauline literature – but that the stories and sayings of Jesus did not come from the Synoptics and John. This is arbitrary. Why should the relations of dependence be this way round, rather than the writer's having known the Synoptics but not Paul? Or why resist the obvious reading, which would make the whole text a second-century derivative product, written by someone who knew both the Synoptics *and* Paul?

The Egerton papyrus, the *Apocryphon of James* and the *Gospel of Peter* all raise similar issues. What exists on paper is more or less clearly later than the New Testament, but Koester tries to use it to infer source documents distinct from the canonical New Testament (and documents like Q which may have lain behind it). His attempts amount only to noting that stories or sayings are told slightly differently and so 'cannot' come from the Synoptics, or John, or wherever.[14]

Koester's difficulties do not come just from the choice he has made among the extracanonical texts: other scholars adopt differing approaches to finding a layer of early material distinct from the canonical New Testament in (mostly) second-century texts, but the methodological obstacles are the same. They end up making equally arbitrary

---

[14] Koester (1990) dates the *Apocryphon of James* at 187–200, P.Egerton at 205–16 and the *Gospel of Peter* at 216–40.

judgments on what 'must' reflect early narratives. Crossan has gone further than most and put forward a theory about a document which he calls the *Cross Gospel*. This, in his view, was a fully elaborated literary text about Jesus, incorporating both sayings and a passion narrative, written earlier than the canonical Gospels (Crossan 1988; 1998: 120, 481–493). He sees the *Cross Gospel* as a source reflected in the extant *Gospel of Peter*, and also in the canonical Gospels. But the few relevant words in the *Gospel of Peter* are nowhere near enough to carry the structure Crossan builds on them: his *Cross Gospel* is wilder speculation than anything in Koester.

One book has become a paradigm case for the extracanonists, because it can be associated more plausibly with an early date than others, and that is the *Gospel of Thomas*. A collection of 114 sayings of Jesus (without narrative), *Thomas* looks like the kind of collection some scholars presume Q was – and this makes it look early. Some date it, or parts of it, to the first century,[15] while others (including Robinson, who dates so many other things early) put it into the second century.[16] There are fragments from *Thomas* on papyri in Greek dated earlier than the Coptic translation from Nag Hammadi.[17] But was Greek the original language? Some argue for Aramaic, while others say the original was probably in Syriac.[18] Most agree that Syria is a likely area of origin for the book (some are more precise, focusing on the city or area of Edessa).

Thomas is esoteric. It begins with the words: 'These are the secret sayings which the living Jesus spoke ... (1)' Later, there are instructions about the passwords which will make possible the return journey of a human spirit to its place of origin:

> Jesus said, 'If they say to you, "Where did you come from?", say to them, "We came from the light, the place where the light came into being on its own accord and established [itself] and became manifest through their image." If they say to you, "Is it you?", say, "We are its children and we are the elect of the living Father." If they ask you, "What is the sign of your Father in you?", say to them, "It is movement and repose" ' (50).

[15] Koester in J. M. Robinson 1998: 125; Patterson 1993: 116–117 (Crossan 1998: 240 adopts Patterson's view); Meyer 1992: 10; Frend 1967: 23–26.

[16] J. A. T. Robinson 1976: 319; Meeks 1993: 52; Valantasis 1999: 60.

[17] P.Oxy. 1, 654–655.

[18] Neller (1989–90: 7–8) surveys views on the language of the original.

Here 'they' are heavenly beings who challenge the spirits of the dead as they ascend through the heavens. When answered correctly, they will allow the spirits of possessors of the secret knowledge to progress upwards.

Most of *Thomas*, however, consists of sayings of Jesus, often expressed much as in the New Testament. This is a difficulty for scholars who think the writer of the *Gospel of Thomas* did not get material from the canonical Gospels. The theory put forward by Stephen John Patterson (1993) and supported by Crossan (1998: 252–255) is that *Thomas* and Q drew (independently) on what Crossan calls a Common Sayings Tradition – not assumed to have been in writing. Their basic argument – that slightly different things are said, and therefore *Thomas* cannot derive from the Synoptics, or even Q – is inadequate in view of the differences between the synoptic Gospels: no-one could plausibly say that later synoptic evangelists had not read and used their predecessor(s), and few would think that John had been written without its author having read the Synoptics. In view of this, the claim in Patterson and Crossan that *Thomas* represents a different 'trajectory' from the pre-synoptic years – with Gnostic ideas added to early Q, rather than apocalyptic ideas added to Q as in the canonical tradition – is on shaky ground.

Klyne R. Snodgrass (1989) proposed a solution which, although it has not been to everyone's taste,[19] has much to commend it. While acknowledging that there is (some) independent tradition in *Thomas*, he argues that the parallels with the Synoptics and John are enough to show familiarity on the writer's part with the canonical Gospels (1989: 38). He adds that if *Thomas* was written about 140, it is difficult to believe that the writer could have been unaware of the synoptic tradition, which by then had been current for seventy years or so: 'Edessa is not *that* far from Antioch' (1989: 27). This last point is weakened only slightly if one accepts (as I do, with Richard Valantasis [1999: 60]), that *Thomas* may have been written as early as 100–10. Snodgrass argues that on ordinary standards for evaluating evidence[20] it is clear that *Thomas* used material drawn from the Gospels, together with additional material, and so constructed (in Pagels' phrase) a Gnostic gospel.

[19] Koester (1990: 85 n. 4) says of Snodgrass's article (1989–90), 'nothing can be learned here'; Crossan (1998) omits to mention Snodgrass at all.

[20] 'I am left with the feeling that no evidence will be sufficient for some of those who favour the hypothesis of independence' (Snodgrass 1989–90: 25).

The extracanonists' case from their other chosen texts is weak. Once a realistic view is taken of *Thomas*, their contention that major modification is needed to the view of first-century Christianity drawn from the New Testament seems improbable. Until at any rate the 90s, the best evidence for Christian life and Christian communities is in the (canonical) New Testament. Not that the ideas which developed into second-century Gnosticism were not there in first-century Christianity: certainly they were (see ch. 8 below). But there is little to be said for the rhetoric of suspicion against the Christians who retained and copied the New Testament, and little reason to think the extracanonists' idea of the shape of first-century Christianity is correct. The bush was already shaggy, but reading the New Testament does not necessarily create a wrong impression of the shape of its core.

New Testament insights on the Christian movement

In this book, then, it will be assumed that the extracanonists are, on the whole, wrong. What can be got out of the New Testament is only a partial view of what went on in first-century Christianity – but the New Testament books are still the best sources we have for their period. Intracanonists, however, who have outlined the first-century church better, have too often given in to the temptation to plot patterns of change over a long period. If the New Testament books were mostly written by 70, the development of theory and practice in the churches must have moved ahead faster than the majority of scholars in the last century or more have supposed.

Many authors have studied the New Testament churches. Anyone who wants a full summary of the growth of Christianity as reflected in the New Testament should turn to them – above all, Meeks' *The First Urban Christians* and *The Origins of Christian Morality*, Ellis' *The Making of the New Testament Documents* and Theissen's *The Religion of the Earliest Churches*. But the following chapters will be directed to solving just one element in the puzzle which the growth of Christianity poses: how did the churches change the religion of the Roman empire? Specifically, what factors produced an organization with the capacity to produce such a great social upheaval?

2
First-generation Christianity

Jesus' church: a sect

The organization which grew into the agent of upheaval started small.
Jesus formed and led a sect, then left it behind to continue what he
had taught. The sect's first leaders were those who had been closest to
Jesus in his life – the Twelve plus relatives of Jesus, especially James.
There were other Jewish sects: indeed, they were an important feature
of Judaism. Josephus, in his *Jewish War* (2.119–166), explains to
Greek and Roman readers what he calls the three 'philosophies' of the
Jews – Pharisees, Sadducees, Essenes. Readers would understand that a
'philosophy' was not just a system of ideas: it was people, loyal to their
teachers and to a particular approach. Jesus laid the foundations of a
sect by choosing the Twelve.

The Gospels say what Jesus did to ensure the continuance of his sect
after his death. As Wright (1996: 104) points out, there are parallel
cases both before and after Jesus, in which a leader aimed 'to leave
behind a community, a renewed Israel, that would continue his work'.
The Teacher of Righteousness referred to in the Dead Sea Scrolls,
Judas the Galilean, Hillel (died AD 10) and Shammai, the founders of
the two 'houses' of Torah interpretation in the first century, and
Simon Bar Kochva, the leader of the Jews in the third Jewish War, all
worked on these lines. As Wright concludes on the same page, 'this is a
thoroughly Jewish intention, which cannot be dismissed by hinting
sarcastically that one can hardly envisage Jesus envisaging the contemporary church'.

Jesus gave Peter a leading role, with access to Jesus' key ethical and eschatological concept – the kingdom of heaven:

'I tell you, you are Peter, and on this rock I will build my church, and the gates of Hades will not prevail against it. I will give you the keys of the kingdom of heaven, and whatever you bind on earth will be bound in heaven, and whatever you loose on earth will be loosed in heaven' (Matt. 16:18–19).

But he also taught that Christian leadership was to be a paradox. Relations within the sect were to be anti-hierarchical:

A dispute also arose among them as to which one of them was to be regarded as the greatest. But he [Jesus] said to them, 'The kings of the Gentiles lord it over them; and those in authority over them are called benefactors. But not so with you; rather the greatest among you must become like the youngest, and the leader like one who serves. For who is greater, the one who is at the table or the one who serves? Is it not the one at the table? But I am among you as one who serves' (Luke 22:24–27).

Cohesion and proper conduct, as well as leadership, were legislated for. Jesus gave instructions on dealing with unacceptable behaviour, with a sanction of exclusion imposed in the worst cases by the *ekklēsia*. This word, given in many English translations as 'congregation' (cf. Septuagint use to translate Hebrew *qāhāl*), may equally well be translated 'church', as in Paul:[1]

'If your brother sins against you, go and tell him his fault, between you and him alone. If he listens to you, you have gained your brother. But if he does not listen, take one or two others along with you, that every word may be confirmed by the evidence of two or three witnesses. If he refuses to listen to them, tell it to the church; and if he refuses to listen even to the church, let him be to you as a Gentile and a tax collector' (Matt. 18:15–17, RSV).

This congregation/church is distinct, not figured on Septuagint lines

---

[1] Septuagint use: e.g. Lev. 4:21; Paul: e.g. Gal. 1:22.

as the collectivity of the whole Jewish people. The analogy of the Qumran sect, as an organization with rules, comes closer to the idea of the congregation in this passage.

Christians, the synagogues and the temple

Any Jewish sect might find tensions arising between itself and the Jewish community at large. In the story of the man born blind, John's Gospel says that the Jews had agreed, in Jesus' lifetime, that 'anyone who confessed Jesus to be the Messiah would be put out of the synagogue' (9:22). Later (16:2) Jesus tells his followers to expect (in future) to be excluded from the synagogue.

But synagogues were one thing, and the temple was another. In Christianity's very early years, it was possible for Christians to worship in the temple, as in the story of Peter and John and the crippled man (Acts 3:1 – 4:22). At the end, the court cautions and discharges Peter and John – leaving them free to come to the temple again, and even preach there (Acts 5:42). When they met in Solomon's Portico, the Christians appeared as a distinct group: 'None of the rest dared to join them'; and they gained respect and converts (Acts 5:12–14); even temple priests – 'a great many', Acts 6:7 says.

The ban from synagogues was not instantly and uniformly effective, even though in some cases it came into existence quickly. Paul, on his journeys, habitually started to preach in a new town at the synagogue or place of (Jewish) prayer. This, however, might last only until the Jews from the last town arrived – as at Lystra, where Paul narrowly escaped being stoned to death (Acts 14:19–20). Jewish reactions to Paul's choice of the synagogue as his starting-place suggest that, at least in Greek-speaking areas, the Christian churches must soon have had to become distinct from synagogue congregations.

Were things different in the Holy Land? Away from the factors at work in Paul's Diaspora-based mission, was there less conflict between 'the sect of the Nazarenes' (Acts 24:5) and Jewish communities? Perhaps; but the Jerusalem church as reflected in Acts and elsewhere in the New Testament is the only case anything is known about.

There, Frend (1984: 88–89) argues for the 'Hellenists', whose complaints were behind the apostles' choice (Acts 6:1–6) of seven deacons (all with Greek names), as evidence that Christian preaching had 'spread to the network of Greek-speaking synagogues in Jerusalem'. He speaks of 'furious dissensions in the Hellenistic synagogues' – inferring that Stephen's preaching brought to the surface disagreements among Greek-speaking Jews over the importance of the temple: hence the charge against him (Acts 6:13–14) of 'saying things against this holy place and the law'. Despite the mention of people from the synagogue of the Freedmen as Stephen's accusers (Acts 6:9), however, Frend's interpretation of the Stephen story as being about Christian preaching in synagogues rests on circumstantial evidence: Acts does not show whether or not Christian preachers were (generally) allowed to speak in synagogues, and does not say how long Christians thought it right to be part of synagogues by attending Sabbath worship.

Wright (1992: 161–162), arguing against the theory that the great split between Judaism and Christianity came with the destruction of the temple, is suspicious of the idea that after 70 'the new rabbinic movement, bitter and grieving over the loss of Jerusalem and the Temple, organized itself ... into a great synod at Jamnia and introduced measures which effectively excluded Christians', while at the same time a new anti-Jewish strand entered Christian thought. He dates the beginning of the break to the time when Saul/Paul received permission from the high priest to act against Christians in the synagogues at Damascus (Acts 9:1–2; Wright 1992: 451–452). But practice probably remained non-uniform after then – and there is no certainty that priests who converted to Christianity were excluded from priestly duties while the temple still existed.

It seems likely that the origin of Sunday worship is a related issue. There is reason to think that Paul assumes Sunday worship. At 1 Corinthians 16:2 (written in 55), he advises his readers each to put aside their money for the collection for the Jerusalem church on Sundays. This may suggest that they worshipped on Sunday (Meeks [1983: 143] notes that the inference is not conclusive). The meeting at Troas (Acts 20:7–9, probably in 56/7) at which Eutychus fell out of the window was on a Sunday. Probably Paul taught his Corinthian converts to meet on Sundays, and did so in 51–2, when he spent eighteen months in Corinth (Acts 18:11–12) while Gallio was proconsul of Achaia. It might be right to project the practice backwards in Paul's teaching to the first missionary journey in 46–8 – or even to guess that the church in Antioch from which he departed on that journey (Acts 13:1–3) met on Sundays.

But even if we assume that Paul went out in 46, and set up churches which worshipped on Sundays as Antioch Christians did, it remains unclear how practice in Antioch might relate to what was done in Jerusalem. The conference presided over by James in Jerusalem in 48 centred on whether, to be Christian, it was necessary also to be Jewish – in the sense and to the degree of being circumcised (Acts 15:1–2). That question had arisen in the Antioch church because 'certain individuals came down from Judea and were teaching the brothers, "Unless you are circumcised according to the custom [better 'law'] of Moses, you cannot be saved."' The answer given was that adherence to proper dietary and moral standards was enough, and circumcision not needed (Acts 15:19–29). The decision made in the conference seems analogous to the broader outlook in Judaism whereby (non-Jewish) Godfearers could take part in some aspects of communal life.

The difference in outlook between the Antioch and Jerusalem churches makes it seem most probable that Jerusalem Christians in the 30s and 40s were still in the synagogues on the Sabbath to hear Moses read (Acts 15:21) – as the Christians whom Saul went to Damascus in 33 to persecute must have been, since he carried letters to the synagogues authorizing him to arrest them (Acts 9:2).

Jerusalem Christianity in the first decade

Jesus' followers began their work in Jerusalem. The decision to base the sect there is made, in Luke, on the ground of Jesus' post-resurrection command and application of prophecy: 'Thus it is written, that the Messiah is to suffer and rise from the dead on the third day, and that repentance and forgiveness of sins is to be proclaimed in his name to all nations, beginnning from Jerusalem ...' (Luke 24:46–47).

The other Gospels describe things differently, but Luke's account is the most important for the shape events were to take: the move from rural mission, as carried out by Jesus, to an urban base, gave Christianity high potential for diffusion. At festivals, Jerusalem was filled with Diaspora Jews, whose importance as potential recruits is evident in the Pentecost story (Acts 2:1–41).

Peter, before his move to Rome during Claudius' reign (41–54),[2] led the Jerusalem church in its first years – as historians of different outlooks agree.[3] Evidence from several directions confirms this: the promise to Peter (Matt. 16:18–19), his leading role in the Pentecost

---

[2] Eusebius, *Ecclesiastical History* 2.14.6.
[3] On the conservative side, Frend 1984: 86; from another angle, Lüdemann 1996: 38.

story (Acts 2:14–41), and the importance of Peter/Cephas to Paul – as the one person he wanted to see when he went to Jerusalem three years after his conversion, about 36 (Gal. 1:18).

The earliest stage of activity in Jerusalem may be when James the brother of Jesus began to take an important part: Paul names him individually in his list of people who saw the risen Christ – separately from the Twelve, after the five hundred who saw Jesus at one time, but before 'all the apostles' (1 Cor. 15:4–7).

The conflict over the daily distribution, which escalated (via a hearing in front of the high priest) as far as Stephen's death by stoning, marked a key moment: 'all except the apostles were scattered throughout the countryside of Judea and Samaria' in a persecution in which Saul participated by 'entering house after house; dragging off both men and women, he committed them to prison' (Acts 8:1–3). The motives of those who decided to move against the Christians were complex. Since the crucifixion (and before), the temple authorities had been hostile to Jesus' sect, but the Roman government had treated issues more even-handedly. The form the eventual expulsion took was eccentric. Why not, after all, expel the leaders, rather than everybody *except* the leaders?

Saul may have helped to talk the Council into the expulsion. Enthusiasm for Saul's anti-Christian plans, however, was probably tempered by the esteem in which the Christians were held (Acts 5:13). The authorities may have calculated that expelling the apostles could cause a backlash. They may have hoped to reduce their influence by removing their followers. As it was, the expulsion gave a fillip to the spread of Christianity. 'Now those who were scattered went from place to place, proclaiming the word' (Acts 8:4). They were not, however, the first outside Jerusalem, as the existence of Christians in Damascus shows.

Acts 8 – 11 tells stories about incidents in the spread of Christianity after the expulsion: Philip in Samaria; Simon Magus; Philip and the Ethiopian; Saul's conversion and preaching in Damascus; and Peter in Lydda, Joppa, and with Cornelius in Caesarea – this last (Acts 10:1 – 11:18) cast by the author as an opening to the debate about whether Gentiles could be Christians. Phoenicia, Cyprus and Antioch are mentioned as destinations outside Judea/Samaria for preachers exiled from Jerusalem (Acts 11:19–20). At Antioch, Gentiles as well as Jews were recruited: Barnabas, a Levite born in Cyprus who had become a Christian in Jerusalem (Acts 4:36–37), was sent to Antioch, probably in or after 36, implicitly to deal with issues raised by there being both Jewish and Gentile Christians in the first wave of Antioch converts – and then Barnabas brought Saul/Paul from Tarsus to join the Antioch venture. He, after being converted, had gone between 33 and 36 to Arabia (meaning probably chiefly the *cities* of the Nabatean client-kingdom, bordering on Damascus – including Petra, Gerasa, Philadelphia and Bostra; Meeks 1983: 10) to preach Christianity (Gal. 1:17).

Simon Magus and his sect

Another informative insight into the religious atmosphere of Judea/Samaria in the 30s comes from the encounter between Christian preachers and Simon Magus. While Philip was preaching in a city in Samaria,

> ... a certain man named Simon had previously practised magic in the city and amazed the people of Samaria, saying that he was someone great. All of them, from the least to the greatest, listened to him eagerly, saying, 'This man is the power of God that is called Great.' And they listened eagerly to him because for a long time he had amazed them with his magic. But when they believed Philip, who was proclaiming the good news about the kingdom of God and the name of Jesus Christ, they were baptized, both men and women (Acts 8:9–12).

The continuation of the story (Acts 8:13–24) is well known. Simon believes and is baptized, but when Peter and John arrive in Samaria and impart the Holy Spirit by laying on hands, Simon offers Peter money in return for the power to do the same: Peter angrily refuses, advising Simon to repent of such a wicked idea.

Here the biblical account ends, but later Christian authors have much to add. The earliest elaborator is Justin, writing in the 150s, ninety or so years after Acts and about 120 years after the event. Arguing that persecuting Christians is wrong, he explains that some people do not get persecuted, despite being called 'Christians'. His example is Simon's sect:

> After Christ's ascent into heaven the demons put forward various men who said that they were gods, and you not only did not persecute them, but thought them worthy of honours. One was a certain Simon, a Samaritan from the village of Gitta, who

in the time of Claudius Caesar, through the arts of the demons who worked in him, did mighty works of magic in your imperial city of Rome and was thought to be a god. He has been honoured among you as a god by a statue, which was set up on the river Tiber, between the two bridges, with this inscription in Latin: SIMONI DEO SANCTO ['To Simon, a holy god']. Almost all the Samaritans, and a few in other nations, confess this man as their first god and worship him as such, and a woman named Helen, who travelled around with him in those days, and had formerly been a public prostitute, they say was the First Concept produced from him. Then we know of a certain Menander, who was also a Samaritan, from the village of Capparetaea, who had been a disciple of Simon's, and was also possessed by the demons ... As we said, all who derive [their opinions] from these men are called Christians, just as men who do not share the same teachings with the philosophers still have in common with them the name of philosophy, thus brought into disrepute ... we are sure that they are neither persecuted nor killed by you, on account of their teachings anyway (*First Apologia* 1:26).

This awkward passage has many points of interest. One difficulty is with Simon's coming to Rome. Possibly he did, and if so it may have been (as stated) in the reign of Claudius (41–54), but Justin's evidence arises from a misunderstanding. There was a Roman god called Semo Sancus Dius Fidius, a god of loyalty and oath-keeping, worshipped jointly with Jupiter at Rome in temples on the Quirinal and on Tiber Island. Justin probably saw a statue of Semo Sancus, read the inscription on the base (there are three such bases preserved, *CIL* 6:567, 568, 30994), thought it was about Simon Magus, and concluded that Simon had been deified at Rome.

Better-informed parts of the account include the point that Simon's followers were (in Justin's time) called Christians. This is put in the background by later heresiologists, and Hippolytus, writing in the early third century, says that Simon 'abjured the faith' (*Refutation of all Heresies* 15). But the fact that his followers described themselves as Christians fits in with Acts 8:20–24, where Simon, after Peter rebukes him for offering to pay for the ability to impart the Holy Spirit, asks the apostles to pray for him: the story implies that Simon was not *really* a Christian ('You have no part or share in this'), without saying that Simon ceased to claim to be one.

How popular was Simon in Samaria? Acts suggests that Philip over-
took him in the popular-preacher stakes. Justin asserts that 'almost all
the Samaritans ... confess this man as their first god'. But even though
Justin was a Samaritan himself and ought to know, what he says may
be only an extrapolation of Acts 8:10 ('All of them, high and low, lis-
tened eagerly to him...'). With Helen, however, Justin brings in
something new. Later writers say more about her. Irenaeus (late second
century) gives her a role in Simon's theology:

> He led about with him a certain Helen, after he had redeemed
> her from a life of prostitution in Tyre, a city of Phoenicia. He
> said she was the First Conception of his mind, the Mother of
> all, through whom in the beginning he had the idea of making
> angels and archangels. This Thought, leaping forth from him
> and knowing what her father willed, descended to the lower
> regions and generated angels and powers, by whom this world
> was made. But after she generated them, she was held captive by
> them because of envy, for they did not want to be considered
> the offspring of anyone else. For Simon was entirely unknown
> to them; his Thought was held captive by the powers and angels
> emitted by her. She suffered all kinds of humiliation from them,
> so that she did not run back upwards to her Father but was
> even enclosed in a human body, and through the ages trans-
> migrated as from one vessel to another, into other female
> bodies. She was in the Helen because of whom the Trojan War
> was undertaken ... Transmigrating from body to body, and
> always enduring humiliation from the body, she finally became a
> prostitute; she was the 'lost sheep'. For this reason he came, in
> order to rescue her first and free her from her bonds, then to
> offer men salvation through his 'knowledge' (*Against Heresies*
> 1:23 – 2:3).

This theory draws on a number of influences. Helen as creative
principle occupies a role like that of wisdom in Proverbs 8 – 9 and in
the Wisdom of Solomon; Helen as Helen of Troy, and the idea of
reincarnation, bring in a Greek strand; and the use of the lost-sheep
parable (Matt. 18:12–14; Luke 15:4–7) indicates direct adaptation of
Jesus' teaching.

Irenaeus next attacks the Simonians as sexually promiscuous, users
of magic, and polytheists. He seems to know more about Simon

Magus than Justin knew thirty or forty years earlier, which is a worry – but some things he says should not be discounted. Tyre, where Helen was from, was a Greek-influenced Phoenician city: this could account for Hellenistic elements in the Helen myth. Samaria, like Judea, was fertile ground for growth of sects. Acts shows Simon as a talented leader, already active 'for a long time', with a big following: there is every reason to expect that his sect would go on beyond its founder's lifetime, and be there for second-century Christian writers to enquire into. Justin names Menander as Simon's successor. The Acts story explains why Simon's sect would have gone by the name of 'Christian' in later decades. Michael Allen Williams (1996: 165–166), arguing that there was no such thing as 'libertine Gnosticism', shows reason to disbelieve the allegations of promiscuity against the Simonians. The past life of Helen, however, was open to no more disapproval than that of some women associated with Jesus (Luke 7:36–50; John 4:1–30).

The Simon sect persisted in the first and second centuries under the Christian umbrella, though Irenaeus was mistaken in thinking that 'all heresies took their rise from [Simon]' (*Against Heresies* 1.23.2). Frend (1984: 195–196) argues that Irenaeus is right, supposing that Simon taught a second-century kind of Gnostic theology decades before anyone else. But in fact, the complex theory ascribed to Simon by Hippolytus[4] may reflect the ideas of Simonians of his own day, as Arland J. Hultgren and Steven A. Haggmark (1996: 20) suggest – and by Hippolytus' day, in the third century, the Simonians may have been innovating (and so leaving Simon's ideas behind), in order to keep up with the times. They were by then a tiny sect, as Origen says:

> The magician Simon also, the Samaritan, wanted to win some through magic, and he deceived them at that time. But now one cannot find thirty all told in the world, and perhaps this number is too high. Even in Palestine they are very few, and nowhere in the rest of the world is his name to be found (*Against Celsus* 1.57).

The Jerusalem church, 41–62

Conditions were soon to change again for Christians at Jerusalem. At the end of the 30s, the temple became the focus of a political crisis.

---

[4] Hippolytus, *Refutation of all Heresies* 6.4, 7, 9, 13–15; see figure 8.1 below, p. 162.

Pontius Pilate ceased to be prefect of Judea in 36, and in 37 Gaius Caligula took over as emperor. In the winter of 39–40, in reprisal for the action of Jews who had destroyed a Greek altar in Jamnia,[5] Caligula sent Petronius, legate of Syria, to Jerusalem with an army to get a statue of himself (Caligula), as a god, set up in the temple. Learning the strength of feeling against the statue, Petronius delayed – and before action could be taken against him, Herod Agrippa I (already allocated territory around upper Galilee to rule, and given the title of king) managed to get Caligula to change his mind.[6] After Caligula's death on 24 January 41, Herod Agrippa took over as ruler of Judea. As befitted a ruler who had averted the imposition of idol-worship in the temple, he encouraged performance of Jewish ritual – 'no day passed for him without the prescribed sacrifice', Josephus said.[7]

Herod Agrippa it was who (about 42) had James the Just, the brother of John, killed (Acts 12:1–3) – a move approved of by 'the Jews' (meaning the temple authorities), who already had substantial reason to thank him. Peter, escaping from jail and the prospect of being next on the execution list, went into hiding, asking people he saw at a prayer meeting at John Mark's mother's house to 'Tell this to James and to the believers' (Acts 12:6–17). This is the first hint in Acts of James's leading role, but by 48, at the conference on the Gentile question, he is clearly the most important man in the Jerusalem church. At Acts 15:19 it is James (personally) who decides on the admission of Gentiles to Christianity ('*Therefore I have reached the decision* that we should not trouble those Gentiles who are turning to God'), and at Acts 21:18 he is the focal point of a meeting between Paul and the leadership of the Jerusalem church.

The adverse political climate did not last: in 44 Herod Agrippa died suddenly. Since the new king, Herod Agrippa II, was only sixteen, the Emperor Claudius put a Roman procurator, Cuspius Fadus, in charge of Judea.[8] He and his successors, Josephus says, 'by abstaining from all interference with the customs of the country, kept the nation at peace' (*Jewish War* 2.220). The effect was to deny the temple leadership, for years to come, the chance of getting civil authority behind it against the Christians. Direct Roman rule in these years was to the Jerusalem church's advantage – as it was soon also to work in Paul's favour.

[5] Philo, *Embassy to Gaius* 30.201–202.
[6] Josephus, *Jewish Antiquities* 18.261–309.
[7] *Jewish Antiquities* 19.331.
[8] *Jewish Antiquities* 19.343–352 (cf. Acts 12:19–23), and 19.360–363.

Paul and the Antioch church

Antioch was where Christians expelled from Jerusalem in 33 first began preaching Christianity to non-Jews (Acts 11:19–20). So the Antioch church, the first to get Gentile converts, and the first to ask what to do about them, became a bridge for Christianity between the Jewish and Greek worlds. There, believers were first called 'Christians' (Acts 11:26). In the Aramaic-speaking world they continued to be called 'Nazarenes' (cf. Acts 24:5). Two centuries later, when captive Romans, with Christians among them (including Demetrianus, bishop of Antioch), were brought to Persia after Shapur I's victory over Valerian in 260, the Greek-speaking Christians among the captives were referred to in Sassanian inscriptions as *klystyd'n*, in contrast to Aramaic-speaking Nazarenes (*n'sl'y*) (Lieu 1992: 95).

Antioch, founded as a city of Greek settlers in Syria, had grown by the first century AD into the third largest city in the Roman empire, with a population perhaps approaching half a million (Meeks 1983: 28), and had as its horizon the Greek and Roman world rather than its own Aramaic-speaking hinterland. Already before Barnabas and Paul set out in 46 to preach Christianity in Cyprus and southern Asia Minor, the Antioch church was a community with unusual advantages and potential, as the list at Acts 13:1 of its early leaders shows. Manaen, *syntrophos* of (i.e. brought up together with) Herod Agrippa, was a Greek-speaking Jew of high educational level. Simeon/Niger, like Saul/Paul, had a Latin alternative name – another Jew with Hellenistic connections.

Lucius of Cyrene, the other person (besides Barnabas) on the list, had a Roman name but was from a Greek city on the African coast. Scholars are cautious about thinking this Lucius could be Luke,[9] the companion of Paul and author of the Gospel and Acts, but 'Luke' (Greek *Loukas*) is a contraction of 'Lucius' (Greek *Loukios*) – and either version of the name might be used of the same person, without explanation.[10] Eusebius (*Ecclesiastical History* 3.4.6) sows confusion by describing Luke as 'by birth one of the people from Antioch' – which

---

[9] Meeks (1983: 216 n. 29), for example, says 'there is no good reason to identify' the Lucius of Rom. 16:21 with Lucius of Cyrene or with the Luke of Philem. 24, Col. 4:14 and 2 Tim. 4:11. Laudable caution: but what if it has led him to make three Lukes out of one (without even mentioning the Gospel writer)?

[10] Cf. Silas, whose name is given consistently in the short form in Acts (15:22, etc.) but as Silvanus in Pauline Epistles (2 Cor. 1:19; 1 Thess. 1:1; 2 Thess. 1:1) and at 1 Pet. 5:12.

if correct would mean he was not Lucius *of Cyrene*, who lived at Antioch but whose home town was Cyrene. But on this point Eusebius may not have had sources any better than ours now. The question remains open, but the identification of Luke, the Gospel writer (and the 'beloved physician' of Col. 4:14), with this Lucius may perhaps be correct. It would be economical to guess in addition that the 'brother whose praise is in the gospel throughout all the churches' (2 Cor. 8:18, AV)[11] – whose identity was so self-evident to recipients of the letter that to mention his name was superfluous – was also Luke.

Paul himself, a Roman citizen (Acts 16:37–38) from Tarsus (Acts 9:11) in Cilicia, had been brought up as a Pharisee and educated at Jerusalem by Rabbi Gamaliel (Acts 22:3). He was born a citizen (Acts 22:22–29). Some (e.g. Meeks 1983: 38) have found difficulty reconciling this with his being Jewish and 'a Pharisee, a son of Pharisees' (Acts 23:6), but such a thing was possible. The most likely route would be (as Meggitt says, 1998: 82 and n. 36) through his father's having been a slave later set free by a Roman citizen. He practised the craft of a *skēnopoios* (Acts 18:3) – a 'tentmaker', though his product range would have run beyond ordinary military tents. Meggitt (1998: 75–97) discusses Paul's economic and social background, and shows what dissonant factors were at work in his life. He was well educated, but not in the dominant (Greek) tradition; of high civic status, but low income; successful in the eyes of intellectual peers (Gal. 1:14), but a manual worker.

The Pauline churches, 46–62

In the fourteen years between the Antioch church's sending Barnabas and Paul out to preach in 46 and Paul's arrival in Rome in 60, Paul travelled in Cyprus, Asia Minor, Macedonia, Greece and 'as far round as Illyricum' [= Albania] (Rom. 15:19), establishing Christian churches. His hope of reaching Spain (Rom. 15:24) was probably not fulfilled. The Pauline Epistles and Acts allow a fairly detailed picture to be built up of what Pauline churches were like, and what kinds of people were in them. Theissen's *The Social Setting of Pauline Chris-*

---

[11] Translated in the NRSV as 'the brother who is famous among all the churches for his proclaiming of the good news' – which gives one possible answer to the puzzle of what *ho epainos en tō evangeliō dia pasōn tōn ekklēsiōn* means, without acknowledging that it is a puzzle. There is no proof that it does not mean 'who has a high reputation in all the churches because of the Gospel he has written', a reading which would date Luke's Gospel before 56 – not impossible, if Acts dates from 62.

tianity (1982), focused on the Corinthian church, and Meeks' *The First Urban Christians* (1983), which draws on the Pauline Epistles (and is sceptical about Acts), have done the most to influence recent discussion of the social makeup of Pauline churches – and by inference also of other first-century Christian communities. The ideas they put forward have come to be called the 'New Consensus'.

The 'new' element is an increased awareness of the importance in Pauline churches of their minority of better-off members. Earlier studies stressed – or had as a premise – that churches were made up of the poor and slaves, and represented (almost exclusively) downtrodden elements.[12] The New Consensus attaches more importance to hints that churches recruited a cross-section, within which patterns of leadership and social relations were not dissimilar to patterns in the wider society. There were people in the Corinth congregation, and elsewhere in the Pauline sphere, who were socially prestigious and presumably rich: for example Erastus (Rom. 16:23), treasurer of the city of Corinth. For a long time, there was discussion over what kind of 'treasurer' Erastus was: a high municipal official, or a public slave? Then, during archaeological excavations in 1929 and 1947, blocks were found with an inscription in Latin recording that a person called Erastus paid for a pavement to be laid in the courtyard east of the theatre at Corinth: 'Erastus in return for his aedileship had [this pavement] laid at his own expense.'[13] Theissen (1982: 79–83) (among others) identifies this Erastus with the 'treasurer of the city' mentioned by Paul. This makes Erastus an office-holder near the top on the city council, with enough money to pay personally for public works (1982: 100).

Meeks goes beyond Theissen's studies on the Corinthian church by bringing status inconsistency into focus: there were people in Pauline churches who were not at the bottom, but among them there was a lack of convergence between the different things which go to shape an individual's status. As far as people mentioned by name in the Pauline Epistles are concerned, Meeks argues that 'their dominant characteristic was social mobility or status inconsistency', and adds:

> May we further guess that the sorts of status inconsistency we observed – independent women with moderate wealth, Jews

[12] For surveys contrasting the New Consensus with earlier perspectives, see Meggitt 1998: 97–101, and John H. Schütz's introduction to Theissen 1982: 3–11.

[13] Meeks 1983: 58–59; inscription: Kent 1966: no. 232 and plate 21.

with wealth in a pagan society, freedmen with skill and money but stigmatized by origin, and so on – brought with them not only anxiety but also loneliness, in a society in which social position was important and usually rigid? Would, then, the intimacy of Christian groups become a welcome refuge, the emotion-charged language of family and affection and the image of a caring, personal God powerful antidotes, while the master symbol of the crucified savior crystallized a believable picture of the way the world seemed really to work? (1983: 191).

The cities of the Roman empire in the first century, he and Theissen argue, provided suitable conditions for the contacts and communication which led to the growth of churches. Along with the response to the gospel from poorer people, the interest generated among those with resources at their disposal (houses, slaves, the means to travel, and so on) was an important element in the success of Christianity.

Meggitt (1998: 135–141) challenges the New Consensus on many points. He argues against the identification of the Corinthian aedile Erastus (or possibly Eperastus, he notes), who paid for the pavement, with the Erastus who was the Corinthian treasurer of the city – though he concedes that if they are one person, he was 'among the most socially powerful of his day' (1998: 136). Individuals whom Theissen sees as well-off and influential, and Meeks as socially mobile and afflicted with status dissonance, Meggitt views (on the same New Testament evidence) as further down the social scale – or rather, in lower layers of a social pyramid which was very wide at the bottom, and supported very few rich individuals at the top. Lydia, for instance, the dealer in purple cloth from Thyatira who had a house in Philippi (Acts 16:14, 40), was probably (Meggitt argues, 1998: 69 n. 164) not one of the few traders in murex purple, the scarce and high-priced dye used for the best purple cloth: Thyatira, her home town, was known for cheap vegetable dyes – so she probably produced ordinary textiles, not luxury goods.

The difficulty with Meggitt's argument, based on questioning every instance of alleged prosperity in Theissen and Meeks and minimizing every item which they (and other New Consensus scholars) take as showing that members of Pauline churches had resources at their disposal, is twofold. First, the cumulative force of the evidence is against him – there is a limit to the number of times it makes sense to say that someone is probably less well off than one would think – and second, he draws too strong a line in his analysis of the Roman world between the rich (and their security and comfort) and everyone else (and the poverty they lived in). He is right to say that Paul and his followers 'faced the same anxieties over subsistence that beset all but the privileged few in that society' (1998: 179), but mistaken to take a measure of insecurity as the same thing as being at the bottom of the heap. In a famine, not only the poorest went hungry; you could be prosperous, without being so far up the scale that fluctuations between good and bad times made no difference.

Some support for the New Consensus comes from comparative considerations brought in by Rodney Stark (1996: 33), who likens first-century Christianity to more recent cult movements – defining these as '*new faiths*, at least new in the society being examined'. Mormonism and Christian Science in the United States, he points out, grew by attracting the relatively affluent, not the poor: and survey evidence shows a skew towards college graduates among adherents of cults – 81% of members of American cult groups having attended college (in a 1989/90 survey), as against (for example) 70% of Episcopalians and 48% of Catholics (1996: 39–43). 'Cult groups over-recruit persons of more privileged backgrounds', Stark generalizes (1996: 46): thus it should not be expected that first-century Christian churches were made up only of the poor and dispossessed.

In their first three decades, then, the churches extended recruitment in two directions: to Judea, by keeping the best profile they could in Jerusalem and staying active in rural areas, and to a constituency of Diaspora Jews and Gentiles reached by itinerant preachers. Two important challenges were met: in Judea, conflict with the authorities was kept within bounds most of the time, and prevented from stemming the Nazarene sect's growth; and beyond the Holy Land, Christianity's initial momentum was retained by a prompt and widely accepted decision on how Gentiles could come into the church. There were Christians in mid-first-century Rome, led by Peter, who moved there between the meeting at Jerusalem in 48 and Claudius' death in 54. Christian churches were separate from synagogues, probably with Sunday worship, at least in the Pauline-influenced ones. Congregations outside Judea were a mix of Jews and Gentiles, rich and poor. As a movement with ambitions to spread empire-wide and beyond, however, Christianity was only at an early stage. Just as it reached that stage, as the next chapter will show, it was outlawed.

3
Initial growth, incipient persecution

Rodney Stark, in his *The Rise of Christianity* (1996), discusses numbers, and the speed of Christianity's expansion. He posits that having started at zero and ended up with about 10% of the population of the Roman empire at the time of Constantine, Christianity must have grown at a rate approximating to 40% per decade. Growth of the Mormon church in the past century has run on average at about 43% per decade, he notes – and argues that there is reason to think a similar growth rate credible for the early church. Putting the population of the Roman empire in AD 300 at about 60 million (as good an estimate as any), he shows that 1,000 Christians in AD 40 would have increased by that date, on his growth rate, to a number consistent with the approximation that 10% of the population was Christian at the turn of the third and fourth centuries. He gives the table reproduced here as figure 3.1 (overleaf).

Parts of this calculation must be right: Christians must have been a good-sized minority by 300 – otherwise, the policy of making their religion into an established church could not have been a realistic option. A Christian percentage of the general population as low as 10% seems a modest estimate, but by 300 Christianity was still stronger in urban areas than in the countryside – and a very high proportion of the population of the Roman empire was rural. To believe that (say) 20 or 25% were Christian before Constantine, one would have to posit a very substantial rural expansion of Christianity before legalization, and this seems improbable; certainly, tangible evidence of it is lacking.

Year	Number of Christians	% of Roman population (60 million)
40	1,000	0.0017
50	1,400	0.0023
100	7,530	0.0126
150	40,496	0.07
200	217,795	0.36
250	1,171,356	1.9
300	6,299,832	10.5
350	33,882,008	56.5

Figure 3.1. Christian growth 40–350 projected at 40% per decade (from Stark 1996: 7).

But Keith Hopkins, in an article responding to Stark's book, draws attention to a striking implication of the low numbers of Christians posited for the first century. If there were about 7,000 Christians in 100, he argues (1998: 212), and about 30% of them were adult males, with a literacy rate (among the adult males) of 20%, then there would have been as few as 420 literate Christians at that date. Given that only a small minority of literates – Hopkins guesses at 10% – went on to an advanced stage of education, he calculates that there may have been as few as 42 'fluent and skilled literates' in the Christian communities empire-wide at the turn of the first and second centuries.

Some of Hopkins' assumptions are contestable. He assumes that the literacy rate among Christians was no higher than the rate in the Gentile population of the Roman empire as a whole – and puts that rate lower than some would think plausible. He considers, and rejects, the possibility that Christians, like Jews, had higher rates of literacy than the general population. He seems to discount two key arguments of Stark's book: that a large proportion of Christians were Jewish (with the literacy rate that that implies), well into the second century; and that Christianity over-recruited well-educated people. Then there is the output to consider: it is difficult to believe that the Christian literature of the 90s and 100s (including Revelation, Clement's letter to Corinth, Hermas' *Shepherd*, the *Gospel of Thomas*, and Ignatius' letters) was written for an audience on such a small scale.

In an article replying to Hopkins, Stark considers the consequences of Hopkins' very low number of literates for what he calls the 'Chaos School of the Early Church' – meaning the work produced by the scholars I have called extracanonists – and concedes that there was 'a lot of variation in the Christianity taught and practiced from place to place in early days (or later for that matter)' (Stark 1998: 261). I do not think his concession goes far enough: if there were only forty-two skilled and fluent literates, there could not have been anything like the variety of trajectories proposed by the extracanonists.

But this is a byway in the debate, since the proper conclusion to draw from Hopkins' argument about numbers of literate people in the churches is that (even allowing for higher literacy rates among Christians than Hopkins uses) the Christian movement worldwide by 100 must have been a lot larger than Stark's table would suggest.

Stark's 40% per decade growth figure is too approximate. In his article, Hopkins (1998: 192–194) mentions some instances of Christian communities getting smaller, and rightly points to differing consequences of supposing that Christianity might have grown faster at first, and slower later, or conversely slower at first, and faster later – or finally of its having had fluctuating growth rates. Fluctuating growth rates are the most probable scenario.

A more general difficulty is that changing Stark's baseline a little makes his calculation implausible: with 2,000 Christians in AD 40 and 40% growth per decade, there would have been 12.6 million, not 6.3 million, in 300 – and so on. If a calculation took numbers of Christians and converts given in Acts (1:15; 2:41; 4:4; 21:20) into account, the figures for 40 and 50 would have to be multiplied by at least five or ten – and that, if Christians were 10% of the population in 300, would imply a lower percentage growth rate per decade.

Stark, like Hopkins, Meeks and others, thinks that figures in Acts such as the 3,000 converted on the day of Pentecost (Acts 2:41) are unreliable. It is not evident, however, that he is right to discount them. Accepting them would, after all, solve Hopkins' conundrum about numbers of literate people. What might be called the 'public-relations purpose' of Acts is clear: Luke aimed to put the development of Christian mission in as positive a light as possible – as much as anywhere, at 21:20, where James and the elders speak to Paul of 'how many myriads[1] of converts there are among the Jews, and they are all zealous

---

[1] My translation: NRSV has 'thousands', but *myriades* means 'tens of thousands'.

for the law'.[2] But excessive caution about evidence yields results as bad as excessive credulity, and a non-Christian text shows that Stark's first-century number estimates are unrealistically small.

In 49 something was going on in Rome, about which the biographer Suetonius says, 'Since the Jews constantly made disturbances at the instigation of Chrestus, he [Claudius] expelled them from Rome' (*Claudius* 25.4). The phrase 'at the instigation of Chrestus' seems to misunderstand the fact that the trouble arose over Christianity being preached – the name *Chrēstos* (Chrestus) being pronounced indistinguishably from *Christos* (Christ) (Stevenson 1987: 2 no. 2). This outbreak of unrest, bad enough to prompt an expulsion of Jews from Rome, shows that Christianity had not only arrived there by 49, but attracted support and provoked opposition. If Christianity caused a stir in Rome, it probably did so in other places, too. The impact of the Chrestus riots implies that when Christianity first started in Judea, it probably attracted support more on the 10,000-adherent scale than the 1,000-adherent scale.[3]

Persecution and illegality

Reimposition of government via procurators in Judea from 44 had halted anti-Christian moves, and given the Jerusalem church breathing-space. But in 62 Festus, the Roman procurator, died in office. In the power vacuum before his successor arrived, Herod Agrippa II deposed Joseph Kabi, son of Simon, recently made high priest, and appointed Ananus son of Ananus instead.

Ananus was a supporter of the Sadducees: he convened the Council, brought James before it, accused him of having broken the law, and had him put to death. Josephus, who tells the story (*Jewish Antiquities* 20.196–200), says this action was unpopular with 'those of the inhabitants of the city who were considered the most fair-minded and who were strict in the observance of the Law' (20.201). This may mean that the Pharisees ('strict in the observance of the Law') were angry at seeing the Sadducees taking action against the Nazarenes (= Christians), who

[2] Cf. Stark 1996: 5, where it is argued that if the statement that 'tens of thousands of Jews' converted to Christianity (Acts 21:20) were numerically accurate, Jerusalem (population approximately 20,000?) 'would have been the first Christian city': but Stark has misread the verse, which does not say that the 'many tens of thousands' are all Jerusalem residents.

[3] Here cf. Wright 1992: 444, arguing that Christianity spread fast: 'as religions and philosophies go, it was exceedingly quick off the starting-line'.

were also 'zealous for the law' (Acts 21:20). Paul, too, in 58, had prevented the Council from reaching a conclusion on the accusations against him by defining his case as being about differences in belief between Pharisees and Sadducees (Acts 23:6–10).

Eusebius, in his *Ecclesiastical History* (2.23.3–18), quotes Hegesippus, who makes scribes and Pharisees the leading figures in the events culminating in James's death, thrown from the temple, stoned, and killed by a blow from a fuller's club. Hegesippus' account, however, as well as being later than that of Josephus, seems to misunderstand the situation: it ends with '... and immediately Vespasian began to besiege them' (which in fact happened five years later); and earlier, Hegesippus had said that 'the seven sects among the [Jewish] people' who 'did not believe either in resurrection or the One who will come to reward each according to his deeds'[4] were behind events – but this contradicts his claim that the Pharisees were to blame, since resurrection and the Messiah were core Pharisaic beliefs. This seems to be a case of a second-century writer pinning responsibility (wrongly) on the *Pharisees*, because of anti-Pharisee polemic in the Gospels, while not seeing the implications of the evidence he had that people who did not believe in resurrection were behind the killing.

Before Lucceius Albinus, the new procurator, arrived, he was informed by Ananus' opponents of what had happened. They stressed the illegality of the high priest's even convening the Council without the procurator's permission. Merely holding a meeting might have seemed excusable, but putting James to death was going too far; only a governor of a province could legally inflict capital punishment. Albinus wrote an angry letter to Ananus, and Agrippa prudently fired him as high priest before Albinus could reach Jerusalem.[5]

So the Roman government in 62 was approaching a crossroads. The killing of James had been illegal, and Albinus did not (strictly speaking) condone it, though the consequences for those responsible were not severe. Paul, awaiting trial in Rome (Acts 28:30–31), had met during the process of his case with mixed treatment from Roman judges: at its worst, it was venal (Acts 24:26–27), but at its best, fairminded (Acts 25:12; 26:31–32). It is not clear what happened to Paul next, or exactly when he and Peter were put to death; but in 64 the fire of Rome happened. The unpopular Emperor Nero was suspected of

---

[4] Eusebius, *Ecclesiastical History* 2.23.8–9.
[5] Josephus, *Jewish War* 201–203.

having planned the fire: many could believe him capable of it – and the fact that dangerous fires were common in the crowded conditions of Rome was not enough to silence the conspiracy theorists. The Roman historian Tacitus, writing about 115, describes what he did:

> Neither human help, nor imperial munificence, nor all the modes of placating heaven, could stifle the scandal or dispel the belief that the fire had taken place by order. Therefore, to scotch the rumour, Nero substituted as culprits, and punished with the utmost refinements of cruelty, a class of men, loathed for their vices, whom the crowd style Christians. Christus, the founder of the name, had undergone the death penalty in the reign of Tiberius, by sentence of the procurator Pontius Pilate, and the pernicious superstition was checked for a moment, only to break out once more, not merely in Judaea, the home of the disease, but in the capital itself, where all things horrible or shameful in the world collect and find a vogue. First, then, the confessed members of the sect were arrested; next, on their disclosures, vast numbers were convicted, not so much on the count of arson as for hatred of the human race. And derision accompanied their end: they were covered with wild beasts' skins and torn to death by dogs; or they were fastened on crosses, and when daylight failed, were burned to serve as lamps by night. Nero had offered his gardens for the spectacle, and gave an exhibition in his circus, mixing with the crowd in the costume of a charioteer, or mounted on his chariot. Hence, in spite of a guilt which had earned the most exemplary punishment, there arose a sentiment of pity, due to the impression that they were being sacrificed not for the welfare of the state but to the ferocity of a single man (*Annals* 15.44).

Tacitus' account is interesting. He gives Christianity a bipolar location in Judea and the imperial capital – thus attacking, in addition to Christianity, the tendency to vice and superstition he sees in Rome. His 'vast numbers' of those convicted, though unspecific, fit with the argument above on the scale of Christianity in Rome, and the nature of the Chrestus riots. There had been Christians in Puteoli as well as Rome when Paul arrived in Italy (Acts 28:13–14), and graffiti in Pompeii, destroyed by volcanic eruption in 79, show that before its destruction there were Christians there, too. One of them *may* read

Bovios audi[t] Christianos sevos o[s]ores ('Bovius is a disciple of the Christians, cruel haters')[6] – but the only word which is certain is *Christianos*. If 'cruel haters' should be read, the graffito would bear on the idea Tacitus has of the Christians' real crime (the 'guilt which had earned the most exemplary punishment'): not arson but 'hatred of the human race'.

It remains uncertain on what basis Christianity became and remained unlawful, but the persecution after the fire of Rome is the moment from which illegality must be counted. T. D. Barnes in his article on legislation against the Christians shows that 'no Roman official in the *Acts of the Apostles* regards Christianity as a punishable offence, still less an offence which had been the subject of recent legislation' (1968: 33).[7] The next evidence on the legal status of Christianity comes from Pliny's exchange of letters with Trajan, almost fifty years after the fire of Rome. Pliny in his letter says he is not sure what should be done at trials of those accused of Christianity (but does not seem to think that Christianity might be legal). Later Christian writers, as Barnes argues, have no independent knowledge of what measure first made Christianity illegal. The nearest thing to possibly useful information appears in Tertullian (writing in the 190s; *To the Gentiles* 1.7.8– 9), who calls persecution of Christians the *institutum Neronianum* ('Neronian institution'/'practice started by Nero').

Barnes' cautious article concludes by arguing that Christianity from its inception had always been likely to come to be regarded as illegal: *mos maiorum*, ancestral custom, he notes, 'was the most important source of Roman law, and it was precisely *mos maiorum* in all its aspects that Christians urged men to repudiate' (1968: 50); foreign religion was always to some degree suspicious in Roman eyes. Therefore, as he sees it, no precise enactment was needed before a provincial governor could punish people for being Christians.

There are two difficulties with this. First, it pays too little attention to the contrast in Roman law between Christianity and Judaism: Judaism was legal. Adherence to it was not countered by officials with demands for sacrifice to Roman deities – although for a while after the Third Jewish War the practice of circumcision was illegal. Secondly,

---

[6] *CIL* IV.679; cf. Berry 1995: 34 and plates 9–10; but Berry's book does not note that the graffito may be *anti*-Christian.

[7] This point is decisive against Tertullian's belief (*Apologeticum* 5.2) that the Senate declared Christianity a *religio illicita* ('illegal superstition') as early as the time of Tiberius (14–37). Sordi's arguments to the contrary (1986: 17–20) are not convincing.

Barnes does not go far enough in recognizing the importance of Trajan's letter back to Pliny, in which the emperor (agreeing that Pliny has acted correctly) lays down conditions under which Christians should be punished. From 112 onward, Trajan's letter, published for the reading public along with Pliny's correspondence, was itself a law, since a letter from the emperor giving instructions to an official had the force of law.[8] A. N. Sherwin-White (1966: 711) argues against the theory that the principles of anti-Christian persecution in Trajan's letter to Pliny could be generalized to all provinces and later governors, and speaks of the imperial letter as 'not a law for the whole empire, though it might be followed as an *exemplum* by governors of other provinces as they saw fit':[9] but even on this minimal view, its persuasive force would be considerable.

Pliny's letter and Trajan's reply will be discussed further in chapter 6, but there is still the fifty-year gap before them to deal with, in which Christianity was illegal – Pliny knew that, even if he was not sure of anything else. Barnes' idea that *mos maiorum* is sufficient to explain and define the illegality of Christianity in this period is too nebulous. There is no other foreign religion whose treatment by the Romans parallels the treatment of Christianity closely enough to support the idea that refusal to practise polytheism or participate in public religious ritual was by itself punishable with death, as a transgression against *mos maiorum*.

What may have happened is that Nero or Domitian (or both) issued a decree or decrees making Christianity illegal. Both those emperors after their deaths were subjected by the Senate to *damnatio memoriae* (condemnation of their memory), and their acts were abolished – that is, all laws they had issued were repealed. If Nero had legislated against Christianity, no copy of the decree would exist now: it would have been excised from all official Roman records, and no Christian would have wanted keep a copy of it – particularly after it ceased to be in force.

---

[8] *Digest of Justinian* 1.4.1 makes this clear, quoting Ulpian: 'That which seems right to the emperor has the force of law ... Therefore, whatever the emperor declared in a letter or a *subscriptio* or a decree in a legal decision, or declared outside of the court of law, or ordered in an edict, is clearly law.' Compare Gaius, *Institutes* 1.5: 'A law of the emperor is what the emperor determined in a decree or an edict or by letter. There is no question that it has the force of law, as this emperor received his *imperium* (emperorship) lawfully.'

[9] On non-universal application of rulings in imperial letters, Sherwin-White instances Pliny, *Letters* 65.2, with his commentary on it. Any flexibility, however, existed in tension with the principle that the emperor's word was law.

But after Nero, even though his acts had (formally) been abolished, there was precedent in the courts for persons being convicted of being Christians; and so, rather than ceasing after Nero's death, persecution continued – intermittently, but without regard to any niceties of repeal consequent on *damnatio memoriae*. Suetonius, after all, in his biography of Nero, lists persecuting Christians as one of the good things Nero did.[10] There would be no practical justification, from that perspective, for ceasing to persecute. Evidence for persecution between Nero and Pliny is not plentiful, but it exists: consider what Clement of Rome said (probably about 96) in his first letter to Corinth:

Owing to the sudden and repeated calamities which have befallen us, we consider that our attention has been somewhat delayed in turning to the questions disputed among you, beloved ... (*1 Clement* 1.1).

These 'sudden and repeated calamities' are probably actions taken against Christians in Rome by Domitian in the 90s. Then, under Trajan and about 106, Ignatius, the bishop of Antioch, was brought to Rome to be put to death for being a Christian.[11] Similarly in Jerusalem, Bishop Simon son of Clopas was executed.[12] The trial of R. Eliezer ben Hyrcanus for *mînût* ('heresy', as the Jewish sources put it, meaning Christianity), of which he was correctly acquitted, also probably took place in this period (see ch. 4 below).

Thus from the 60s Christianity was illegal. Paul and Peter died in Rome under Nero. On the Vatican hill, just under a century later, there was a little shrine (the 'Aedicula') built into a pre-existing wall of a family tomb (the 'Red Wall'). This was found in excavations in the 1940s under the high altar of St Peter's basilica (Frend 1996: 271–275), and identified (probably correctly) with the 'trophy' which Caius, a Roman presbyter, spoke of in the 190s in a written dialogue with Proclus the Montanist, reported by Eusebius:

Caius ... speaks as follows of the places where the sacred relics of the apostles in question [Peter and Paul] are deposited: 'I can

---

[10] 'During his reign a great many public abuses were suppressed by the imposition of heavy penalties ... Punishments were also inflicted on the Christians, a sect professing a new and mischievous religious belief' (Nero 16.2).

[11] Ignatius, *Romans* 5.2–3.

[12] Eusebius, *Ecclesiastical History* 3.32.6; cf. Bauckham 1990: 91.

point out the trophies of the apostles, for if you wish to go to the Vatican or to the Ostian Way, you will find the trophies of those who established this church' (*Ecclesiastical History* 2.25.6–7).

The Christian graffiti which cover nearby walls are probably mostly from between 312 (when Christianity was legalized) and 322 (when work began on building the first basilica of St Peter on the site) (Frend 1996: 273). This is the place which, a century after his death, Roman Christians treated as the last resting-place of Peter – though (as Frend notes) it cannot be certain that fellow-Christians at the actual time of Peter's death succeeded in 'securing his body for burial among those of other criminals destined for the Tiber or a common grave' (1996: 274).

A threshold

Christianity was more popular in its earliest decades than academic studies in recent times have wanted to allow. The balance of evidence for its first-century rate of growth tends to point in the same direction as Acts, the biblical text most often suspected of exaggerating the size and importance of the apostles' following. In Jerusalem, where conflict had originally been sharpest, and Jesus, Stephen and two Jameses had died, the Nazarene sect – perhaps surprisingly – came out on Roman government's right side. But Rome proved to be the flashpoint. Perhaps the original introduction of Christianity, which provoked the Chrestus riots, was not planned, or not by Christianity's most import-ant leaders. But Peter's decision to base himself in Rome must have been strategic – possibly based on an observation that Christianity was taking off well there (this was what Tacitus observed – in his case, dis-approvingly).

And Christianity did not avoid imperial attention. Even if Nero did not remember the Chrestus riots, he had Paul's case to prompt him. Acts ends by saying that Paul spent two full years in Rome teaching (and waiting for his court date) (28:30–31), but eventually he must have come up before Nero. Whatever the decision, it is a fair guess that memories of the accusations were in Nero's mind when he decided that the Christians were a suitable group to blame for the fire. The persecution of 64 was a defining moment. Whatever the mechan-ism, Christianity had become unlawful, and was to remain so for two

and a half centuries. But illegality did not make the Christians of
the following generation abandon their efforts to change the religion
of the empire. The story of those years, told in the next chapter, is
one of the further broadening of Christianity's base.

4

The second Christian generation

Another graffito, from the last years of Pompeii, gives a glimpse of Christianity in Italy but away from Rome: but it is deliberately cryptic, which makes it difficult to draw conclusions – and some scholars have even hypothesized that it may not in origin be Christian. It is a palindromic word-square, found on a pillar of the west wall of the Herculaneum wrestling-school, and at Pompeii on the wall of a house (see Frend 1996: 131). The letters are:

R O T A S

O P E R A

T E N E T

A R E P O

S A T O R

The same words are read left to right downwards and right to left upwards. It is more or less possible to 'read' the square as a Latin sentence, though it is an obscure one: 'Arepo [person's name] the sower [*sator*] holds [*tenet*] the wheels [*rotas*] with care [*opera*].' But the point is revealed by rearranging the letters (see overleaf). They yield 'Pater noster', which means 'Our Father' and begins the Latin Lord's Prayer, twice over, with just one letter N, which both the phrases use and so form a cross shape. The letters left over are two As and two Os, which correspond to alpha and omega, the first and last letters of the Greek alphabet. In Revelation 1:8 the Lord says, 'I am the Alpha and the Omega.'

```
                 P
                 A
             A   T   O
                 E
                 R
   P A T E R N O S T E R
                 O
                 S
             O   T   A
                 E
                 R
```

Arguments against the square as a Christian sign are weak;[1] its presence in Pompeii and Herculaneum shows that someone in those two towns by 79 (when they were destroyed) was Christian, familiar with the Lord's Prayer, the cross and the idea of God as Alpha and Omega. All this is to be expected, if Matthew and Luke (which record the Lord's Prayer) were written before 62, and large numbers of Christians were put to death by Nero in Rome in 64. Illegality perhaps turned Christians' minds to indirect ways of communicating their message – Christianity in the last third of the first century did more than merely hold on and go underground. Key texts show the direction things were taking.

Second-generation church order: the *Didache*

Robinson's early dating for the *Didache*, between 40 and 60,[2] has in its favour that there is nothing in the *Didache* which seems to show influence from either the Pauline or Johannine books of the New Testament; and Crossan (1998: 363, cf. 605) places the *Didache* earlier than Matthew and Luke: but on balance the second Christian generation, in the last third of the first century, seems the most probable period for its composition.

The first and shorter part of the *Didache* is an explanation of the Way of Life and the Way of Death. Christianity was called 'The Way'

---

[1] Frend (1996: 131 and n. 53) argues for a Jewish origin, which might be consistent with 'Pater noster', but leaves AO/OA unexplained. ROTAS, 'wheels', as he says, may echo Ezek. 1:16 – but Christians as well as Jews knew Ezekiel.
[2] Robinson 1976: 327. See ch. 1 above.

(e.g. at Acts 19:23). Thus by explaining 'The Way of Life', the *Didache* answers the question 'What is Christianity?' In its first paragraphs (1.1–3), it rehashes and comments on the Sermon on the Mount:

> There are two Ways: a Way of Life and a Way of Death, and the difference between these two Ways is great. The Way of Life is this: 'Thou shalt love first the Lord thy Creator, and secondly thy neighbour as thyself; and thou shalt do nothing to any man that thou wouldst not wish to be done to thyself.' What you may learn from these words is to bless them that curse you, to pray for your enemies, and to fast for your persecutors. For where is the merit in loving only those who return your love? Even the heathens do as much as that. But if you love those who hate you, you will have no enemy ...

This brief opening to the book draws briskly on a range of ideas from the Gospels. It uses Jesus' summary of the law (Mark 12:29), combined with the Golden Rule (Matt. 7:12) expressed negatively ('Do nothing ... that thou wouldst not wish to be done to thyself'), then follows up with a cento on Matthew 5:44–46. The sentence 'But if you love those who hate you, you will have no enemy' brings in a new idea, expanding on Matthew.

In its second part, the *Didache* gives instructions on baptism, the Lord's Prayer, fasting, the Eucharist, Sunday worship and church leadership. Baptism should be carried out after a fast has been kept, and 'in the Name of the Father, and of the Son, and of the Holy Spirit' (7.1). On fasting, the *Didache* says: 'Do not keep the same days for fasting as the hypocrites. Mondays and Thursdays are their days for fasting, so yours should be Wednesdays and Fridays' (8.1). The 'hypocrites' here are the Jews.[3] This is the earliest reference to the idea of Friday as a regular Christian fast-day.

In the section on the Eucharist (9.1 – 10.7), the eucharistic prayer gives thanks first for the wine, then for the bread. When the *Didache* was first discovered, this forced scholars to try to work out where, and in what period of church history, it was ever customary not to begin

---

[3] See to the contrary Crossan 1998: 367: 'a fairly recent split within the *Didache* group itself': but his argument that this 'is the moderate calling the more conservative position hypocrisy' (368) is unsatisfactory – both are fasting two days a week.

with the bread. The most likely explanation is that the *Didache* is so early that there was no settled practice when it was written.

The Eucharist is spoken of as a full meal, rather than a meal eaten in symbolic quantities: the *Didache* says, 'when all have partaken sufficiently, give thanks in these words ...' A change from a full meal to a symbolic meal is suggested in 55 to the Corinthian church by Paul at 1 Corinthians 11:20–34, in response to bad behaviour at eucharistic meals ('one goes hungry and another becomes drunk'). But the reference in the *Didache* to the Eucharist as a full meal does not necessarily date the text to the 50s or earlier: outside Corinth, celebration of the Eucharist as a full meal may have persisted longer.

A liturgy is prescribed, with prayers for the celebrant and responses for the faithful. This is the earliest unambiguous quotation of part of a liturgy for worship in Christian churches, though scholars argue that fragments of liturgy are quoted at many places in the New Testament. The wording given is not compulsory for all celebrants: 'Prophets ... should be free to give thanks as they please.' Prophets, and apostles, are envisaged as itinerant preachers, and the *Didache* gives instructions on how local congregations should provide for them:

> As regards apostles and prophets, according to the Gospel directions this is how you are to act. Every apostle who comes to you should be welcomed as the Lord, but he is not to stay more than a day, or two days if it is really necessary. If he stays for three days, he is a false prophet. And an apostle at his departure should accept nothing but as much provisions as will last him to his next night's lodging. If he asks for money, he is a false prophet (11.3).

A cautious attitude to money is in evidence. Some congregations may have been worried about people who arrived as 'apostles' or 'prophets', then lived on the generosity of the community. The *Didache*, however, also spells out expectations about local leadership:

> You must choose for yourselves bishops and deacons who are worthy of the Lord: men who are humble and not eager for money, but sincere and approved; for they are carrying out the ministry of the prophets and the teachers for you. Do not esteem them lightly, for they take an honourable rank among you with the prophets and teachers (15.2).

This bipartite ministry (bishops/deacons) is close to the pattern in Titus 1:5–9, where there seems to be no distinction between elders/presbyters and overseers/bishops. There began to be a difference not many decades later: in Ignatius of Antioch, writing about 106, bishops rank above presbyters (*Ephesians* 4.1; *Magnesians* 6.1). In the *Didache*, however, the bishops' role is analogous to that of itinerant prophets: a hint that the *Didache* was produced as the church was heading into a second generation and needing to make its new leadership take up the functions of people who had been there in Jesus' own lifetime. It is taken for granted in the *Didache* that bishops and deacons are paid: otherwise, there would be no need to ensure that they were not after the job for the money. At the same time, church hierarchy was being spelt out: note, 'they take an honourable rank among you'.

The geographical background of the *Didache* is uncertain. The argument that it must be from a hilly wheat-growing area (Syria has been canvassed), because it speaks of 'this broken bread, once dispersed over the hills' (9.4), is not compelling. Crossan's reason for thinking that it came from a rural, not urban, background ('the *Didache*'s rhetorical serenity, ungendered equality and striking difference from so many other early Christian texts', 1998: 373) is not satisfactory, because it arises from an unrealistic view of rural life in the Roman empire – not necessarily a life of pastoral calm, still less of gender equality. If the *Didache* came from Syria and was first written in Greek, it would be from an urban background, since most country-dwellers in Syria spoke Aramaic or its dialect Syriac. But Syria is not the only possibility. Other parts of the eastern half of the Roman empire, with early Christian mission but peripheral to the Pauline area – such as Bithynia and Pontus,[4] Galatia or the Nabatean kingdom – would be equally plausible candidates.

Second-generation discipline: Clement of Rome

There is a more metropolitan view of church life in Clement of Rome's letter to the Corinthian church. This letter is important not only for what Clement says, but also as an example of the way letter-

---

[4] Though Paul did not preach in Bithynia (Acts 16:7), Pontus and Bithynia are mentioned at 1 Pet. 1:1, and there were Christians in Pontus by Pliny's time in 112.

writing continued to shape Great Church Christianity. In the New Testament it is easy to see how the Epistle-writers meant their work to draw people together and develop a unified outlook. Clement had the same purpose, as did Ignatius, and the writers of the *Didache* (although it is not a letter), the *Epistle of Barnabas*, the *Epistle to Diognetus*, and (well into the second century) the writer of *2 Clement*. Continual communication by letter, an 'almost obsessional mutual interest and interchange' (as Rowan Williams calls it, 1989: 11), was a hallmark of mainstream Christian congregations. By contrast, Williams notes, there is no evidence for regular and significant contact between congregations established by heterodox teachers.

Eusebius (*Ecclesiastical History* 3.4.8–9) records Clement as third bishop of Rome after Peter and Linus. Clement wrote in Greek, probably in the 90s or earlier,[5] and he refers to people in Corinth who were appointed there to lead the church by 'our apostles' themselves:

> Our apostles also knew through our Lord Jesus Christ that there would be strife for the name of bishop. For this reason, since they had received perfect foreknowledge, they appointed those mentioned above, and afterwards added the codicil that if they should fall asleep, other approved men should succeed to their office. We think therefore that it is not just to remove from office those who were appointed by them, or later on by other respected men with the consent of the whole church, and have held office blamelessly over Christ's flock, with humility, peacefully and disinterestedly, attaining the good opinion of all for a long time (*1 Clement* 44.1–3).

The reason for sending the letter was that long-serving bishops/presbyters in Corinth had been deposed by younger leaders: a coup which was a side-effect of growth:

> All glory and enlargement was [*sic*] given to you, and that which is written was fulfilled: 'My beloved ate and drank, and he was enlarged, and waxed fat, and kicked.' From this arose jealousy and envy, strife and sedition, persecution and disorder, war and captivity. Thus 'the worthless' rose up 'against those who were

---

[5] Ellis (1999: 280 n. 236), agreeing with Robinson, prefers a date as early as 69–70; but his arguments are not conclusive.

in honour', those of no reputation against the renowned, the foolish against the prudent, 'the young against the old'. For this cause righteousness and peace are far removed ... (*1 Clement* 3.1–4).

Clement aims to persuade the Corinthians to reverse their decision to sack the old leadership. Campbell (1994: 213–216), following Robert M. Grant, argues that the event discussed is a move by one bishop to take control from a number of elders (each the leader of a house church), centralizing along the lines of a monarchical episcopacy. But this interpretation cuts a full-blown overthrow of leaders down to a reorganization of elders under a single bishop – whereas surely, if the church had been taken over by an individual, Clement would have said so. Instead, he lists examples to show God on the side of the victims of jealousy, which he says motivates the new leaders, and ends the list by referring to Peter and Paul:

Let us come to those who contended in the days nearest to us; let us take the noble examples of our own generation. Through jealousy and envy the greatest and most righteous pillars of the Church were persecuted and contended unto death. Let us set before our eyes the good apostles: Peter, who because of unrighteous jealousy suffered not one or two but many troubles, and having thus given his testimony went to the glorious place which was his due; and through jealousy and strife Paul showed the way to the prize of endurance: seven times he was in chains, he was exiled, he was stoned, he was a herald both in the East and the West, he gained the noble fame of his faith, he taught righteousness to all the world, and when he had reached the limits of the West he gave his testimony before the rulers, and thus passed from the world and was taken up to the Holy Place – becoming the greatest example of endurance. To these men with their holy lives was gathered a great multitude of the elect, who suffered many assaults and tortures through jealousy and became a very fine example among us (*1 Clement* 5.1 – 6.1).

This is earlier evidence on Peter and Paul and their connection with Rome than the Red Wall and Aedicula: the 'great multitude of the elect' who were martyred would be the 'vast numbers' Tacitus says were killed by Nero. The point of foregrounding Paul is to put his

authority behind Clement's prescriptions: indeed, the whole letter is
structured to resemble Paul's 1 Corinthians, with (for instance) two
chapters (49 – 50) on love, full of parallels to 1 Corinthians 13.
Apparently the letter achieved its aim: it was read aloud in church at
Corinth for decades afterwards,[6] which would hardly have happened if
the Corinthians had not accepted its advice.

Clement is conservative, in church and civic matters. He says that
Jesus 'commanded us to carry out offerings and services, and ordered
that this should not be done randomly or without order, but at set
times and hours. He has himself fixed by his supreme will where and
by whom he wants these things to be carried out ...' (*1 Clement*
40.2–3).

Since Clement argues for fixed times and places for worship,
perhaps the coup had its origins in a group who met apart from Corinthian Christians in general. Clement stresses that no-one should
transgress the 'rule of his own office', saying how the high priest
inspected offerings at the temple (*1 Clement* 41.1–3). Everything must
go through the official leadership. Earlier, he had likened the Christian
life to army service:

> Let us serve as soldiers, brethren, with all earnestness, following
> his blameless commands. Let us consider with what good order,
> habitual readiness and submissiveness those who serve carry out
> the instructions of our leaders. Not all are prefects or tribunes or
> centurions or 'rulers of fifties' and so on, but each in his own
> rank carries out the commands of the King and of his leaders.
> The great cannot exist without the small, nor the small without
> the great; there is a certain mixture among all, and herein lies
> the advantage (*1 Clement* 37.1–4).

Conservatism in Clement extends beyond church hierarchy to
support for government, developing Paul's view that the authorities are
instituted by God (Rom. 13:1). Just before ending his letter, Clement
puts in a long prayer, with intercessions for peace and the well-being of
rulers:

> Give concord and peace to us and to all that dwell on the earth,
> as thou didst give to our fathers who called on thee in holiness

---

[6] Eusebius, *Ecclesiastical History* 4.23.11.

with faith and truth, and grant that we may be obedient to thy almighty and glorious name, and to our rulers and governors upon the earth. Thou, Master, hast given the power of sovereignty to them through thy excellent and inexpressible might, that we may know the glory and honour given to them by thee, and be subject to them, in nothing resisting thy will. And to them, Lord, grant health, peace, concord, firmness that they may administer the government which thou hast given them without offence (*1 Clement* 60.4 – 61.1).

This is a long way in sentiment from Revelation, written at the same period, in which Babylon the Great (= Rome) is apocalyptically overthrown: 'in her[7] was found the blood of prophets and of saints, and of all who have been slaughtered on earth' (Rev. 18:24). Living in Rome, and possibly connected with the imperial palace and the heart of Roman administration (see ch. 7 below), Clement saw reasons to pray for the government.

Second-generation prophecy: Hermas

Unity and hierarchy, for Clement, are the path to righteousness and holiness. In the church at Rome at the same time or a little later,[8] however, another assessment of where Christianity had got to found expression in Hermas' book *The Shepherd*. In one of the visions he describes, Hermas is asked if he has given his book to the elders/presbyters yet; when he says no, he is instructed to make additions, then give it to Clement and Grapte: 'Clement shall then send it to the cities abroad, for that is his duty; and Grapte shall exhort the widows and orphans; but in this city you shall read it yourself with the elders who are in charge of the church' (Visions 4.3).

It is not certain that the Clement to whom Hermas was told to give his book was the Clement who wrote to Corinth – but it probably is he, even if Hermas wrote as late as about 120, where Frend (1984: 132) and Peter Brown (1988: 69), for example, place his work.

Hermas records a series of visions, commands ('Mandates') and parables ('Similitudes'). Concern with the length of time since Christianity began comes out in three visions of the church as an old

[7] NRSV mg. translating the Greek; NRSV main text 'in you'.
[8] Robinson (1976: 319–323) gives the arguments for a date close to *1 Clement*; see also Campbell 1994: 222–224.

woman. In the first, Hermas says, 'I saw before me a white chair of great size made of snow-white wool; and there came a woman, old and clothed in shining garments with a book in her hand, and she sat alone and greeted me, "Hello, Hermas"...' (Visions 2.2). In a later vision (4.1), a young man explains that the old woman is the church, 'because she was created the first of all things'.[9] But the infirmity which forces her to sit in a chair is mysterious until another vision (3.11.1–3), in which the young man says:

> Listen, concerning the forms which you are asking about: why did she appear to you [singular] in the first vision as old and seated on a chair? Because your [plural] spirit is old and already fading away, and has no power through your weakness and double-mindedness. For just as old people, who have no longer any hope of becoming young again, look for nothing but their last sleep, so also you [plural], who have been weakened by the occupations of this life, have given yourselves up to worry, and have not "cast your cares upon the Lord".'

The singular 'you' is Hermas: the plurals speak to Hermas' church in general. Worldly concerns, the vision urges, have made Christianity old and tired. There are Christians 'who are engaged in many and various businesses [and] do not cleave to the people of God' (Similitudes 9.20.1–4): they are figured as a mountain covered in thorns and thistles, and Hermas says that busy lives separate them from the Christian community. Well-off Christians were cutting back involvement in church life.

Hermas is more critical of high-status people than is Clement. But the state the church has reached is not hopeless. The old woman appears standing up in Hermas' second vision of her, and young and beautiful in the third. The point is that repentance will rejuvenate the church: 'they ... who have repented, shall completely recover their youth and be well founded ...' (Visions 13.4).

Hermas spoke about himself, as well as the church. He starts his book by describing an encounter which caused him anxiety:

> He who brought me up sold me to a certain Rhoda at Rome. After many years I made her acquaintance again, and began to

[9] Equating the church with wisdom (Prov. 8:22).

love her as a sister. After some time I saw her bathing in the river Tiber, and gave her my hand and helped her out of the river. When I saw her beauty I reflected in my heart and said: "I should be happy if I had a wife of such beauty and character." This was my only thought, and no other, no, not one' (Visions 1.1–2).

He outlines the situation only sketchily. Brought up as a slave, he was sold to Rhoda, but probably she subsequently freed him, and their paths did not cross until he 'made her acquaintance again'. By saying that he 'began to love her as a sister' he may mean to indicate that they met the second time at church. This is not the only possible reading: Peter Brown (1988: 70) assumes Hermas was still a slave when the bathing incident happened (a view which fits less well with his making Rhoda's acquaintance *again*), and says that 'his Christian owner, when bathing in the Tiber, had once asked Hermas (a mere slave, at that time, whose sexual feelings counted for little) to help her, stark naked, out of the river ...'

Hermas was married, and the bathing incident made it harder for him to keep his love for Rhoda in the brother-sister frame. His feeling that he had entertained an improper thought resulted in a vision in which Rhoda reproached him: 'Yes, it is a sin, and a great one, for the righteous man has righteous designs ...' (Visions 1.1.8). Unhappy with his wife and children, Hermas had come to an internal crisis over Rhoda, but later visions reassure him about his family ('the Lord will heal all the past evil things in your house', 1.3.1), who have not turned to Christianity (2.3.1), and advise him that his wife 'shall in future be [his] sister' (2.2.3) – meaning that she will be converted.

The Rhoda narrative shows Hermas overcoming sexual temptation. Virginity is a connected theme in *The Shepherd*, as a metaphor for Christian virtues. In a long parable, twelve virgins carry stones through a gate, to be used in building a tower: stones not brought through the gate by the virgins cannot be part of the tower (Similitudes 9.2.1 – 4.8). The virgins take brooms, sweep the dirt away from the tower and sprinkle water (9.10.3).[10] It is revealed to Hermas that the virgins are Faith, Temperance, Power, Long-suffering, Simplicity, Guilelessness,

---

[10] Readers of John Bunyan will remember that he quotes 'I have used similitudes' (Hos. 12:10) at the beginning of *Pilgrim's Progress*.

Holiness, Joyfulness, Truth, Understanding, Concord and Love (9.15.1–2). Hermas's concern, as Brown says, is with 'the sins of a sophisticated community that needed not continence but the more sociable and elementary virtue of singleness of heart' (1988: 72).

Clement and Hermas illustrate the issues affecting the church at Rome at the turn of the century. An established leadership, some of whom at Rome (like their deposed counterparts at Corinth) had apparently been in place since the apostles' time,[11] faced new challenges from a larger church, where busy adherents might be reluctant to pull their weight, and deacons could be suspected of financial corruption (Similitudes 9.26.2). Clement's answer for Corinth stressed staying in touch – across the water with Rome, and back in time with the way the apostles set the Corinthian church up. Hermas is more urgent about moving ahead. He is conscious of his own faults – as Brown says, 'few figures in the Early Church are as delightful or as open-hearted as Hermas' (1988: 69) – but confident of the results of repentance, and sure that success and joy will result from a disciplined life.

Second-generation growth: Alexandria and Egypt

At the other end of the Mediterranean, the second largest city in the Roman empire, Alexandria, had contact with Christianity early. The crowd in Jerusalem at Pentecost (Acts 2:10) included Jews from Egypt – and although there were Jews throughout Egypt, Alexandria had by far the largest community. Apollos, whom Priscilla and Aquila updated on Christian baptism at Ephesus in the 50s, was from Alexandria: previously he 'had been instructed in the Way of the Lord' (Acts 18:25) – and a variant reading of this verse in the Codex Bezae adds 'in his own country'. As Birger A. Pearson says, 'this reading, if historically accurate, would presuppose the existence of a Jewish Christian community in Alexandria by the late 40s or early 50s' (Pearson & Goehring 1986: 136). But the Codex Bezae reading is certainly a later addition to the original: it does not prove that there were Christian teachers in Alexandria as early as 50.

Summarizing the then available knowledge about the earliest Christian activity in Alexandria, Pearson concludes (quoting Roberts 1979: 1) that we may never be able to lift the 'obscurity that veils the early

---

[11] Hermas, Visions 3.5.1; cf. Robinson 1976: 321.

history of the church in Egypt' (1986: 156). His pessimism, however, is not total: he points out details in the Greek *Acts of Mark* which apparently correspond with circumstances and places which would fit the context of a Christian preacher arriving in Alexandria and commencing a mission with a focus on the Jewish community. Mendion/ Bendidion, the place where Mark in the *Acts of Mark* goes to a cobbler named Ananias to have a broken sandal-strap fixed, Pearson identifies as in Delta, a Jewish quarter on the north-west side of the city (1986: 152–153). Ananias, hurting his left hand while mending the sandal, shouts, '*Heis theos!*' ('One God!'). He is Jewish, as his name and his exclamation imply, but a hellenized Jew: he does not know the Bible – only the *Iliad, Odyssey* and so on (1986: 140). Another location mentioned in the *Acts of Mark*, Boukolou ('Cow-pastures'), was in the city's other and larger Jewish quarter, in north-east Alexandria near the palace and the beach (1986: 153–154). 'Christian activity in that area and at that time', Pearson concludes, 'would have been carried out under the shadow of the great synagogue, the "glory of Israel"' (1986: 154). That there were some Christians in that area in the first century is probable.

But despite plausible features in the *Acts of Mark*, the work is pious fiction, not history. The details of location show that the writer knew Alexandria, not that he knew anything from local sources about Mark. One of the gaps in his knowledge shows when he says Mark was martyred when Gaius Tiberius Caesar (14–37) was emperor:[12] in fact, Mark was still alive to help Paul during his imprisonment (Philem. 24), probably at Ephesus in 54 or 55. But this mistake does not disprove the Mark–Alexandria connection: Mark was a missionary, who parted company with Paul (Acts 15:37–39) and went to Cyprus with his cousin (Col. 4:10) Barnabas; later he was in Rome (1 Pet. 5:13). As an itinerant evangelist, he might well have visited Alexandria, a quick and easy sea voyage away from Cyprus.

The earliest source linking Mark and Alexandria is Eusebius (early fourth century).[13] In Jerome's Latin version of Eusebius' *Chronicle*, Mark's arrival in Alexandria is plausibly placed in 43 (cf. Pearson & Goehring 1986: 139 and n. 30) In the *Ecclesiastical History*, however,

---

[12] Surianus' Latin translation of the *Acts of Mark* says 'Claudius Nero Caesar', which shows that the translator noticed the difficulty: Nero (54–68) was a better guess. See Pearson & Goehring 1986:142.

[13] Quesnell (1975) argues convincingly that the letter of Clement of Alexandria quoting a secret gospel of Mark, published by Morton Smith in 1973, is a twentieth-century forgery.

Eusebius' reference to Mark carries on into an issue on which he seems confused:

> They say that this Mark was the first to be sent to preach in Egypt the Gospel which he had also put into writing, and was the first to establish churches in Alexandria itself. The number of men and women who were there converted at the first attempt was so great, and their asceticism was so extraordinarily philosophic, that Philo thought it right to describe their conduct and assemblies and meals and all the rest of the manner of their life ... (2.16.1–2).

From somewhere – a lost work of Clement of Alexandria, David T. Runia (1993: 7) suggests – Eusebius has learnt of Mark going to Alexandria: but the reminiscence is combined with a claim that the Therapeutae, a Jewish ascetic community at Alexandria which Philo describes in *On the Contemplative Life*, were Christian. In fact, they were Jewish – as Sozomen, a fifth-century church historian, knew.[14] Runia argues that the misidentification of the Therapeutae (and Philo) reached Eusebius from Clement, along with the Mark story. This may be right, but it is also possible that Eusebius' own reading convinced him that Philo (who lived from about 15 BC to AD 50) and the Therapeutae were Christian. As bishop of Caesarea, he had a library which included books which Origen had brought to Caesarea in 231 – and among them was a set of Philo's works (Runia 1993: 16–22, 212–214). The Christian reading of Philo's *On the Contemplative Life* may be Eusebius' own idea.

The fact that the Mark–Alexandria connection is first attested so late has led modern authors to ask in what form Christianity first reached Alexandria. Walter Bauer (1971: 44–53) argued that the earliest Christianity in Egypt was Gnostic, and that the story of Mark's connection with Alexandria originated in late second-century attempts by Great Church Christians to create a local tradition for themselves. He argues that the situation developed in Alexandria as it did in Edessa, where (orthodox) Palûtians came on the scene later than the

---

[14] At Sozomen, *Ecclesiastical History* 1.12, Therapeutae are viewed as Jews who have converted to Christianity and retained their Jewish practices. Most Christians before AD 50 fell into that category. Pearson & Goehring (1986: 150) hint at an inclusive solution by arguing that the earliest Christians in Alexandria 'can be presumed to have participated in the life of the synagogues' as well as having attended house churches.

Marcionites. On Edessa Bauer was probably right,[15] but there are difficulties transferring the Edessa model to Alexandria – a larger city, with
easier communications to Judea. Roberts (1977: 12–14) observed that
of fourteen Christian papyri of second-century date found in Egypt,
seven are Old Testament, three New Testament (fragments of John,
Matthew and Titus), and four non-biblical (P.Egerton 2; Hermas, *The
Shepherd*; *Gospel of Thomas*; and Irenaeus, *Against Heresies*).[16] Of these,
only the *Thomas* fragment is clearly Gnostic, while Irenaeus' book is
anti-Gnostic. Roberts' finding calls into question Bauer's idea of a
Gnostic main stream in the earliest Egyptian Christianity.

It has often been guessed that the little post-apostolic treatise called
the *Epistle of Barnabas* came out of Alexandrian Christianity, in the late
first or early second century. The Two Ways sermon, preserved in the
Didache, is also in *Barnabas*, though not in the same words. This suggests a comparably early date. In addition, *Barnabas* uses allegorical
exegesis, similar to the method of reading and understanding the Bible
commended by Philo. Allegory, for Philo, is a basic tool. One of many
places where he asserts and applies the method is in *The Worse Attacks
the Better*, at the place where he discusses the 'sevenfold vengeance'
promised to anyone who kills Cain (Gen. 4:15):

> We must make up our minds that all such language is figurative
> and involves deeper meanings ... the irrational side of the soul
> is divided into seven parts, seeing, hearing, smelling, tasting,
> touching, speaking, begetting. Were a man to do away with the
> eighth, mind, which is the ruler of these, and here called Cain,
> he would paralyse the seven also. For they are all strong by
> sharing the strength and vigour of the mind, and with its weak-
> ness they wax feeble ... (167–169).

The writer of *Barnabas* had similar assumptions. He interprets
dietary regulations from the Pentateuch allegorically:

> Moses spoke in the Spirit. He mentions pigs for this reason:
> 'You shall not consort', he means, 'with *people* who are like
> pigs,' that is to say, who, when they have plenty, forget the
> Lord, but when they are in want they recognise the Lord, just as

[15] See Introduction, above, p. 18.
[16] For a more recent listing of papyri see Comfort & Barrett 1999.

the pig when it eats does not know its master, but when it is
hungry it cries out, and after receiving food is again silent
(10.2–3).

This technique is flexible. The *Barnabas* writer uses it broadly in
giving ethical applications to food laws. The prohibition on eating the
hyena is explained as being about avoidance of adultery – and as for
the weasel:

> Moses abhors the weasel rightly. 'Thou shalt not', he says,
> 'become the kind of person that we hear of committing law-
> lessness in their mouths because of their impurity; nor shalt
> thou cleave to impure women who commit lawlessness in their
> mouths.' For this animal gives birth with its mouth (10.8).

The ban on eating the weasel is read as forbidding oral sex.

Philo would have thought this writer an apt pupil. The possibility
that *Barnabas* was written by someone who had been in Alexandria, or
at least read Philo, is strong. But the case cannot be proved on style of
biblical teaching alone. Paul read the Bible allegorically, too: at 1 Corinthians 9:9–10 he expounds 'You shall not muzzle an ox while it is
treading out the grain' as meaning that an apostle is entitled to receive
payment. Allegorical exegesis had a track record in Christian understanding before *Barnabas*, and Alexandria was not the only place the
technique could be learnt.

At two places in *Barnabas* there are indications of date. The letter
was written after 70, since it refers directly to the First Jewish War and
the destruction of the temple: some date it close to the Bar-Kochva
rebellion in the 130s, on the basis of a reference to rebuilding the
temple:

> 'And furthermore he says again [Is. 49:17], 'Behold, those who
> destroyed this temple shall themselves rebuild it.' This is hap-
> pening. For owing to the war it was destroyed by the enemy;
> and now the servants of the enemy are themselves going to
> rebuild it (16.3–4).

But even though, at the time of the Bar-Kochva rebellion, rebuilding momentarily seemed possible, the reference to 'the servants of
the enemy' rebuilding the temple remains obscure. The Roman

government, before or after the war, was never going to sponsor reconstruction. More likely *Barnabas* is, as usual, not speaking literally: referring to Gentiles (Roman subjects, so 'servants of the enemy') building a *spiritual* temple, in a way he goes on to detail:

> Now give heed, in order that the Temple of the Lord may be built gloriously. Learn in what way. When we received the remission of sins, and put our hope on the Name, we became new, being created again from the beginning; therefore God truly dwells in us, in the habitation in which we are (16.8).

The second possible dating-point in *Barnabas* is even more difficult. He warns that the 'last stumbling-block' is at hand, quoting Daniel 7.24:

> ... the prophet also says this: 'Ten kingdoms shall reign upon the earth and there shall rise after them a little king, who shall subdue three of the kings under one' (4.4).

The writer of *Barnabas* may have the eleventh Roman emperor in mind as the 'little king' – but which was the eleventh? Vespasian (emperor 69–79) came to power at the end of a year in which three short-lived emperors seized power after the death of Nero (54–68): so the 'three kings' *might* be Galba, Otho and Vitellius. Alternatively, 'three kings under one' *might* refer to Vespasian and his sons Titus and Domitian, who were associated with their father as subordinate rulers in his lifetime. If the writer thought Daniel pointed to either of these sets of three kings, it would indicate that *Barnabas* was written in the 70s (soon after the temple was destroyed; see J. A. T. Robinson 1976: 313–319). But in the next century when the Roman biographer Suetonius wrote his *Twelve Caesars*, beginning with Julius Caesar (adoptive father of Augustus, the first emperor), Vespasian was tenth, not eleventh, in his sequence.[17] Suetonius' later idea of who counted was not binding on the writer of *Barnabas*: he might have counted Mark Antony after Julius Caesar and before Augustus, which would make Vespasian eleventh.

Despite the difficulty, I think *Barnabas* was probably written in the

[17] Julius Caesar, Augustus, Tiberius, Caius Caligula, Claudius, Nero, Galba, Otho, Vitellius, Vespasian, Titus, Domitian.

70s, either in Alexandria, or at least by someone familiar with the kind of biblical interpretation best known there. The church situation *Barnabas* implies fits in with the picture in the *Didache* of travelling preachers and their relations with local churches: 'You shall love "as the apple of your eye" all who speak to you the word of the Lord', says the writer (19.9) – with no mention of bishops or presbyters. This points towards the late first century. The socially mixed character of congregations found in the Pauline context seems also to be reflected – and placed in an egalitarian context – when the writer says:

> I beseech those of you who are in high positions, if you will receive any advice from my goodwill – have among yourselves those to whom you may do good: do not omit this ... I beseech you again and again: be good lawgivers to each other, remain faithful advisers to each other, remove all hypocrisy from among you (21.2–4).

The second generation in Jerusalem and the Jewish churches

Five years of tension in Jerusalem and Judea followed the illegal execution of James in 62. In 66, seeing war coming, the Jerusalem church (Eusebius says) moved out of the city, north-east across the Jordan to Pella:

> The people of the church in Jerusalem were commanded by an oracle given by revelation before the war to those in the city who were worthy of it, to depart and dwell in one of the cities of Peraea which they called Pella. To it those who believed on Christ migrated from Jerusalem, so that when the holy men had completely deserted the royal metropolis of the Jews and the whole land of Judaea, the judgement of God might at last come upon them for so many lawless acts against Christ and his apostles, and wipe out that generation of sacrilegious persons from the human race (*Ecclesiatical History* 3.5.3).

The historicity of the Pella migration has been doubted, but it fits in with the fact that the Jerusalem church apparently ceased to be influential with other churches from this time. Frend (1984: 120) argues that Jerusalem Christians 'suffered the fate of many historical moderates' – the initiative passing out of their hands.

Judaism after 70, instead of being weakened by not having the temple, underwent a rebirth which took the synagogues forward stronger than before. An important factor in its development was Jamnia: Rabbi Johanan ben Zakkai, who escaped from Jerusalem before or during the siege (hidden in a coffin, according to a later account)[18] established with others a school, where interpretation of the Bible continued to develop, along lines pioneered by the Pharisees. The teachers' greatest concern was to define how the law ought to be applied in daily life – a key task, now that the temple, where worship had been based on exact performance of biblically prescribed ritual, no longer existed. Rabbinic teachers over the following generations up to the time of the Mishnah (c. 200) included some from priestly and aristocratic backgrounds – including the school's second leader Rabbi Gamaliel II, son of Simeon ben Gamaliel (and grandson of the Gamaliel who taught Paul), and Rabbi Eliezer ben Hyrcanus – but others from poor families. Rabbi Aqiba ben Joseph, born about 40, kept up a scholar's life by living on his wife's earnings. His teacher Nahum of Gimso had taught Aqiba that every letter and tittle of the law was of direct significance, so that a meaning must be deduced from it. Allegory was not on the agenda: in Jamnia teaching, the style of biblical interpretation favoured by Philo (and the Christians he influenced) was left behind.

For Judean rural Christianity, the Pella migration and the fall of Jerusalem were less of a watershed. Bauckham argues for activity through the first century in the Judean countryside, with relatives of Jesus taking an important role. Symeon son of Clopas, second bishop of Jerusalem (after James), was a cousin of Jesus, according to Eusebius (*Ecclesiastical History* 3.11; 4.22.4; cf. Bauckham 1990: 79–90); and others in Eusebius' list may also have been members of Jesus' family, on the hypothesis that twelve of the fifteen names preserved (more 'bishops' of Jerusalem than necessary for the years up to 135) are actually names of twelve elders who presided over the Jerusalem church together with James in the first generation (1990: 70–79).

Outside Jerusalem, relatives of Jesus lived in Nazareth and Kokhaba, and were itinerant Christian preachers, according to a third-century letter by Julius Africanus, quoted in Eusebius (*Ecclesiastical History* 1.7.14), about the genealogies of Jesus in the Gospels:

A few who were careful ... gloried in the preservation of the

---

[18] *The Fathers According to Rabbi Nathan* A 4, 6.

memory of their good birth; among these were those mentioned above, called *desposynoi*, because of their relation to the family of the Saviour, and from the Jewish villages of Nazareth and Kokhaba they travelled around the rest of the land and gave expositions of the genealogy of their descent (mentioned above), and from the book of Chronicles, wherever they went.

Africanus appears to be talking about the first Christian generation. His information may be reliable, though it is worth thinking about the place-names – Kokhaba recalls the Star (*kôkāb*) of Jacob (Num. 24:17), while Nazareth 'was probably related' (Bauckham notes), 'by means of the pesher-like pun, to the prophecy of the messianic branch (*nēṣer*) from the roots of Jesse' (Is. 11:1) (Baukham 1990: 64; see 62–66). Did members of Jesus' family *choose* to live in villages called 'Star' and 'Branch', as Bauckham concludes (since coincidence seems un-likely), or did a later writer – who felt it *should* have been so – make the story up?

Separation between Christianity and Judaism

It may be that Judaism and Christianity, in a hostile relationship in some quarters, coexisted with tolerance elsewhere. There is one source which can perhaps be taken as implying that before the des-truction of the temple, Christian sensibilities about Sunday were being taken into account in the development of thought about Jewish reli-gious observance. A third-century rabbi, asked a question about fast-days, said: 'On the eve of the Sabbath they did not fast, out of respect for the Sabbath; still less [did they fast] on the Sabbath itself. Why did they not fast on the day after the Sabbath? R. Yohanan says, "Because of the *Notzrim* [Nazarenes]"' (Babylonian Talmud *Ta'anit* 27b).

Martinus C. de Boer (1998: 247–248), following Ray A. Pritz, notes that since Friday and Saturday are avoided as fast days out of respect, consistency would dictate that avoiding Sunday indicated respect for Sunday, or for Christian sensitivities about Sunday. This is a possible way of understanding the rabbi's answer, but Reuven Kimel-man (1981: 241–243) argues that R. Yohanan meant that those who decided what days of the week were suitable for fasting wanted to avoid giving religious significance of any kind to Sunday, 'because of the Nazarenes'. By the time of the *Didache*, Christians, for their part, were being told to avoid characteristic Jewish fast-days.

After 70, the split was clear. R. Ishmael (early second century) said, 'The *Notzri* day' [Sunday] 'is forbidden for ever' (Babylonian Talmud *Avodah Zarah* 6a). At the request of R. Gamaliel II as Patriarch in Jamnia, Samuel the Small composed a prayer called the 'Benediction against the Heretics' (*birkat ha-mînîm*) to be added as the Twelfth Benediction of the Tefillah:[19] the names of persons involved fix the time of this move between 80 and 100. This prayer seems to be behind Justin's assertions in the mid-second century that the Jews curse Christ in the synagogues.[20] Until the discovery of a huge deposit of medieval Jewish manuscripts in the Cairo Genizah in the late nineteenth century, it was not known how the Benediction against the Heretics was worded, partly because rabbinic tradition prohibited writing prayers down:[21] they were recited from memory. The Cairo Genizah text, however, reads:

> For the apostates let there be no hope, and may the arrogant kingdom be uprooted speedily in our days, and may the Nazarenes (*Notzrim*) and the heretics (*mînîm*) perish as in a moment and be blotted out of the Book of Life, and not be inscribed with the righteous. Blessed art thou, O Lord, who humblest the arrogant (Schechter 1998: 657, 659).

Some argue that *Notzrim* is an addition, and the earliest form of the prayer cursed only *mînîm*.[22] Jack T. Sanders (1993: 59) argues that the effect of the Benediction against the Heretics was (only) to bar Christians from serving as precentors (whose duties included saying the Benedictions) in synagogues. His view is partly persuasive: in the third and fourth centuries Christian leaders including Origen, Jerome and John Chrysostom took it upon themselves to urge Christians not to go to synagogue or join in Jewish festivals.[23] Not all Christians were either excluded from synagogues or disinclined to go there.

Kimelman (1981: 228–232) makes the point that *mînîm* must be Jewish heretics, conceding that Christians were the most significant group of these (cf. Sanders 1993: 64), but arguing that Gentile

[19] Babylonian Talmud *Berakoth* 28b–29a; cf. Horbury 1998: 67, and de Boer 1998: 251.

[20] Justin, *Dialogue with Trypho* 137, mentioning prayers in the synagogue. The point that the Jews curse Christ is made repeatedly in the dialogue (16, 47, 93, 95, 96, 108, 123, 133).

[21] See Safrai 1987: 1: 45–49, discussing Tosefta *Shabbat* 13.4.

[22] See for instance Kimelman 1981: 233, noting apparent redundancy in referring to both *Notzrim* and *mînîm* – but hendiadys is common in the Bible.

[23] Evidence summarized at Kimelman 1981: 239–240.

Christians were not the target of the Benediction. This is a possible reading from the Jewish side: on the other side, by the later first century, the distinction between Jewish and Gentile Christians was becoming less important. Wright (1992: 164) thinks Christians were not the main issue, arguing that 'the "heretics" in view included many groups of whom the Christians were only one': but evidence is thin for other late first-century Jewish groups so heretical that rabbis would want to pray for them to be excluded from the Book of Life. Justin was probably right to believe that the rabbis would think worse of him for being a Christian than just for being a Samaritan. As several scholars say, it is possible that not all synagogues used the added Benediction (or not immediately).[24] Hard words, however, were used on both sides in these years: Revelation, written in the 90s, refers to 'the synagogue of Satan, who say they are Jews and are not, but are lying' (3:9).

After the fall of the temple, being associated with Christians could be embarrassing, certainly for a rabbi. When R. Eliezer ben Hyrcanus was arrested on suspicion of Christianity, he got the charge dismissed, but went on feeling bad:

> R. Eliezer was once arrested because of *mînût*, and the governor took him and made him ascend a dais to be tried. He said to him, 'Rabbi, can a great man like yourself occupy himself with those idle matters?'
>
> He answered, 'Faithful is the judge concerning me.'
>
> He [the governor] thought that he was alluding to him, but in fact he said it with reference to God. He thereupon said to him, 'Since I have been acknowledged right by you, I too have been thinking, and say, "Is it possible that these academies should go astray with such idle matters?" You are consequently acquitted and free.'
>
> After R. Eliezer had left the dais, he was sorely grieved at having been arrested because of *mînût*. His disciples visited him

---

[24] See Wright 1992: 165 n. 68, arguing that Ignatius (*Magnesians* 8.1; 10.3; *Philadelphians* 6.1) would not have advised against associating with Jews in the terms he did 'if a binding anti-Christian decree had been in force in the synagogue community ... for twenty or thirty years'. Ignatius' warnings, however, are mainly against 'practising' or 'living according to' Judaism, and attending a synagogue service did not amount to that (non-Jews, who by definition were not 'practising Judaism', were allowed to be present). He does advise (*Magnesians* 10.3) against listening to Jewish preachers, who were most easily found in synagogues; but it is not always redundant to advise someone against going somewhere where (in theory) he or she would not be admitted.

to console him, but he would not accept [their words of comfort].

R. Aqiba visited him and said to him, 'Rabbi, perhaps one of the *mînîm* expounded something in your presence which was acceptable to you.'

He answered, 'By heaven, you have reminded me! Once I was walking up the main street of Sepphoris when there came towards me a man named Jacob of Kephar Sikhnaya who told me something in the name of *Yesû ben Pndr'* which pleased me, namely, "It is written in your Torah, *You shall not bring the hire of a harlot, or the wages of a dog, into the house of the Lord your God in payment for any vow* [Deut. 23:18]. What is to be done with them?" I told him that they were prohibited [for every use]. He said to me, "They are prohibited as an offering, but is it permissible to destroy them?" I retorted, "In that case, what is to be done with them?" He said to me, "Let bath-houses and privies be made with them." I exclaimed, "You have said an excellent thing," and the law [not to listen to the words of a *mîn*] escaped my memory at the time. When he saw that I acknowledged his words, he added, "Thus said *Yesû ben Pndr'*: 'From filth they came and on filth they should be expended: as it is said, *From the hire of a harlot she gathered them, and to the hire of a harlot they shall return* [Mic. 1:7]'"' (*Ecclesiastes Rabbah* 1.8.3).[25]

Yesû ben Pndr' is 'Jesus son of Panthera' – the patronymic referring to the anti-Christian story (known from Celsus) that Jesus' father was a Roman centurion called Panthera.[26] In the Babylonian Talmud parallel, Jesus is called *Yesû han-Notzri*, 'Jesus the Nazarene'. Kephar Sikhnaya/Sikhnin is modern Sakhnin, 4 miles (6 km) from Kokhaba, where (according to Julius Africanus) Jesus' relatives lived: it is not surprising that a Christian teacher should be from there.[27]

This interesting exchange shows a Christian teacher debating the law with a rabbi in terms like those of the Jamnia tradition. Eliezer and Aqiba seem content with Jacob's legal argument – the problem is his

[25] Cf. parallels at Tosefta *Hullin* 2.24 and Babylonian Talmud *Avodah Zarah* 16b–17a; cf. also Bauckham 1990: 109–111.

[26] Origen, *Against Celsus* 1.32: cf. Bauckham 1990: 114.

[27] Bauckham (1990: 116) identifies Jacob of Sikhnin as probably James, the grandson of Jude, Jesus' brother: but Jacob/James was such a common name that there is no certainty.

Christianity, and the point of the story is not to associate with Christians, however attractive what they have to offer may seem. The principle enunciated in a treatise in the mid-third century Tosefta is that they are equivalent to Samaritans (with whom Jews do not associate, John 4:9), and worse than Gentiles:

> Flesh which is found in the hand of a Gentile is allowed for use; in the hand of a *mîn* it is forbidden for use. That which comes from a house of idolatry, lo, this is the flesh of sacrifices of the dead, because they say, 'slaughtering by a *mîn* is idolatry, their bread is Samaritan bread, their wine is wine offered [to idols], their fruits are not tithed, their books are books of witchcraft, and their sons are bastards. One does not sell to them, or receive from them, or take from them, or give to them; one does not teach their sons trades, and one does not obtain healing from them, either healing of property or healing of life' (Tosefta *Hullin* 2.20–21).

A story with the same point as the R. Eliezer/Jacob of Kephar Sikhnaya story, but more radically expressed, attaches itself to Jacob's name immediately after this passage in the Tosefta, and again has parallels in *Ecclesiastes Rabbah* (1.8.3) and Babylonian Talmud *Avodah Zarah* (27b):

> The case of R. Eleazar ben Dama, whom a serpent bit. There came in Jacob, a man of Kephar Sama, to cure him in the name of *Yesuaʿ ben Pntrʾ*, but R. Ishmael would not allow it. He said, 'You are not permitted, Ben Dama.' He said, 'I will bring you a proof that he may heal me.' But he had not finished bringing a proof when he died. R. Ishmael said, 'Happy are you, Ben Dama, for you have departed in peace, and have not broken through the ordinances of the wise; for upon every one who breaks through the fence of the wise, punishment comes at last, as it is written, *Whoever breaks through a fence, a serpent shall bite him* [Eccles: 10.8]' (Tosefta *Hullin* 2.22–23).

In the Talmud parallel, Jacob is called 'the *mîn* of Kephar Sikhnaya'. In Bauckham's judgment (1990: 117–121), Jacob of Kephar Sama may not be the same person as Jacob of Sikhnin – and he notes that others besides Christians used Jesus' name in healing – but even if his caution is justified, the point about the unacceptability of healing in the name of Jesus remains. Whether offering to perform miraculous healing as Jesus did, or representing Jesus as discussing the law point by point in a quasi-rabbinical way, Christian teachers in the wake of the destruction of the temple were subject to the exclusion implicit in the Benediction against the Heretics.

Bar-Kochva at the time of his rebellion (132–35) went further than exclusion. Justin, twenty years or so after the event, accuses him of anti-Christian persecution:

> For in the Jewish war which lately raged, Barcochba, the leader of the revolt of the Jews, gave orders that Christians alone should be led to cruel punishments, unless they would deny Jesus Christ and utter blasphemy (*First Apologia* 31).

But Jewish Christians in this war had even more to fear from the Romans. After the Roman victory, and the law banning Jews from entering the city and district of Jerusalem, Eusebius begins a new sequence of Gentile bishops:

> Thus when the city came to be bereft of the nation of the Jews, and its ancient inhabitants had completely perished, it was colonized by foreigners, and the Roman city which afterwards arose changed its name, and, in honour of the reigning emperor Aelius Hadrianus, was called Aelia. The church, too, in it was composed of Gentiles, and after the Jewish bishops the first who was appointed to minister to those there was Marcus (*Ecclesiastical History* 4.6.4).

So the Jewish Jerusalem church, already reduced in importance since the Pella migration, ceased to exist.

Nor was that all. Hadrian's campaign in Judea was ruthless. His destruction of 985 villages and killing of 580,000 men make him arguably the worst perpetrator of genocide against Jews before Hitler: 'nearly the whole of Judaea was made desolate', says Dio Cassius (69.13.3 – 14.2). Probably Hadrian and his soldiers made no distinction between Christian and non-Christian Jews (although Bar-Kochva had) in the final campaign – Christianity was illegal in any case, and punishable under Roman law by death, so that no Jewish Christian caught by the advancing Roman army would escape by appealing to religion. The province of Judea was renamed Syria Palaestina – Palestine, after the Philistines instead of the Jews. The Jewish, Aramaic-speaking church of Judea was, on the most optimistic guess, severely reduced in numbers and strength.

This change had the effect of reinforcing Christianity's move to become a cosmopolitan religion. During the second century, the writer of *To Diognetus* was to comment that Christians live in any Greek or foreign city, and 'conform to ordinary local usage in their clothing, diet and other habits' (5).[28] Holding on to Jesus' message and adapting its implementation to up-to-date conditions was a task whose complexity continued to increase. Geographically widespread and socially mixed churches had generated the diverse needs which were behind Clement's and Hermas's books. At the same time, broad engagement with the non-Christian world resulted in new challenges to Christians' abilities to explain and persuade. In Hadrian's reign (117–38) Christian intellectuals made the first efforts at ecclesiastical diplomacy, offering books about Christianity to the emperor. At the same time, new stories were being told about the apostles.

Chapter 5 will discuss what the new outpouring of writing from the second century onwards shows about mission and church growth.

---

[28] Those who originally ruled on what non-Jewish converts had to do (Acts 15:19–29) might have been surprised at this acceptance of ordinary Gentile foods.

5

Second- and third-century Christianity: another source debate

Memories and apologia

Polycarp, who died in the 150's aged eighty-six (a Christian all his life), was old enough to remember people who had met Jesus himself. Irenaeus, copied by Eusebius, records that Polycarp had been appointed bishop of Smyrna 'by apostles' – and indeed it was Polycarp who told the story (whether he was there or not) of John the apostle going to the bath-house at Ephesus for a bath, but leaving hurriedly when he saw Cerinthus, saying, 'Let us flee in case the bath-house falls down, since Cerinthus, the enemy of the truth, is in it.'[1] That incident would perhaps have happened during the second Christian generation, in the 80s or 90s.

Polycarp's John and Cerinthus story, with controversy to the fore, is a corrective against a view of the apostolic age that would differentiate it from everything which followed. Right from the second century, Christians began to think there had been something special and irreplaceable about the time when people who had been alive in Jesus' lifetime were still around. They wanted to look back to a better time. In the second half of the second century, a writer called Hegesippus, in his *Five Memoirs of the Acts of the Church*, lamented the loss of the church's virginity, which had been secure as long as the apostles, its original guardians, lived – but after they died (says

[1] Irenaeus, *Against Heresies* 3.3.4; Eusebius, *Ecclesiastical History* 3.26.1 and 4.14.3–6.

93

Hegesippus) the pure Christian message had been polluted by false teachers.[2]

In fact, despite Hegesippus' appeal to nostalgia, there had always been disagreements between Christian teachers. Robert L. Wilken (1971: 158) warns against privileging Christianity's earliest days over against what came later: 'The apostolic age is a creation of the Christian imagination. There never was a Golden Age when the church was whole, perfect, pure – virginal. The faith was not purer, the Christians were not braver, the church not one and undivided.'

So no great threshold is crossed with the turn of the first and second centuries. As before, there is little to be learnt from archaeological evid-ence, and less the earlier one goes. Written texts are the most import-ant sources. Non-Christian and anti-Christian books are more numerous and more important than in the first years: even Suetonius and Tacitus, whose interesting snippets about first-century Christianity are discussed above, actually wrote after 100; and with Christianity growing and making more impact, second-century non-Christians found more occasion to mention it.

The growth of anti-Christian polemic as a sub-section of the Greco-Roman literary scene was provoked in part by second-century Christian apologetic[3] writing. In some New Testament texts there is concern to attract readers to Christianity – John, for instance, says he wrote his Gospel 'so that you may come to believe' (20:31) – but the surviving Christian literature of the later first century (*Didache*, Clement, Hermas, *Barnabas* and the rest) is nearly all directed, like the New Testament Epistles, to people who are Christians already. In the second century, a number of Christian writers used their literary talents in evangelism. The writer of *To Diognetus*, mentioned at the end of the last chapter, addressed his treatise to a social superior ('my lord Diognetus...')[4] – but Diognetus was a minnow in the big picture. Others went right to the top. Two Christians, Quadratus and Aristides, had each written a book to defend and commend Christianity. When the Emperor Hadrian visited Athens in 124, they presented him with

---

[2] Eusebius, *Ecclesiastical History* 3.32.7–8 and 4.22.1–9; on the date of Hegesippus' work, Eusebius, *Ecclesiastical History* 4.11.7.

[3] Greek *apologia* means primarily 'a speech for the defence in a trial', and generally 'a written explanation/justification of a course of action'. Hence an 'apologia' for Christianity, or 'Christian apologetic writing', is not an 'apology' (in the sense of an expression of contrition) but an explanation of the truth and value of Christianity.

[4] *To Diognetus* 1. Luke's Theophilus (Luke 1:1–3) is addressed in a similarly respectful way.

copies. And the addressee was not the only target – each author also meant his book for the reading public (Eusebius, *Ecclesiastical History* 4.3.1–3).

Quadratus, described in Jerome's Latin translation of Eusebius' *Chronicle* as a disciple of the apostles, was presumably old by 124 – but little else is known of him, and only a few lines of his *Apologia* survive, quoted by Eusebius, arguing that Jesus' miracles had long-lasting results. Aristides' *Apologia*, on the other hand, long believed lost, is preserved in two versions: a Syriac translation, published by J. Rendel Harris in 1893, and a Greek version, not identical to the Syriac, included (but not ascribed to Aristides) as a Christian sermon in *Barlaam and Ioasaph*, a story adapted by John Damascene, bishop of Damascus in Muslim-ruled eighth-century Syria. *Barlaam and Ioasaph* itself is a lightly christianized retelling of the tale – by then over a thousand years old – of the Buddha and his journey in search of enlightenment (see Grant 1988: 35–39). The anonymous embedding of Aristides' work in this story illustrates both how texts from the early church could be lost without trace, and how texts might be copied and handed on in unexpected ways.

Apologetic and mission

As the second and third centuries progressed, a steady stream of apologetic writers came forward: in Greek, Justin Martyr, Athenagoras, Tatian, Apollinaris of Hierapolis, Melito of Sardis, Theophilus[5] and, above all, Origen; in Latin, Tertullian, Minucius Felix, Cyprian and Arnobius.[6] It remains unclear how much impact they made: 'So far from people agreeing with our writings,' said Tertullian, 'no-one even reads them unless he is a Christian already' (*The Testimony of the Soul* 1.4). Modern scholars are inclined to agree that Christian literature circulated mostly among Christians, not reaching many readers in the majority culture. This view may not be wholly justified – Averil Cameron (see below) mentions an important reservation – but it probably is true that Christianity travelled mostly along lines defined by personal networks. That dynamic is illustrated in Minucius Felix's *Octavius*, which is cast as the record of a conversation about religion between a Christian and a non-Christian who are friends; as they walk

[5] On these writers see Young 1999.
[6] On Tertullian, Minucius Felix and Cyprian see Price 1999; on Arnobius, Simmons 1995.

along the beach, the Christian explains the drawbacks of polytheism and advantages of Christianity (2.4 – 4.6). But personal networks were not always important. Justin, in his *Dialogue with Trypho* (3.1 – 8.1), speaking about his younger days, recalls a moment of dissatisfaction in his search for a philosophy to live by, at which time a mysterious old man mentioned Christianity to him and put him on the path to conversion.

Christian apologetic and anti-Christian literature, then, represent the to and fro of argument in the public sphere. Disparagement of Christian literature was part of the game. In fact, the Bible and the works of Christian writers were not stylistically plain or poor, as their critics claimed. Eusebius, in the fourth century, distinguishing the writer of Revelation from the writer of the Gospel and Epistles of John, would say that the Gospel and Epistles were 'written in faultless Greek' and showed 'the greatest literary skill in expression, reasoning and the constructions in which they are expressed' (*Ecclesiastical History* 7.25.25). Just as importantly, Paul, despite disclaimers (e.g. 1 Cor. 2:1), was a well-educated writer of great rhetorical ability – and later authors were as concerned to convince as he had been. And yet Christians did not usually defend the literary quality of the Bible. Cameron (1991: 33–36) notes how it suited both sides to claim that Christians communicated in 'the language of fishermen'. She casts doubt on the idea that Christian apologists in the second and third centuries wrote only for the converted (1991: 44–45): as she sees it, the debate was no mere shadow.

It is worth remembering that there is a bias in what is now available: Christians won the long-term argument, and part of the result, from the fourth and fifth centuries, was that production and storage of books came overwhelmingly into Christian hands. That situation lasted throughout the Middle Ages, until the invention of movable metal type radically altered the factors bearing on whether a book would survive. Monks made copies (which would last a century or so, if they were scrolls, or as much as several hundred years if they were codices), and they had no motive to copy a work like Celsus' *True Word* or Porphyry's *Against the Christians*. Even so, the intellectual world of medieval Europe did not suppress all non-Christian texts: classical literature – Virgil and Terence, Sallust and Cicero (in the West), Homer, Greek tragedy and comedy, and Plato (in the East) – remained basic to the education system.

Because of medieval Europe's selection of the books it thought it needed, a good deal of writing against heretics is preserved, while the texts which provoked it are gone. Thus Marcion, whose sect in the middle of the second century had a vigorous programme of mission, is known mostly from Justin's and Tertullian's attacks on his version of Christianity; and Justin's pupil Tatian is known from denunciations of his opinions, while the *Diatessaron*, the book he wrote in Syriac combining the four Gospels, is lost, except for quotations. But other Christians, with the same zeal which motivated Hegesippus to travel the Roman world identifying the authentic successors to the apostles, took to writing apologetic literature aimed not only at converting polytheists and Jews to Christianity, but also at defending Christianity against heresy.

Justin Martyr, put to death in the 150s, was an apologist, and the doyen of heresiologists. Based in Rome, he addressed his *First Apologia* and *Second Apologia* to Antoninus Pius (138–61), and also wrote the *Dialogue with Trypho*, a version of a debate with a Jewish teacher. A Greek-speaker from Flavia Neapolis (Nablus/Shechem), Justin calls himself a Samaritan[7] – a background which may account for his knowledge of Simon Magus' sect. Equally important with the Jews as a target, however, was Marcion – still alive when Justin wrote (*First Apologia* 1.26). The last thing he wanted was to win converts to Christianity, only to have them join the Marcionites. Later apologists, too, might combine the project of defending Christianity with a concern to focus attention on what was, and was not, authentic. Thus Tertullian, from the 190s, wrote both apologetic (including his *Apologeticum*) and anti-heretical books (including *Against Marcion* and *Against the Valentinians*).

Other writers made opposition against heresy their only task. Irenaeus of Lyons, in the last quarter of the second century, wrote *An Examination and Refutation of 'Knowledge' Falsely So Called* (aimed against Gnosticism, a book soon referred to simply as *Against Heresies*), while in the next generation Hippolytus, at Rome, wrote a *Refutation of all Heresies*. Hippolytus' book reflected an apologetic agenda by going back beyond variant Christian systems to include Jewish and Greek theories – a decision by the author which makes the book into an important source today for the beliefs of little-attested Greek philosophers of the pre-Socratic period, whom Hippolytus catalogues alongside other purveyors of (to him) unsatisfactory ideas.

---

[7] Justin, *Dialogue with Trypho* 120.6. Some have doubted his claim to Samaritan ethnicity, not for very good reason.

Both Hippolytus and Tertullian ended up as opponents of the Great Church: Hippolytus out of discontent over the choice of Callistus as bishop of Rome (he tells a long story of Callistus' past failings),[8] and Tertullian as leader of the Carthage version of the Montanist sect (see ch. 8 below).

Besides heresiology and apologetic, second- and third-century writers began to deal with theological questions in new forms – not yet in decades-long debates of the kind engaged in by fourth-century theologians, but in treatises which came out of the teaching given to new Christians, out of ongoing controversy between Christians and Jews, and out of matters in dispute between the Great Church and proponents of Gnosticism. Clement of Alexandria, who taught catechumens (candidates for Christian baptism) in Alexandria, until he left town in the persecution of 203, recorded his theology in three extant works, the *Protrepticus* ('Exhortation to Study'), the *Paedagogus* ('Tutor') and the *Stromateis* ('Miscellanies') – each aimed at more advanced students than the last. Origen, who at the age of eighteen succeeded Clement in Alexandria, was still more prolific: given the services of shorthand writers and copyists by a patron,[9] he turned out commentaries (thirteen books on Genesis, thirty-six on Isaiah, twenty-nine on Ezekiel, twenty-five on Matthew, thirty-two on John, and so on) and theological treatises, steadily over about fifty years – and hundreds of his regular sermons, first recorded in shorthand, were made available and preserved for future use.[10] Far from all his huge output is extant, but what remains amounts to a great deal. Clement and Origen wrote in Greek, but in Latin Tertullian ('first theologian of the West', in the title of Eric Osborn's book, 1997) and Cyprian, both from Carthage, left substantial writings – including, in Cyprian's case, four volumes (in G. W. Clarke's translation, 1984–9) of letters on church matters.

Apocryphal stories

A less easily circumscribed category of literature was that of apocryphal stories: Acts of named apostles, infancy gospels, the pseudo-

---

[8] Hippolytus, *Refutation of all Heresies* 9.11.1 – 12.26. In the introduction to his edition, Marcovich (1986: 8–17) establishes that the writer of the *Refutation* was Hippolytus the sect-leader.

[9] Eusebius, *Ecclesiastical History* 6.23.

[10] Jerome, *Letters* 33; cf. Crouzel 1985: 38–39.

Clementines (stories starring Clement of Rome) and (in the long run most influentially) the *Protevangelium of James*, a narrative of the family and girlhood of the Virgin Mary. Often hard to pin down to dates and places, these tales, Cameron argues (1991: 89–90), were an important part of Christian writing throughout the second and third centuries ('the very time when story was enjoying a prominence unusual in the ancient world'), until in the fourth century and after- wards they were superseded as the liveliest genre of Christian literature by Lives of saints. 'We cannot escape the fact', Cameron adds, 'that these fanciful narratives contributed more than their critics would like to admit to the total Christian world-view.' The tales had something to offer to both believers and preachers:

> On the level of story, the apocryphal *Acts*, together with the infancy gospels and the *Protevangelium* of James ... constitute a world of discourse complementary to and filling the many gaps left blank in the Gospels. Officially recognized or not, it was this body of material on which later generations of preachers dwelt so often and so lovingly, and indeed we can sometimes detect the gentle exasperation that nearer-contemporaries evid- ently also felt when the details they would have liked – the upbringing of the Virgin, for instance – are simply omitted from the Gospel stories (Cameron 1991: 98).

Stevan L. Davies (1980: 6–10)) examines six apocryphal Acts, of John, Paul, Peter, Andrew, Thomas and Xanthippe, observing that there is a consensus among scholars on dating them between about 160 and 225. A large part of the message of all these books, which theologically bear varied relations to an orthodox outlook (Davies 1980: 11; James 1924: 270, 300), is one of absolute sexual continence: celibacy for the unmarried and an end to sexual relations for married people. Not unreasonably, Davies argues that, although at the time of writing there was no monasticism, nor any requirement for clerical celibacy, the writers of these Acts 'valued sexual continence above almost everything else' (1980: 50). He jumps ahead further than subsequent writers have been prepared to follow when he infers that communities of con- secrated widows in the churches produced the books.

The chief difficulty for his theory is lack of positive evidence, but there are also other concerns: Davies (1980: 108) dismisses Tertullian's claim (*On Baptism* 17) that a (male) priest in Asia was responsible for

Paul and Thecla, on the ground that Tertullian probably was not well enough informed about Asian churches to know this – and perhaps he was not, but we have less information than he did: disbelieving Tertullian is one thing, believing something contradictory is another. The general claim that an identifiable group, of the female gender, was behind all pro-continence Acts also runs counter to probability (see e.g. Cooper 1996: 62). There must have been people of both sexes practising and idealizing sexual continence, for continent lifestyles to work in churches. Davies' observation (1980: 111) that male apostles in the stories do not positively help wives to leave their husbands or avoid sex does not prove what he wants to deduce (that women enrolled as widows/virgins insisted on continence, while men in church leadership found ordinary married life religiously unproblematic). This element arises from a moral ambiguity in the narrative. Each story has to show the apostles preaching a pure life – rather than stealing wives from their husbands – and each story must persuade readers that the husbands are unfair to be angry at being deprived of sex. For dramatic reasons, the decision in the story must be the woman's: a man who told his wife he would no longer have sex with her would not face consequences as frightening.

The storytelling in these works has much in common with the non-Christian Greek and Latin novels which were being written in the same centuries. Cameron (1991: 91) points out features which they share – 'damsels in distress, the quest theme, the miraculous escape, and so on' (the theme of continence is in the secular novels too, in that heroes and heroines postpone sex with each other until they are married) – but she warns against categorizing them straightforwardly as novels, despite their stories having originated in the imagination of the writer rather than in historical records. Christianity 'built up its own symbolic universe by exploiting the kind of stories that people liked to hear' (1991: 93). Stories filling in the gaps in biblical accounts, and foregrounding elements (including sexual continence and the importance of virginity) which were increasingly central to second- and third-century Christian preaching, came to have a truth value attached to them – perhaps inevitably, considering the loose ends in the stories of particular characters left by some biblical narratives.

Cameron stresses how seriously the apocryphal stories were taken, especially over time, and most especially in the case of the Mary material: 'their audiences were disposed to accept them as true', she says (1991: 93), and 'in some sense, if not in the same sense as in the case of history, they are different from fiction in the matter of their relation to truth' (1991: 118). Her last (carefully phrased) comment, however, goes as far as anyone can: there remained for Christians in the fourth century (when lists of New Testament books were made) a divide based on critical consciousness of differences between the origins of books – reserving canonical status for a selection of first-century books, and not making every story of the Virgin or the apostles into *that kind of* sacred text.

Gnostic writing

Another kind of book being written in the second century, and into the third, was the Gnostic treatise. The 1945 Nag Hammadi find of thirteen codices filled with numerous books of cosmic and theological theorizing, reflecting a variety of viewpoints on the Gnostic spectrum, added enormously to what is known about what Gnostics thought and taught. Michael Allen Williams (1996: 51–53) points out the difficulty in generalizing about Gnostic systems: many draw a distinction between a creator god and the supreme being – but theories about the relations of the two and other divine/angelic beings go in various directions. Williams shows flaws in the modern view which in the past has made 'anticosmic world-rejection' a fundamental feature of Gnosticism (1996: 96–115), or classified systems as 'Gnostic' if they reinterpret biblical creation-narratives according to particular patterns. Different Gnostic sects saw things differently. Williams uses a table to illustrate the difference in reactions in Nag Hammadi texts to elements of the Genesis story: the serpent in the Garden of Eden is valued positively in the *Origin of the World*, but negatively in the *Apocryphon of John*; and Cain is a good thing in the view of the Cainites, but a bad thing as the Sethians saw him (no surprise there) (1996: 61–62). These contradictory outlooks, in evidence in the Nag Hammadi collection, prompt the overall argument of Williams' book, that it is unhelpful to speak of any such thing as 'Gnosticism', as if it were a category comparable to 'Judaism' or 'Platonism' or 'Christianity'. He prefers 'biblical demiurgical traditions'.

Williams is unlikely to succeed in getting the -ism word out of the vocabulary of Gnostic studies, but his book may make scholars less lazy about speaking of 'protest exegesis' or 'anticosmic world-rejection'. While in many places Gnostic writers reinterpreted biblical narrative against the grain of ordinary Christian or Jewish reading, elsewhere their concerns are close to those found in the apocryphal Acts, or in Great Church writers like Hermas.

Not everything in the Nag Hammadi collection is closely related to mainstream Christian moral teaching; but Williams disproves the long-held theory that there were two kinds of Gnostic system, ascetic and libertine (1996: 163–188). Proponents had argued that all Gnostics hated the flesh and the physical world: most thought self-denial was the way to free the divine spark trapped in a human person, but some thought the flesh was so evil that it did not matter what the body did (since the flesh could not affect the spirit) – while others even claimed it was *necessary* to commit every type of physical sin in order to attain release from the physical world. Williams shows, however, that accusations of libertine theorizing or behaviour came only from the heresiologists (1996: 168–169, 179–182): Gnostics themselves theorized asceticism in an amended Christian framework.

Eusebius

Against this background, with Christian writers beavering away at encouraging chastity, telling stories, making converts, educating catechumens, proving the wrongness of Christian views they did not like, and appealing to rulers for tolerance, it may seem strange that for so long no-one thought of writing a history of Christianity. But the first large-scale attempt was made under Constantine, by Eusebius, whose *Ecclesiastical History* aimed to record the history of Christianity from the time of Christ to his own day. He begins in the forty-second year of Augustus (1 BC), and ends with the surrender of Licinius and Constantine's victory in the civil war which reunited the Roman empire in 323.

Why no-one beforehand had written a history of Christianity remains a question about which one can only speculate. Wilken (1971: 27) comments on the possible role of the nearness of the end of the world: 'At first, Christians gave little thought to their own history. The Lord would return soon, they believed, and put an end to all history. When men give up their jobs, gaze into the heavens, and look for the end of the world, they write no history. Why record the past if there will be no one to remember it?'

This is a relevant consideration, but it must be kept in proportion. It was 280 years from Jesus to Eusebius, and many Christians in the interval wrote without apparent short-term apocalyptic expectations.

The case of Papias is relevant: bishop of Hierapolis in the second century, he is quoted by Eusebius as source for some narrative items, including the distinction between John the Evangelist and John the presbyter (*Ecclesiastical History* 3.39.5–7). Since he believed in 'a Millennium after the resurrection of the dead, when the kingdom of Christ will be set up physically on this very earth' (3.39.12),[11] Papias presumably suffered no anxiety about lack of a future in which his books could be read. But although he recorded some events in his work, Papias was not a historian: his five books were called *Interpretation of the Sayings of the Lord* (3.39.1).

There must have been other factors. One was that Christian literature by the second century was establishing its own directions, which did not point towards history. A Christian with a literary education and an urge to communicate was more likely to write apologetic, or to put the Christian past in novelistic form. Cameron (1991: 74) observes that after Tacitus, Roman senators stopped writing history for some time. History was out of fashion. Part of its job on the literary scene was taken over by biography, whose Christian counterpart was in apocryphal Acts, and then in Lives of saints. The use of imagery which typified Christian language, for Cameron, was another element which led implicitly to Lives: quoting 1 Corinthians 2:7 ('we speak the wisdom of God in a mystery, even the hidden wisdom, which God ordained before the world to our glory'), she comments that

> ... it is important to realize also that their way of interpreting the lives they wrote about was part of the wider realm of Christian discourse and illustrates its figural character particularly well. Written *Lives* were mimetic; real ascetic discipline in turn imitated the written *Lives* ... The proclamation of the message was achieved by a technique of presenting the audience with a series of images through which it was thought possible to perceive an objective and higher truth (1991: 57–58).

Thus Christianity could most obviously be conveyed through nonhistorical writing. In addition, there was a standard perception in the ancient world of what history was, or should be, about. As Wilken says:

---

[11] 'He was a man of very little intelligence', Eusebius editorializes (3.39.13).

... in antiquity people wrote histories of peoples, of nations, of empires, but not of religions ... the glorious deeds of ancient history – kings victorious in war, statesmen triumphant in politics – hardly suited the small religious sect that began in Palestine. By the historical standards of antiquity, Christians had produced little in the first century – one or two charismatic leaders, a few literary works of graceless prose and doubtful distinction, a few thousand people gathered in conventicles in the larger cities of the empire. There were no glorious deeds. By the end of the third century, however, *gloria* abounded. Christians could look back on brave martyrs, courageous bishops, brilliant teachers, sophisticated literary works of charm and elegance, controversies and conflicts, legends and romances and adventure stories. All that was needed was the vision, imagination, and order a historian could give to the story (1971: 52–53).

If Wilken is right, composing a history of the church was a project whose time had come. Eusebius, however, gave himself the task of telling the story right through what Wilken sees as the period of obscurity, before coming to the changes his own lifetime had brought.

He begins Book 1 of his *Ecclesiastical History* with a statement of the purposes of the work. The assumption that history was about peoples, nations and empires is in evidence, but the church's relation to government and politics is not the only thing Eusebius wants to record:

Having decided to hand on in writing the successions of the holy apostles, together with the enumeration and dating of as many deeds as are said to have been accomplished in the history of the Church during the times which have passed between our Lord and us, and how many people led and presided over it outstandingly, in its most famous places of sojourn, and how many in each generation whether orally or in writing were the ambassadors of the divine Word, and what people, how many, and at what times, advanced in their desire for innovation to the furthest point of error and announced themselves as the introducers of 'Knowledge' (falsely so called), unsparingly ravaging Christ's flock like grievous wolves; and besides this, to hand on what has come upon the whole nation of the Jews ever since their plot against our Saviour, and how many wars, of what kind and at what times, have been carried on against the divine Word by the

Gentiles, and the stature of the people who in their times went through the contest of blood and tortures, and also the martyrdoms in these our own times, and the merciful and gracious aid of our Saviour towards all the martyrs, I will start nowhere else but with the dispensation of God in our Saviour and Lord, Jesus the Christ (*Ecclesiastical History* 1.1.1–5).

This impressive piece of Greek rhetoric, a single sentence, sets out seven themes Eusebius will write about: first, the 'successions of the holy apostles' – who came after whom in Christian leadership, city by city; second, who the great preachers and writers were; third, who the leading Gnostics ('introducers of "Knowledge" [falsely so called]') were; fourth, what happened to the Jews; fifth, how the Gentiles persecuted the divine Word; sixth, who the old martyrs were; and seventh, the martyrdoms of the Great Persecution (303–12).

Apostolic succession was at the top of the agenda for a reason. There was at Eusebius' time no settled New Testament canon: discussion was still proceeding about which books were and were not authoritative. Eusebius gives his own opinions, offering a list not identical with other fourth-century writers' lists, and lumping pseudepigraphic gospels and acts together as 'put forward by the heretics' (*Ecclesiastical History* 3.25.1–7; cf. Johnson 1986: 537–538). Therefore authentic Christian teaching at his time could not be identified solely on the basis of adherence to the Bible. In any case, recognition of others' loyalty to biblical precept was complicated by the varying methods of interpretation followed: Eusebius thought Papias' belief in a literal and earthly millennium evidence of 'a misunderstanding of the apostolic accounts' on his part (*Ecclesiastical History* 3.39.12), though he does not allege heresy; but dealing a few pages later with Marcus (another second-century teacher) and his rituals of bridal chamber and baptism, he accuses him of 'magical trickery', and speaks of 'initiations which do not initiate, and loathsome mysteries'. Eusebius' criterion for acceptability is not agreement on everything, but a teacher beyond a certain line is branded a heretic and sorcerer.

Hence the importance of apostolic succession: with no self-validating written interpretation (and only a partially agreed corpus of sacred text), the question of who could claim to be in a line of teachers commissioned by legitimate predecessors back to the time of the apostles was vital. The concern is already evident in Clement of Rome's wish for the Corinthians to stick with their old leaders, and appears on a broader scale in the work of Hegesippus. On his tour, ending at Rome, he 'met many bishops and found the same doctrine among them all'. He compiled lists of episcopal succession, concluding that 'in each succession-list and in each city it is as the Law and the Prophets and the Lord preach' (Eusebius, *Ecclesiastical History* 4.22.1–3).

So Eusebius' plan to base his work around apostolic succession was directed to producing a unifying history, with the church opposing the Gnostics, advancing against a background of Jewish misfortune and Gentile attack, and producing the former and latter martyrs. Unusually among historians in the Greek and Roman world, Eusebius regularly quotes named authors and incorporates official documents into his narrative. He was consciously doing something new:

> ... I am the first to attempt it, as if I were travelling some deserted and untrodden road. I pray that I will have God as my guide, and the power of the Lord as my helper, since I am quite unable to find even the bare footsteps of people who have travelled it before, except that there are slight indications by which in different ways they have left us partial accounts of the times they went through ... So whatever I think profitable for the purpose in hand, out of the scattered records left by those people, I have collected, as if I were picking like flowers the appropriate voices of the ancient writers, out of the meadows of their words (*Ecclesiastical History* 1.1.3–4).

The resulting story became for Eusebius' fourth- and fifth-century successors both the first and the last version: no competitor tried to redo Eusebius' job, though three fifth-century writers (Socrates, Sozomen and Theodoret) set themselves to continue from where he ended.

Political interests are never far from the surface in Eusebius. In this respect Wilken's assertion that the church in the earliest period lacked potential as a subject for a Greek or Roman historian misses the mark: Eusebius found material all right – if sometimes at a cost in accuracy. A forged correspondence between Jesus and King Abgar, which was on file at Edessa, attracted him, overcoming the well-developed critical sense which led him to disbelieve all late gospels and apocryphal Acts – and it would make sense to think that the political point of his Abgar story (a king being converted and commanding his citizens to listen to a Christian preacher) had made Eusebius want to believe it.

The third century, as Wilken surmised, offered more political scope, and there Eusebius records among other things that Julia Mamaea, mother of the emperor Severus Alexander (222–35), invited Origen to visit her and speak about Christianity (6.21.3–4), that the emperor Philip the Arab (244–9) was (his source tells him) a Christian (6.34.1), that Gallienus issued an edict of toleration in 261 (7.13.1), and that Aurelian (emperor 270–5) gave a legal ruling in favour of Domnus, the new bishop of Antioch, against Paul of Samosata, his deposed predecessor, who had refused to relinquish possession of the house church (7.30.18–19).

He occasionally stretched a point in order to relate Christianity to leading figures in the Roman empire. It is not likely that Philip was a Christian, for example, though he may have gone to church once or more, and adopted a pro-Christian attitude.[12] But Eusebius was trying to record things which did happen, rather than simply tell a story which he thought ought to have been so. His plan to write about true and false teachers gives him villains (like the Montanists) and heroes (Origen, for instance), and because he wrote so long after most of the disputes he records, his firm position-taking and strong anti-heretical rhetoric (seen above in his attack on Marcus) can imply a situation less fluid than it would have seemed at the time. The reader must make allowance for hindsight – and for the fact that Eusebius, a loyal and admiring fan of Constantine, presents the whole story with the assumption that Christian history has progressed logically, despite apparent setbacks, to reach a high point represented by the official adoption of Christianity by the Roman empire.

Indispensable to anyone who aims to understand what happened in the early churches, Eusebius needs to be read in the context of all other evidence which can be brought to bear. His sixth and seventh aims, to tell the stories of the martyrs, focus attention on the place where the rubber hit the road in the Christian–polytheist conflict. Eusebius' own early life had been in the quiet late third-century period, but from the late first century until then, as the next chapter will show, anti-Christian violence was endemic to the religious policy of Roman rulers.

[12] See Rives 1999: 140 n. 28, arguing that Philip may have been interested in Christianity, without being a Christian himself. Sordi, however (1986: 96), argues that Eusebius was right on Philip.

6
Persecution and anti-Christian polemic

The way Eusebius tells it, the reader would think the Christian church leapt into existence pretty well in its fourth-century form as soon as Christ ascended into heaven. He recounts a tale of Tiberius (14–37) making a favourable report on Christianity, and the Senate rejecting it and making Christianity illegal.[1] All the same, he says,

> ... by the power and assistance of Heaven, the saving Word began to flood the whole world with light like the rays of the sun. At once, in accordance with the divine Scriptures, the voice of its inspired evangelists and apostles 'went forth to the whole earth and their words to the ends of the world'. In every city and village churches were established, completely full of tens of thousands of people, like a teeming threshing-floor. Those who by hereditary succession and original error had their souls bound by the ancient disease of the superstition of idols were set free as if from fierce masters and found freedom from fearful bondage by the power of Christ ... (*Ecclesiastical History* 2.3.1–2).

All this, on Eusebius' chronology, before the word 'Christian' had even been invented. Gentile bishop of Caesarea in Palestine, he has nothing to say here about Jewish Christians: he sees the Gentile church

---

[1] Eusebius, *Ecclesiastical History* 2.2.6. As noted in ch. 3 above, no-one in Acts says Christianity is illegal in Roman law: this is enough to show that Sordi (1986: 17–20) cannot be right to think the Tiberius incident really happened. It was anyway virtually unheard-of by Tiberius' time for the Senate to act directly counter to an emperor's expressed wish.

('freedom from the superstition of idols') as the heart of post-ascension Christianity.

In fact, conflict with polytheism, implicit from the beginning, entered a new phase in the first quarter of the second century. From the Christian side a symbolic challenge was issued by Aristides – the Aristides who gave his *Apologia* to Hadrian in 124. He was the first apologist to continue to dress as a philosopher – claiming a place for Christianity among the philosophical systems. Justin Martyr, in the next generation, also dressed as a philosopher, and when he describes how he turned to Christianity, he ends by saying, '... in this way, then, and for these reasons, I am a philosopher' (*Dialogue with Trypho* 8.2).

Philosophy represented the heart of Greek and Roman *ethical* teaching. Many writers have pointed out that Greco-Roman religion does not have much morality in it. Performance of ritual, public or private, was the main requirement. But to the Romans and (especially) the Greeks the moral life was the concern of philosophers. Christianity did what both religion and moral philosophy did in the Greek model. Meeks (1993: 66–71) discusses how New Testament writers drew on the Greek and Roman moral thought of their day to construct a model of Christian behaviour – for instance, by using lists of virtues and vices. Aristides' and Justin's follow-up was logical. By putting Christianity forward in the philosophical arena, they acted consistently with their aim of offering a 'totalizing discourse' (Cameron 1991: 58, 220–221): a system to which everything in life can be related.

Pliny and Trajan

Even before Aristides and Justin, polytheists were noticing the pressure which Christians' outlook on life could put on the Greco-Roman religious system. A feeling of having encountered something which made people fail to react normally to threatened punishment runs through Pliny's letter to the Emperor Trajan, written in 112, and the emperor's reply. It is worth studying the exchange of letters:

> Pliny to the Emperor Trajan:
> It is my custom to refer all my difficulties to You, my lord, for no one is better able to resolve my doubts and inform my ignorance.

I have never taken part in investigations of Christians; hence I do not know what is the crime usually punished or investigated, or what allowances are made. Nor am I at all sure whether any allowance should be made on grounds of age, or if young people and adults should be treated alike; whether a pardon ought to be granted to anyone retracting his beliefs, or if he has once professed Christianity, he shall gain nothing by renouncing it; and whether punishment attaches to the mere name apart from secret crimes, or to the secret crimes connected with the name.

In the meantime, this is the course I have taken with those who were accused before me as Christians. I asked them whether they were Christians, and if they confessed, I asked them a second and third time with threats of punishment. If they kept to it, I ordered them for execution; for I held no question that whatever it was that they admitted, in any case obstinacy and unbending perversity deserve to be punished. There were others of like insanity: but as these were Roman citizens, I noted them down to be sent to Rome.

Now that I have begun to deal with this problem, as so often happens, the charges are becoming more widespread and increasing in variety. An anonymous pamphlet has been circulated which contains the names of a number of accused persons. As to those who said that they neither were nor ever had been Christians, I thought it right to let them go, since they recited a prayer to the gods at my dictation, made supplication with incense and wine to your statue (which I had ordered to be brought into court for this purpose along with the images of the gods) and moreover cursed Christ: things which (so it is said) those who are really Christians cannot be made to do.

Others, whose names were given to me by an informer, first admitted the charge and then denied it; they said that they had ceased to be Christians two or more years previously, and some of them even twenty years ago. They all did reverence to your statue and the images of the gods in the same way as the others, and reviled the name of Christ. They maintained, however, that the amount of their fault or error had been this, that it was their habit on a fixed day to assemble before daylight and recite by turns a form of words to Christ as a god; and that they bound themselves with an oath, not for any crime, but not to commit theft or robbery or adultery, nor to break their word, and not to deny a deposit when demanded. After this was done, their custom was to depart, and to meet again to take food, but ordinary and harmless food; and even this (they said) they had given up doing after the issue of my edict, by which in accordance with your instruction I had forbidden the existence of clubs. On this I considered it the more necessary to find out from two maidservants who were called deacons (*ministrae*), by applying tortures, how far this was true; but I discovered nothing apart from a perverse and extravagant superstition.

I have therefore adjourned the case and hastened to consult You. The matter seemed to me worth deliberation, especially on account of the number of those in danger; for many of all ages and every rank, and also of both sexes, are brought into present or future danger. The contagion of that superstition has penetrated not only the cities, but also the villages and the country; yet it seems possible to stop it and set it right. At any rate it is certain enough that people have begun to throng the temples, which had been almost entirely deserted for a long time; and that long disused ceremonies are restored, while there is a general demand for sacrificial animals, which up to now have found very few buyers. It is easy to work out from this that a great many people could be reformed, if they were given an opportunity of repentance (*Letters* 10.96).

Two batches of accused persons have been dealt with. Pliny is unsure of the legal position: is just being a Christian a crime, or is a governor supposed to investigate the crimes popularly associated with Christians? Incest and infanticide – allegations concocted from partial knowledge of the ideas of brotherly love and of eating the body and drinking the blood of Christ in the Eucharist – would be the crimes of which Pliny had heard: hence the reference to 'ordinary and harmless food'.

The first batch of accused, apart from the Roman citizens among them (who were sent to Rome for trial), were put to death for recalcitrance. Pliny did not demand that they should sacrifice to the Roman gods: this he required only later, from suspects who claimed not to be Christians. Explaining the procedure to the emperor, he says, 'I held no question that whatever it was that they admitted, in any case obstinacy and unbending perversity deserve to be punished.' In a *cognitio extra ordinem* ('special investigation'), the governor of a province, when satisfied of the guilt of the accused, had discretion over the penalty. Christianity could attract the death penalty, but lesser sentences could be imposed instead (see Sherwin-White 1966: 695–696). Pliny, unclear about what is wrong with being a Christian, falls back on the idea that failure to comply with exactly what he, as governor, demands, is itself a capital offence.

Better knowledge of precedent would have given Pliny a stronger legal argument: earlier in Trajan's reign Symeon son of Clopas had been put to death for Christianity at Jerusalem,[2] and Ignatius of Antioch had been sent to Rome for execution (Ignatius, *Ephesians* 1.2). Christianity was in itself illegal, and had been for decades. Against that background, Pliny's uncertainty over what it was about Christianity that was illegal might seem a relatively minor issue.

Tertullian, the Christian apologist, pointed out in 197 in his *To the Gentiles* (1.2.1–3) the peculiarities in proceedings against Christians. Normally, when arrested criminals deny their crimes, he says, torture is used to make them confess; but with people accused of Christianity, torture is used to make them deny the accusation against them. Criminals who deny their crimes are disbelieved, but Christians who claim not to be Christians are immediately believed. Criminals are normally punished for past actions, but when a suspect denies being a Christian (now), anything he or she did in the past is disregarded: there is no punishment for *having been* a Christian (1.3.4). What is punished (Tertullian agrees with Pliny) is the name: and a harmless name, too, he says (1.3.5–10). Tertullian's programme in these chapters comes from Pliny's letter.

The accused in Pliny's second batch are dealt with less summarily. Victims of an anonymous allegation, they all deny being Christians and comply with Pliny's requirements: polytheistic prayers, offerings to the statue of the emperor, cursing Christ. Their stories do not quite add up: they claim to have ceased being Christians two or more years ago, but also say they gave up attending meetings when Pliny (who took up the governorship less than two years before) issued his decree against the existence of clubs.

---

[2] Eusebius, *Ecclesiastical History* 3.32.3–6, and Bauckham 1990: 91–95. Smallwood (1962) dates the governorship of the official named in Eusebius between 99 and 103.

The anonymous allegation had followed on Pliny's action against the first batch: this shows up a difficulty for governors. One known to be ready to persecute Christians might face a flood of accusations from anyone who wanted to cause trouble for a personal enemy. Some refused to be manipulated: four of the six governors of Africa mentioned in Tertullian's *Ad Scapulam*, and a governor of Asia, responded either by refusing to hear prosecutions against Christians, or by devising new procedures favourable to the accused (see Sherwin-White 1966: 782).

Trajan's briefer reply approves Pliny's handling of the issue, but (without open reproach) rules against making use of anonymous allegations, as Pliny has done:

Trajan to Pliny:
The method you have pursued, my dear Secundus, in sifting the cases of those denounced to you as Christians, is extremely proper. It is not possible to lay down any general rule which can be applied as the fixed standard in all cases of this nature. These people should not be sought out; when they are denounced and found guilty, they must be punished – but with the reservation that whoever denies that he is a Christian, and proves it effectively, by worshipping our gods, shall gain pardon as a result of that repentance, regardless of how suspect his previous conduct has been. Anonymous denunciations must not be accepted as evidence in any case, since that would be a very bad example, and not in accordance with the spirit of Our age (Pliny, *Letters* 10.97).

Tertullian again, this time in his *Apologeticum* (2.8), attacks the legal reasoning: 'What a decision, how inevitably entangled! He says they must not be sought out, implying they are innocent; and he orders them to be punished, implying they are guilty.' But if the logic is convoluted, the effect is clear: Trajan's aim of leaving a governor with full powers to persecute Christians, while not allowing the inconveniences which could come from letting ordinary people inform against Christians without fear of reprisal, is achieved – hence Sherwin-White's view that 'there is administrative genius in Trajan's solution' (1966: 711).

The image of the good emperor and his honest official projected in some recent discussion of the Pliny–Trajan exchange about Christians is due for a rethink.[3] Trajan shows himself as an arbitrary ruler, refusing to commit to a definite regulation – and because he is arbitrary, he supports the authoritarian stance Pliny has taken against the first batch of Christians, whom he has put to death for disagreeing with him ('obstinacy and unbending perversity deserve to be punished').

Pliny ends his letter justifying his actions by reference to the damage he says Christianity has done to established religion in Pontus (temples deserted, ceremonies abandoned, no market for sacrificial animals). He congratulates himself on a revival of observance. Modern writers think his account exaggerated,[4] and are reluctant to think that the church Pliny attacked could have been big enough – even locally – to make the impact on public, and economic, life which he sketches. But even though Eusebius' generalization about the instant popularity of Christianity cannot be given much weight, automatic scepticism has difficulties too: why would Pliny report that Christians committed no moral crimes, then argue for suppressing them because livestock merchants were not making profits? It is better to assume that he was not trying to misrepresent the situation to his master, and conclude that Christianity had enjoyed a wave of local popularity. Not that people who failed to participate in polytheistic ritual were all Christian: deciding to skip a sacrifice or a festival, because one has heard someone preach against idolatry, or just knows others are questioning it, is different from being converted to Christianity – even if logically it is a first step. Pliny found many who denied being Christians: some, presumably, because they could expect torture and death if they admitted it, but others, surely, who were really not Christian, but had been listening (perhaps sympathetically) to Christian ideas.

The general popularity or unpopularity of Christianity, an issue which swayed governmental and judicial decisions from Acts onwards, played an unpredictable role. Pliny made persecution part of his plan

---

[3] Trajan is more widely admired, but for hero-worship of both see Crossan 1998: 7: 'with human decency triumphing over legal logic, it shows us Pliny, Trajan and Rome at their best'. Well, *something* had triumphed over legal logic, as Tertullian showed. And yet Crossan (same page) has not forgotten about the torture: 'that torture in pursuit of information', he says, 'was carried out by as humane a Roman governor as we have on record'. Even Sordi (1986: 62–63), a writer with a very different outlook from Crossan's, suggests that Pliny wanted Trajan to allow him to exercise mercy towards Christians: but in fact Pliny wants only to be allowed not to punish people who turn away from Christianity.

[4] See e.g. Sherwin-White 1996: 709, who simply does not believe that scheduled (public) sacrifices could fail to be performed in response to Christian influence at this date.

to put things right in Bithynia and Pontus, where he, as a financial expert, had been made governor to sort out years of mismanagement: a return to conventional religion suited him in his drive for probity – and he did not care about popularity, having been appointed to the province exactly in order to tread on toes. At the same time, the issue of informers might be complex: Eusebius, drawing on Hegesippus, claims that Symeon son of Clopas at Jerusalem about the turn of the first and second centuries was informed on by 'the sects' – his Christian rivals (*Ecclesiastical History* 3.32.3–6). If he is right, this was a case of Christians manipulating the government to further their disputes with other Christians. Governors would not have been acting intelligently if they had got into the habit of executing Christian leaders on the basis of the latest demand for action.

Hadrian: deterring informers

This is the political point behind a letter the Emperor Hadrian sent to Minucius Fundanus, governor of Asia, about 125. Fundanus' predecessor had asked for advice, but before the answer came, the change-over had happened:

> I received the letter written to me by your predecessor, the most illustrious Serenius Granianus, and it is not my pleasure to pass by without inquiry the matter referred to me, lest both the innocent should be disturbed, and an opportunity for plunder afforded to slanderous informers. Now, if Our subjects in the provinces are able to sustain by evidence this their petition against the Christians, so as to accuse them before a court of justice, I have no objection to their taking this course. But I do not allow them to use mere clamorous demands and outcries for this purpose. For it is much more equitable, if anyone wishes to accuse them, for you to take cognizance of the matters laid to their charge. If therefore anyone accuses and proves that the aforesaid persons do anything contrary to the laws, you will also determine their punishments in accordance with their offences. You will on the other hand, by Hercules, take particular care that if anyone demands a writ of accusation against any of these Christians merely for the sake of libelling them, you proceed against that man with heavier penalties, in accordance with his heinous guilt (Eusebius, *Ecclesiastical History* 4.9).

The background to the procedure Hadrian lays down is that the property of people convicted of capital crimes was forfeited to the state, and informers received a share – hence the 'opportunity for plunder'. Granianus, it seems, had faced an anti-Christian demonstration calling for action against Christians without legal process. Hadrian's reply to Granianus' letter does not modify Trajan's non-principle ('it is not possible to lay down any general rule'), and so leaves the legal jeopardy Christians faced unchanged; which is why, when Tertullian came to discuss the law on Christianity in the *Apologeticum*, he turned to the Pliny–Trajan letters. What is new, however, is that Hadrian puts informers at risk: the penalty for falsely accusing someone of Christianity is to be a fine in excess of the amount the informer would have gained on conviction of the accused. This made the financial prospects of an accuser depend on the fortitude of the accused: unless he or she was ready to admit the charge and face martyrdom, the accuser was on the road to financial ruin.

Not all informers were deterred: in the story of Ptolemaeus and Lucius, told by Justin (*Second Apologia* 2) in the 150s under Antoninus Pius, a woman married to a 'licentious husband' is converted to Christianity, and at first continues to live with him; but then he goes to Alexandria, and she, hearing that his behaviour there is worse than ever, divorces him. He informs on her for being a Christian. She succeeds in getting the divorce, and in getting the hearing on the allegation of Christianity deferred, but her ex-husband hits back by accusing Ptolemaeus, her Christian teacher, of Christianity – and even gets a centurion to arrest and question him. Ptolemaeus admits that he is a Christian, and is brought up before Urbicus, prefect of the City of Rome, who (in accordance with the Pliny–Trajan precedent) merely asks, 'Are you a Christian?' He sentences Ptolemaeus to death on receiving a positive answer. Lucius, a bystander who objects to Ptolemaeus' conviction for 'the name of Christian' in the absence of actual crimes, is also sentenced to immediate execution.

Peregrinus: when politics dictated tolerance

Provincial governors did not always follow the toughest anti-Christian precedent. The satirical writer Lucian, whose *Passing of Peregrinus* treats Christians and Christianity without respect, describes the philosophical career of Peregrinus the Cynic philosopher, also known as Proteus, who shortly before the time of writing had burnt himself to death on a pyre at the end of the Olympic Games of 165 (*Peregrinus* 1). Earlier in life, probably in the 140s,[5] he had gone through a Christian phase, until discovered eating forbidden food. A citizen of Parium, a small city on the Hellespont, he had undertaken an extended tour after the death of his father (whom Lucian alleges he murdered). 'It was then', Lucian says, 'that he learned the wonderful wisdom of the Christians, by associating with their priests and scribes in Palestine.' An able convert, he had advanced quickly. Lucian's description balances attacking Peregrinus as a charlatan and portraying the Christians who welcomed him as lacking intellectual sophistication:

> ... in a short time he made them look like children, and he alone was the prophet, cult-leader, head of the synagogue and everything. He expounded and clarified some books of theirs, and others he himself wrote, and they revered him as a god, and had him as a lawgiver, and enrolled him as their protector – obviously, after the one whom they still worship, the man who was crucified in Palestine because he brought this new cult to life (*Peregrinus* 11).

After a time, Peregrinus was arrested for Christianity. The governor of Syria, however, did not bring him to trial, and finally had him released. Lucian makes it sound surprising that Peregrinus was not even whipped (*Peregrinus* 14), but since Peregrinus was rich and probably a Roman citizen, it would have been unusual for a governor to inflict a beating without trial. And there was another political factor besides Peregrinus' status: in prison, Lucian says, he was made much of by the Christian community:

> ... from daybreak old women and widows and orphan children could be seen waiting by the prison, and their officials bribed the prison guards and slept inside with him. Then elaborate meals were brought in, and their holy books were recited, and

[5] After the Christians threw him out, Peregrinus spent time in Egypt undergoing instruction in Cynicism (Lucian, *Peregrinus* 17), and then was at Rome until expelled by the prefect of the city (18); following this, he went to Greece and, at the Olympic Games of 153, criticized the aqueduct recently built by Herodes Atticus ('the spectators of the Olympic Games ought to endure their thirst ...', 19). On the completion date of the aqueduct see Tobin 1997: 321. Allowing a reasonable time for his philosophical retraining and his sojourn in Rome puts his involvement with Christianity before 150.

the excellent Peregrinus (for that was still his name) was called by them 'the new Socrates' (*Peregrinus* 12).

Socrates had been imprisoned and put to death for his convictions, but the analogy goes further. Peregrinus, like Socrates, was a Greek philosopher – Aristides' claim for Christianity as philosophy was gaining momentum. Nor was that all: Christians were sent from Asia at the churches' expense to visit and support Peregrinus (*Peregrinus* 13). Lucian is keen to show what this meant to Peregrinus in money terms (and interprets his later decision to give his valuable inherited property in Parium to the city on the assumption that Peregrinus did not need it, expecting to continue making a high income out of fellow-Christians; *Peregrinus* 14–16), but the crowds of visitors made his imprisonment a sensitive issue. From the governmental viewpoint it may have seemed that putting Peregrinus to death would risk un- necessary unpopularity – and not only among people who did not matter.

The setting of the story is either Aelia Capitolina (ex-Jerusalem) or Caesarea, in the years after the Third Jewish War. Peregrinus, initially a visitor from outside Palestine, and later (Lucian says) a leading figure in the local Christian scene, would have been held in one of the main cities. The church involved is Greek-speaking, with connections west- ward to Asia Minor where Peregrinus' visitors come from. It is de- lighted to get a Greek intellectual in the congregation. Against that background the governor's decision to release Peregrinus without charge makes sense as a pro-Gentile move, at a time when the Palest- inian situation must have seemed to demand ongoing action favourable to the non-Jewish population, which included Gentile migrants brought in to secure long-term support for Rome. An anti-Jewish stance took priority over possible anti-Christian action.

Polycarp: the crowd demands a victim

The unnamed governor of Syria, then, exploited the lack of a legal principle and applied his discretionary powers to take no further action in Peregrinus' case. But political exigencies could cut either way. The Asian churches which in the first decade of the century had received Ignatius' letters of encouragement, written on his way from Antioch to Rome for execution in the amphitheatre, and which a generation later sent representatives to Palestine in support of Peregrinus, faced in 155 or 156 a loss of their own in the martyrdom of Polycarp of Smyrna. Political conditions brought that martyrdom about.

A young bishop when Ignatius addressed one of his letters to him personally, Polycarp at the age of eighty-six was well known by non-Christians as well as Christians. The view in some recent literature that he was a haughty aristocrat may not be right: the *Martyrdom of Polycarp* (13.2) does say that he was not used to having to take his own shoes off, but adds that this was because the faithful were so keen to touch him (i.e. not because he always had a slave to help him dress and undress). Polycarp offers to discuss Christianity with the proconsul, but not the crowd at the arena – but he gives as his reason the Christian teaching that authorities established by God should be treated honourably: as for the crowd, he refuses to be accountable to it (10.2). On the other hand, he did have slaves, one of whom under torture revealed his whereabouts to the police (6.1), and he was a famous man. When the result of his questioning by the proconsul is announced, the crowd in the arena shouts, 'This is the teacher of Asia, the father of the Christians, the destroyer of our gods, who teaches many not to sacrifice or worship!'

Here, as in the Pliny–Trajan exchange, polytheist anxiety about the popularity of Christianity is to the fore. The gladiatorial games, coming to a close when Polycarp is brought in, are a ritual of unity around Greco-Roman religion, and one in which Christians will not join, although (the *Martyrdom* says) Jews are there. Eleven Christians, besides Polycarp, are killed – one, Germanicus, forcing a spiritless wild beast to kill him; but a person called Quintus avoids death by agreeing to take the oath by the emperor and offer incense.[6] The people are in a mood to assert their identity, purify their community and assuage their fears by participating in burning 'the father of the Christians'. Christian visitors from Philadelphia are martyred together with Polycarp (19.1): their presence may have triggered the Smyrnaeans' impulse to act against him. The threat which they perceive, however, has built up slowly – Polycarp has had decades, apparently undisturbed, in which to become 'the teacher of Asia'[7] – and just as Pliny in 112 claims that the threat to established religion in Pontus has passed, now that he has acted against the Christians, so the Christians in Smyrna

---

[6] *Martyrdom of Polycarp* 3.1 – 4.1; eleven plus Polycarp: *Martyrdom of Polycarp* 19.1.

[7] A phrase with Pauline resonance: for two years in Ephesus (Smyrna's rival city) Paul had spoken daily in the hall of Tyrannus, 'so that all the residents of Asia, both Jews and Greeks, heard the word of the Lord' (Acts 19:10).

find that once Polycarp has died, the persecution against them comes to an end (1.1).

After Polycarp's death, Smyrnaean Christians employed two techniques, neither wholly new but both with potential for further development, to make his death a rallying-point against the secular community's view of them. His story was written out as a martyr-act (and the copy from which the extant version descends was sent to the church at Philomelium), and the day of Polycarp's death was made into a regular celebration. The recovered parts of the saint's charred bones would be used as a reminder of his qualities, and his example as a martyr enunciated to Christians who might be called to do as he did. The impulse to touch him, which had made it unnecessary for him to remove his own shoes, was translated into part of his commemoration (18.1–3). Later martyr-stories, too, were written out and collected – and contemporary accounts can usually be distinguished from the elaborate fictional stories of martyrs produced after the end of the persecutions.

Intellectual attacks

Among the first martyr-stories like the *Martyrdom of Polycarp*, a very few years later, was the *Martyrdom of Justin*. Justin, the apologist, was arrested with others. Questioned in court, he denied knowing of any Christian meeting-places in Rome apart from his own lodging above a bath-house (*Martyrdom of Justin* 3) – which seems surprising, but perhaps he was economical with the truth to make it difficult for the prefect to persecute more widely. The six named Christians are put to death, their bodies recovered by fellow-Christians and 'laid ... in a convenient place' (6) – a place not known among the many Christian sites of Rome; the earliest Christian catacombs are datable about twenty years later.

Christian efforts, such as those in Justin's books, to invade élite knowledge, began to result in more literary attention being paid to Christianity. Pliny spoke of an 'extravagant superstition' (*Letters* 10.96), and Tacitus looked down on Christianity as a nasty fashion from Judea which took root in the capital because of Rome's moral decadence (*Annals* 15.44.4), but Pliny and Tacitus had not seen Aristides, Quadratus, Peregrinus or Justin dressing and speaking as philosophers, or heard Polycarp described as 'the teacher of Asia'. Lucian made light of the intellectual level of Christians, but he was in the humour business.

Lucian was also a provincial intellectual, whose friends were not right at the top. But his attitude did mirror what was being said in the very highest circles. Fronto, former tutor of Marcus Aurelius, delivered a speech in the 160s against Christianity at Cirta in his home province of Africa, repeating the old allegations of infanticide and incest (Minucius Felix, *Octavius* 9.6; 31.2). Galen, Marcus' court doctor, picks Christians as his example of people who cannot understand philosophy:

> Most people are unable to follow any demonstrative argument consecutively; hence they need parables, and benefit from them ... just as now we see the people called Christians drawing their faith from parables [and miracles], and yet sometimes acting in the same way [as those who philosophize]. For their contempt of death [and of its sequel] is patent to us every day, and likewise their restraint in sex. For they include not only men but also women who refrain from sex all their lives; and they also number individuals who, in self-discipline and self-control in matters of food and drink, have attained a pitch not inferior to genuine philosophers (Galen, *Summary of Plato's Republic*, quoted in Frend 1965: 319).

The emperor himself was equally anti-Christian. He would not count Christians as an authentic case of people ready to die for their beliefs:

> That soul which is ever ready, even right now (if need be) to be separated from the body, whether by way of extinction, or dispersion, or continuation in another place and estate – how happy it must be! But this readiness must proceed not from an obstinate and peremptory resolution of the mind, violently and passionately set upon opposition, as in the case of Christians, but from a peculiar judgement, with discretion and gravity ... (Marcus Aurelius, *Meditations* 11.3).

This chorus of bile from an intellectual emperor and his underlings shows that Christians were making their mark in the philosophical market-place. Then, in the late 170s, Celsus wrote a full-dress literary attack on Christianity: his treatise *The True Word*. The title is sometimes translated *The True Doctrine*, which underestimates Celsus' knowledge of Christian teaching: John's Gospel begins 'In the beginning was the Word...' (referring to Christ) – so Celsus' attack is, provocatively, *The True Word*. The book itself is lost, but much of it survives in quotations used by Origen two generations later in his reply, *Against Celsus*.

Only a tiny minority in the churches was on an intellectual par with Polycarp, or Justin and the apologists, and indeed the whole idea of philosophy became controversial in Christianity. By the beginning of the third century, Tertullian saw it as 'the material of the world's wisdom, the rash interpreter of the nature and the dispensation of God' – and specifically, the source of Gnostic theories (*Ruling out of Court of the Heretics* 7). Celsus in his book, accordingly, could use distrust of philosophy, and reliance on faith, as a stick to beat Christians with:

> ... he compares those who believe without rational thought to the 'begging priests of Cybele and soothsayers, and to worshippers of Mithras and Sabazius, and whatever else one might meet, apparitions of Hecate or some other demon or demons'. For just as among them scoundrels frequently take advantage of the lack of education of gullible people and lead them wherever they wish, 'so also,' he says, 'this happens among the Christians'. He says that 'some do not even want to give or receive a reason for what they believe, and use such expressions as "Do not ask questions, just believe," and "your faith will save you".' And he affirms that they say, 'The wisdom in the world is an evil, and foolishness a good thing' (*Against Celsus* 1.9).

Celsus had evidently heard Pauline paradoxes on wisdom (1 Cor. 1:18–25) and saw a line of attack. Origen found plenty to say in reply, but *The True Word* had many other objections: Christians worship Christ as well as God the Father – does that not compromise their claim to be monotheists (*Against Celsus* 8.12–14)? Why should God come down to earth – did he not know enough about the place (4.2–3)? Who saw the resurrected Christ? 'A hysterical female ... and perhaps some other one of those who were deluded by the same sorcery...' (2.55).

Along with more plausible objections, Celsus repeated anti-Christian stories which had circulated for decades. The birth of Jesus offered an obvious opportunity:

After this he represents the Jew as having a conversation with Jesus himself and refuting him on many charges, as he thinks: first, because 'he fabricated the story of his birth from a virgin; and he reproaches him because he came from a Jewish village and from a poor country woman who earned her living by spinning'. He says that 'she was driven out by her husband, who was a carpenter by trade, and she was convicted of adultery'. Then he says that 'after she had been driven out by her husband and while she was wandering about in a disgraceful way she secretly gave birth to Jesus' ... (1.28).

A little further on, the identification of Jesus' father as a Roman soldier called Panthera is attributed by Celsus to the Jew he has mentioned (1.32). As for Jesus' miracles, Celsus argues, they are explained by the time he spent in Egypt (1.28), where he learned 'certain magical powers on which the Egyptians pride themselves' – they are on a par with tricks performed by sorcerers and illusionists in market-places (1.68).

Celsus' knowledge of the New Testament was good, and only partly concealed by the fact that it did not suit him to quote its writers by name; and he tackled Christian preaching head on: Christians say Jesus was born of a virgin, but really he was an illegitimate child; Christians say Jesus did miracles, but really he was a cheap magician. These arguments are reinforced with attacks on Christianity as being spread in underhand ways by people who have no right to be taken seriously: the resurrection narrative originated, Celsus says, with someone who 'wanted to impress the others by telling this fantastic tale, and so by this cock-and-bull story to provide a chance for other beggars' (2.55). The Christian message, he says, is passed on by subversive elements who would not venture to measure up their teaching against the wisdom of authorized representatives of the dominant culture:

In private houses also we see wool-workers, cobblers, laundry-workers, and the most illiterate and bucolic yokels, who would not dare to say anything at all in front of their elders and more intelligent masters. But whenever they get hold of children in private, and some stupid women with them, they let out some astounding statements such as, for example, that they must not pay attention to their father and teachers, but must obey them; they say that these talk nonsense and have no understanding, and that in reality they neither know nor are able to do anything good, but are taken up with mere empty chatter. But they alone, they say, know the right way to live, and if the children would believe them, they would become happy and make their home happy as well. And if just as they are speaking, they see one of the teachers coming, or some intelligent person, or even the father himself, the more cautious of them flee in all directions; but the more reckless urge the children on to rebel. They whisper to them that in the presence of their father and their school-teachers they do not feel able to explain anything to the children, since they do not want to have anything to do with the silly and obtuse teachers who are totally corrupted and far gone in wickedness, and would have them punished: but if they wish, they should get away from their fathers and teachers and come with the women, and the little children who are their playmates, to the wool-worker's shop or the cobbler's shop or the laundry, in order to attain perfection. And by saying this they persuade them (3.55).

Celsus ridicules the idea that perfection could be gained through something learnt in a non-élite workplace: he is concerned to preserve the tradition of high-status knowledge represented in his argument by the father, the teacher and the 'intelligent person'. This passage can (rightly) be read as picturing Christianity as a lower-class movement, but, vitally, it is a lower-class movement which teaches students/young men whose attention ought to be kept on traditional knowledge: the Christian knowledge-system challenges polytheism in areas it values (élite male hearts and minds) by occupying places – workshops, women, children – which it despises.

The True Word became a fixture on the literary scene; in a world with fewer books than today, it was topical enough seventy years on to justify Origen's efforts in writing against it. But its success came from negative energy – there was little positive argument for polytheism. Other writers, however, had ideas in that direction. Philostratus' *Life of Apollonius of Tyana*, written around 217, is an attempt to reoccupy ground on which Christianity was making gains and winning converts.

Apollonius, born at Tyana in Cappadocia within a decade or so of when Jesus was born, had been a polytheist holy man. A temple to him had been set up in his home town (1.5). A Pythagorean, he consumed no wine or meat, wore no shoes, and went long-haired and unshaven (1.8). He was celibate, as Philostratus explains: 'as Pythagoras was commended for his saying that "a man should have no intercourse except with his own wife", he declared that this was intended by Pythagoras for others than himself, for he was resolved not to marry, nor ever to come to the intimacy of sex' (1.13).

He made and kept a five-year vow of silence (1.14), opposed the luxury of hot baths (1.16), and claimed to understand all human languages without having studied them (1.19). Philostratus, a member of the literary circle surrounding the Empress Julia Domna, wrote about him at her request, but did not finish the work in her lifetime (1.3).

Philostratus' picture of Apollonius has a series of correspondences with the story of Jesus. There is a miraculous birth:

> To his mother, just before he was born, there came an apparition of Proteus, who changes his form so much in Homer, in the guise of an Egyptian demon. She was in no way frightened, but asked him what sort of child she would bear. He answered, 'Myself.' 'And who are you?' she asked. 'Proteus,' answered he, 'the god of Egypt' (1.4).

Apollonius teaches people how to pray:

> 'Since [the gods] know everything, it appears to me that a person who comes into the house of god and has a good conscience, should pray the following prayer: "O gods, grant to me what I deserve." For,' he went on, 'the holy ... surely deserve to receive blessings, and the wicked the contrary ...' (1.11),

and makes a point of teaching with authority:

> When a certain quibbler asked him why he asked no questions, he replied, 'Because I asked questions when I was a lad; but now I must not question, but teach what I have found out.' 'How then,' the other asked again, 'shall the wise man converse?' 'Like a lawgiver,' he said, 'for the lawgiver must make the things of which he has persuaded himself into instructions for the many.' This was the line he pursued during his stay in Antioch, and he converted to himself the most unrefined people (1.17).

He heals a youth bitten by a mad dog (6.43), spots and leads the community against an evil demon (4.10), raises a girl from the dead

(4.45),[8] and so on. Philostratus even puts in a story of dogs eating the scraps which fall from the table, appearing to echo Matthew 15:27, when he refers to Damis of Babylon, who (so he says) wrote the first book about Apollonius:

> It was a lazy and malignant fellow who tried to pick holes in him, and remarked that he had recorded well enough a lot of things, for example the opinions and ideas of his hero, but that in collecting such trifles as these he reminded him of the dogs who pick up and eat the fragments which fall from a feast. Damis replied thus: 'If there be banquets of gods, and gods take food, surely they must have attendants whose business it is that not even the bits of ambrosia which fall to the ground are lost' (1.19).

How deliberate is the anti-Christian agenda of the *Life of Apollonius*? Was Philostratus borrowing out of the Gospels and reusing the stories in his Apollonius narrative? Christians in the ancient world were in no doubt, and a century after the *Life of Apollonius* was written, Eusebius of Caesarea produced a reply called *Against Philostratus on Apollonius of Tyana*.[9] Much of this pedestrian book is devoted to summarizing what Philostratus said, and its objections, Celsus-style, are to particular loopholes: if Apollonius was divine, why did he need schooling (9)? Where Philostratus protests that Apollonius was not a wizard, Eusebius retorts that he really was (27; our mighty deeds are miracles, yours are cheap tricks – both sides took that position). Eunapius, a fourth-century polytheist historian, says in his *Lives of the Philosophers* (454) that Philostratus' book should have been called *The Visit of God to Mankind*.

Where persuasion fails: anti-Christian violence

By the turn of the second and third centuries, Christianity appeared increasingly successful. From time to time there was persecution: the brief *Martyrdom of the Scillitans* from 180, for example, provides the earliest evidence for Christianity in Africa outside Egypt, describing the trial at Carthage, the provincial capital, of twelve small-town

[8] On the possibility that Philostratus wrote 'with an eye on the Gospels' cf. Swain 1999: 194.
[9] Also referred to as *Against Hierocles*.

Christians, seven men and five women. They refuse to take an oath by the genius of Caesar, and refuse to accept a thirty-day deferral of their case – so Saturninus, proconsul of Africa, condemns them to death:

> The proconsul Saturninus read out the sentence from a tablet: 'Whereas Speratus, Nartzalus, Cittinus, Donata, Vestia, Secunda and the others have confessed that they live in accordance with the religious rites of the Christians, and, when an opportunity was given them of returning to the usage of the Romans, persevered in their obstinacy, it is our pleasure that they should suffer by the sword.'
>
> Speratus said, 'Thanks be to God.'
>
> Nartzalus said, 'Today we are martyrs in heaven: thanks be to God.'
>
> The proconsul Saturninus commanded that the proclamation be made by the herald: 'I have commanded that Speratus, Nartzalus, Cittinus, Veturius, Felix, Aquilinus, Laetantius, Januarius, Generosa, Vestia, Donata, Secunda be led forth to execution.'
>
> They all said, 'Thanks be to God.'
>
> And so all were crowned with martyrdom together, and reign with the Father and Son and Holy Spirit for ever and ever. Amen.

Other martyr-acts illustrate some of the unifying features (on the polytheist side) evident in the burning of Polycarp. Amphitheatre killings such as that of Blandina and others at Lyons in 177, and of Perpetua and others at Carthage in 203, dramatized government action against Christianity as community rejection of deviance. Elsewhere, as in Peregrinus' case, governors sometimes found reason to avoid being drawn into action. Tertullian before 200 was confident that Christianity was not only growing, but gaining influence: 'we have filled everything you have,' he says, 'cities, tenements, forts, towns, exchanges – yes, and army camps, tribes, palace, senate, forum. All we have left you is the temples!' (*Apologeticum* 37.4–5). Fifteen years or so later, in a pamphlet directed at dissuading the proconsul of Africa from persecuting, he describes how a proconsul of Asia had declined to be drawn into wholesale violence:

> When Arrius Antoninus was persecuting in Asia, all the Christians of the city in question, in one united band, presented themselves before his judgment seat; on which, ordering a few to

be led forth to execution, he said to the rest, 'You wretches! If you want to die, you have cliffs and ropes.' If we should take it into our heads to do the same thing here, what will you make of so many thousands, of so many men and women, persons of every sex and every age and every rank, when they present themselves before you? How many fires, how many swords will be required? (*To Scapula* 5).

The Decian persecution

Forty years later, however, the large-scale attack on Christianity which Tertullian claimed was practical was tried under the Emperor Decius (249–51), who decreed that everyone in the empire must make a sacrifice and obtain a certificate to record that the sacrifice had been made. D. S. Potter's (1990: 43) suggestion that Decius simply intended to reaffirm Rome's relations with the gods, did not intend to eradicate Christianity, and may not even have been aware of a problem, is not realistic:[10] Christians were numerous enough for any emperor, even one who was (in Potter's phrase, 1990: 41) 'quite stupid', to be aware that they existed and dissented from polytheism.

The economic strain and external pressure the Roman empire was under were important factors. Since 238/9, the Persians had been occupying Armenia (usually a Roman client kingdom), and some cities and territory actually inside the Roman empire. Expeditions led by the boy-emperor Gordian III (238–44) drove the Persians back, but after Gordian's suspicious death in 244, his successor Philip the Arab made concessions which left some Roman territory – it is not clear how much – in the hands of Shapur I of Persia (Dodgeon & Lieu 1991: 32–49 and nn. 13–34).

Shapur apparently meant to keep the territory he conquered: Kartir, a trusted minister, was set to establishing Zoroastrian fire-altars with Magi priests in ex-Roman areas, and discouraging non-Zoroastrian worship. In the annexed Roman provinces he discouraged worship of the devs. Kartir left an inscription at Naqsh-i Rustam describing his achievements, in which he says:

... in every province and place of the whole empire the service of

---

[10] Rives (1999: 141), by contrast, says that 'an emperor who required universal sacrifice in the mid-third century A.D. could hardly be oblivious of its implications for Christians'.

Ohrmazd and the yazads [subordinate Zoroastrian deities] was exalted, and the Mazda-worshipping religion and its priests received much honour in the land. And the yazads, and water and fire and cattle, were greatly contented, and the devs suffered great blows and harm. And the creed of Ahriman and the devs was driven out of the land and deprived of credence. And Jews and Buddhists and Brahmins and Nazarenes and Christians and Baptizers and Manichaeans were assailed in the land. And images were overthrown, and dens of demons were thus destroyed, and the places and abodes of the yazads [i.e. fire temples] were established. And from the first I, Kartir, underwent much toil and trouble for the yazads and the rulers, and for my own soul's sake. And I caused many fires and priestly colleges to flourish in Iran, and also in non-Iranian lands. There were fires and priests in the non-Iranian lands which were reached by the armies of the King of kings. The provincial capital Antioch and the province of Syria, and the districts dependent on Syria; the provincial capital Tarsus and the province of Cilicia, and the districts dependent on Cilicia; the provincial capital Caesarea and the province of Cappadocia, and the districts dependent on Cappadocia, up to Pontus, and the province of Armenia, and Georgia and Albania and Balasagan up to the Gate of the Alans – these were plundered and laid waste by Shapur, King of kings, with his armies (in Boyce, ed., 1984: 112–113).

Some of Kartir's inscription is about achievements later in his long career. But it is possible that Decius' move to persecute Christians in 250 was prompted by Kartir's attacks on non-Zoroastrian religions in Persia, and on Greco-Roman polytheism in conquered territory. The 'devs' Kartir refers to included Greco-Roman gods, the 'images' included statues of gods, and Greco-Roman temples, in Kartir's vocabulary, would be 'dens of demons'.

The Decian persecution made a very sharp impact on the churches. The requirement was for all Romans (the whole free population of the empire had been made Roman citizens in 214)[11] to attend sacrifices

[11] The surviving fragment (P.Giessen 40) of the *Constitutio Antoniniana*, the decree the Emperor Caracalla (211–17) issued to extend Roman citizenship, gives religious unity as the reason for the move: 'I consider that in this way I can ... render proper service to their [the immortal gods'] majesty ... by bringing with me to the worship of the gods all who enter into the number of my people. Accordingly I grant Roman citizenship to all aliens throughout the world ...'

arranged under the supervision of commissioners, satisfy them that they had complied with the requirements of the ritual, and then obtain a certificate proving that they had done so. Some of these certificates survive in Egypt, and similar ones were issued all over the empire during 250. Aurelius Diogenes got his certificate on 26 June:

> (First hand) To the commission chosen to superintend the sacrifices at the village of Alexander's Isle. From Aurelius Diogenes, son of Satabous, of the village of Alexander's Isle, aged 72 years, with a scar on the right eyebrow. I have always sacrificed to the gods, and now in your presence in accordance with the edict I have made sacrifice, and poured a libation, and partaken of the sacred victims. I request you to certify this below. Farewell. I, Aurelius Diogenes, have presented this petition.'
>
> (Second hand) I, Aurelius Syrus, saw you and your son sacrificing.
>
> (Third hand) ...]onos[...
>
> (First hand) The year one of the Emperor Caesar Gaius Messius Quintus Traianus Decius Pius Felix Augustus, Epeiph 2 [26 June, 250] (Stevenson, ed., 1987: no. 193.1).

As J. B. Rives notes (1999: 137, 141), the bishops of great cities were attacked promptly. Fabian, bishop of Rome, was put to death on 20 January 250 (Eusebius, *Ecclesiastical History* 6.39.1), and Babylas, bishop of Antioch, on 24 January (6.39.4). At Alexandria, the Prefect of Egypt sent a soldier after Bishop Dionysius as soon as he received the edict (6.40.2), and at Carthage Bishop Cyprian was declared an outlaw (Cyprian, *Letters* 66.4.1). These were the four biggest cities of the empire. Evading arrest, Cyprian left Carthage early in 250, not to return until after Easter 251. His evasion of persecution was to prove controversial with other Christians; and meanwhile his flock did not stand up to the pressure well, in their bishop's opinion – some of them queuing to sacrifice:

> Alas! ... They did not even wait to be arrested before they went up, or questioned before they made their denial. Many fell before the fight, many were laid low without meeting the enemy; they did not even give themselves the chance of seeming unwilling to sacrifice to the idols. They ran to the market-place of their own accord, they hastened to death of their own will; as

if they had always wished it, as if embracing an opportunity which they had fervently desired. How many the magistrates put off at the time, as night was at hand! How many there were who even entreated that their undoing might not be delayed! How can anyone make violence an excuse for his guilt, when the violence was rather on his own part and to his own destruction? (Cyprian, *On the Lapsed* 8).

By the time of writing, Cyprian was facing the question of how to deal with Christians who had sacrificed and now wanted to be forgiven and readmitted to the church. While the persecution was going on, it cannot have seemed certain that there would be a church left.

At Smyrna a presbyter called Pionius, realizing that he and two companions, Sabina and Asclepiades, would be arrested the next day (23 February, the anniversary of Polycarp's martyrdom – not coincidentally, but because the proconsul of Asia's assize tour brought him to hear cases in Smyrna at the same time every year),[12] put symbolic woven chains round his own and the others' necks in advance – so that no-one would think they were going to sacrifice (*Martyrdom of Pionius* 2.1–4; Lane Fox 1986: 461). He was afraid that the officials would bundle him to the temple of Nemesis where the sacrifices were happening (6.3), force him through a hurried ritual and push him out with a certificate – compromising his claim to be a loyal Christian. Some aimed to avoid sacrificing by getting a certificate through bribery – but the verdict in the churches was that having a certificate was as bad as having sacrificed. A confrontation in front of a festival-swollen crowd in the market-place followed, with Pionius insisting that Smyrna faced a fiery Day of Judgment which would lead to punishment worse than any he could be subjected to for being a Christian (4.1–24).

Officials did their best to persuade him and the others to sacrifice, but they refused and were put in prison to await the arrival of the proconsul – hotheads in the crowd having to be reminded that only he had the right to sentence a prisoner to death (10.4). But before the proconsul's arrival, the officials succeeded in getting the bishop of Smyrna, Euctemon, to sacrifice. While he was still worshipping at the altar (and to show willing, he had provided his own lamb, 18.13–14),

[12] Lane Fox 1986: 483–486. On the *Martyrdom of Pionius*, as well as Lane Fox 1986: 460–492, see Robert 1994.

Pionius and the others were brought. Pionius resisted being taken from the jail, and when they arrived in the market-place they threw themselves on the ground and shouted that they were Christians, to avoid being brought inside the temple. Six policemen were required to get Pionius to where the sacrifices were being made (1–7). Again he and the others refused to sacrifice. They were taken back to jail (16.1 – 19.12). When Quintilianus the proconsul finally arrived, not much was left to be said: he tried to talk Pionius into sacrificing, then, when he failed, sentenced him to be burnt alive (19.1 – 20.7). At his next stop, in Pergamum, Quintilianus had Carpus, Papylus and Agathonice put to death for Christianity (*Martyrdom of Carpus, Papylus and Agathonice*, cf. Lane Fox 1986: 490–491).

By November 250 persecution was easing off at Carthage. The lapsed, Cyprian ruled by letter, were not to be readmitted to church too quickly, and certainly not while he himself was still out of town (*Letters* 17.1–3) – but, cautious as he was, even Cyprian was confident enough to return before Decius' death in battle against the Goths in May or June 251. This was the end of the first empire-wide persecution of Christians, and the most dangerous one: by the time of the Great Persecution, between 303 and 312, numbers had increased to a point where wiping Christianity out empire-wide was not a realistic political project.

Still, the Emperor Valerian, on his accession in 253 apparently friendly to Christians (Eusebius, *Ecclesiastical History* 7.10.3), changed tack and announced a second empire-wide persecution of the Decian type in 257. Eusebius blames Macrianus, a financial official in Egypt, for poisoning Valerian's mind against the Christians and persuading him to persecute (7.10.4). Cyprian says Valerian's edict focused on clergy, and Christians from high-status backgrounds:

... Valerian had sent a rescript to the Senate directing that bishops, presbyters and deacons should forthwith be punished; that senators and men of rank, and Roman knights, should lose their dignity and be deprived of their property, and if, when deprived of their possessions, they should still continue to be Christians, then they should lose their heads also; that matrons should be deprived of their property and banished; and that whosoever of Caesar's household had either before confessed, or should now confess, should forfeit their property, and be sent in chains as conscripts to Caesar's estates (*Letters* 80.1).

Before writing this letter, Cyprian had been arrested. At a hearing on 30 August 257 he was sent in exile to Curubis; then a year later he was recalled and tried by Galerius Maximus, proconsul of Africa. On 14 September 258 at Carthage, after avoiding arrest long enough not to be tried at the lesser assize-centre of Utica (see Lane Fox 1986: 487), he was beheaded. Some other clergy in Africa were also put to death.[13] Valerian's persecution, which lasted until 260, was not as intense as that under Decius. Eusebius knows of just three men in Caesarea who died (*Ecclesiastical History* 7.12); but they went to the judge of their own accord – a deed not approved by the churches, though excusable if the doer then became a martyr.

Through the 250's, despite the shock of Antioch falling to the Persians in 252, the Romans won back lost lands. In 260, however, Valerian was captured in battle by the king of Persia. Neither military action nor offers of concessions could secure his release, and he died in captivity. His colleague and successor Gallienus ended the anti-Christian campaign, and instructed that buildings confiscated from Christians should be returned. His original edict does not survive, but Eusebius preserves a letter Gallienus sent to some bishops who, presumably to overcome bureaucratic reluctance, requested confirmation that they were to have the buildings:

The Emperor Caesar Publius Licinius Gallienus Pius Felix Augustus, to Dionysius and Pinnas and Demetrius and the other bishops. I have given my order that the benefit of my bounty should be published throughout all the world, to the intent that the places of worship should be given up, and therefore you also may use the ordinance contained in my rescript, so that none may molest you. And this thing, which it is in your power to accomplish, has long since been conceded by me; and therefore Aurelius Quirinius, who is in charge of the exchequer, will observe the ordinance given by me (*Ecclesiastical History* 7.13).

The provision against molestation did not overturn the principle that Christianity was illegal. Eusebius tells a story from Gallienus' reign of a soldier at Caesarea called Marinus, who was due for promotion to centurion: a rival denounces him as a Christian and says that he does not sacrifice to the emperors. When Marinus admits that he is a Chris-

---

[13] Cf. the *Martyrdom of Montanus and Lucius* and the *Martyrdom of Marianus and Jacobus*.

tian and refuses to sacrifice, he is put to death (7.15.1–5). But forty quiet years were to follow, and the Great Persecution, which began in 303, was to be the last river to cross before Christianity was not only legal, but the official religion of the Roman empire.

Some recent writers (e.g. Goodman 1997: 328) have supposed that the overall number of Christians martyred cannot have been very large, at least before Decius. Their implicit assumption that the martyrdoms known now are a good proportion of all there were is disputable. The writer of *To Diognetus* assumes his readers will have seen Christians thrown to the beasts (7) – and says that the more are killed, the more Christianity grows. Eusebius, for his part, thought the *lack* of persecution in his lifetime had made the churches slack (*Ecclesiastical History* 8.1.7–9). And yet there were practical advantages in not being persecuted – and there was a whole category of Christians, who held an important place in Roman society, who throughout the first three centuries could almost always count on a degree of safety from persecution. These were the emperor's own servants. Chapter 7 will examine the exceptional circumstances applying to them.

7

An enclave: Caesar's palace

Government officials

During the process I have been describing whereby the Christians changed the religion of the Roman world, it was a strange anomaly which made the emperor's personal service possibly the safest place for a Christian to be. And not merely strange – the resulting situation was one a hypothetical strategist for Christian mission could hardly have planned better. The emperor's servants were the people who really ran the empire. The long-term effects of Christian influence in this context were considerable.

These servants were not only the people who staffed the palace on the Palatine hill in Rome, but the whole *familia Caesaris* ('household of Caesar'), the organization of slaves and freedmen (= former slaves) who staffed all the places (residential, bureaucratic, commercial, industrial) owned personally by the emperor throughout Rome, and his estates across the whole empire.

As well as ruling, collecting tax and presiding over public life, the emperor was a landowner on a grander scale than anyone in his domains. His staff ran to many thousands, and as well as supplying his needs and caring for his affairs in every way from managing vast estates down to sweeping leaves, they formed nearly all the lower and middle levels of the civil service, and important parts of its higher reaches. The empire's ministers of finance, for example, for more than a century after Augustus, were all freedmen. Money was too important to leave to a senator or a Roman knight – officials who would be less dependent on the emperor. Most officials below the level of a Roman knight in government offices were either freedmen or slaves of the emperor.[1] So the imperial service divided into two sections: the domestic side, where clothes and food and other daily requirements of great households were produced, and the administrative side, a cadre of officials who did government work. These officials were often talented and highly educated. The household had its own school in Rome, in the region called Caput Africae, where young slaves of the emperor learnt the skills needed to administer Rome.

Christian mission made inroads into the palace in the first generation. Paul sent to Philippi a greeting (Phil. 4:22) from Christians in the *familia Caesaris*: 'All the saints greet you, especially those of the emperor's household.' There may already have been more than a few: von Harnack (1905: II.195–196) argued for a possible connection with the greetings in Romans 16:10–11 to members of the households of Aristobulus and Narcissus. Following J. B. Lightfoot, he identified Narcissus with the Emperor Claudius' freedman of that name, and Aristobulus with the uncle of Herod the Great. Narcissus had his own great house, and slaves and freedmen, but his assets (including slaves) would have been absorbed into imperial ownership after his death in 54/5, and the same may have happened to Aristobulus' household (though Aristobulus' date of death is not known).

The second generation

The next trace of Christianity at court comes from AD 96 with the fall of Flavius Clemens (consul 95) and Flavia Domitilla – assuming that 'Jewish customs' referred to by Suetonius are actually Christianity – which may be so.[2] Peter Lampe (1987: 166–171), after discussing the possibility that there were two Flavia Domitillas, argues that in any event a Christian Flavia Domitilla of senatorial rank was exiled – but he notes that no source earlier than Syncellus in the ninth century calls Flavius Clemens a Christian.

It has been argued that Clement of Rome was a dependant of a member of the imperial family, possibly Flavius Clemens (see e.g.

---

[1] But note that in the provinces a great deal of 'civil service' work was done not by civilians but *soldiers* on detachment from their units.

[2] Dio Cassius 67.14; Suetonius, *Domitian* 15, 17. Eusebius (*Ecclesiastical History* 3.18.4) records Flavia Domitilla's exile as 'a witness to Christ', and says that Domitilla was Clemens' niece – whereas Dio Cassius says she was his wife (and also comments that they were related).

Wong 1977: 87). Lampe (1987: 172–173) is sceptical: he points out that Clemens is not a family name (slaves, once freed, took their ex-master's family name), so that Clement of Rome's name proves nothing; and he adds (rightly) that arguments based on the style of writing in *1 Clement* cannot prove that its author was trained in producing government documents: he need only have had a literary education. But still, Clement's social ties are suggestive: his letter was carried to its destination at Corinth by two men whose names were Claudius Ephebus and Valerius Bito. As von Harnack points out, Ephebus' family name (Claudius) suggests that he may have been a freedman manumitted by Claudius or Nero, while Bito could have gained his name by being a freedman of Claudius' wife Messalina, whose family name was Valeria (*1 Clement* 65.1; cf. von Harnack 1905: II.197).

James S. Jeffers (1991: 63–89) suggests that a house church associated with Clement may have met in a warehouse building which has been excavated beneath the church of San Clemente. He pictures it as a place with *cachet*, saying of the churchgoers: 'They were in effect a social elite among the congregations of Rome and had greater wealth, more education, and more hope for a comfortable life on earth' (1991: 89). He analyses differences of outlook between Clement and Hermas, pointing up Clement's social conservatism (1991: 90–144, esp. 132).

Inferring tension between parties in Roman Christianity, with the priorities of each side encapsulated in the writings of Clement and Hermas, perhaps reads too much between the lines. But Jeffers' model of Clement and Christian members of the *familia Caesaris* as socially confident, and strangers to the alienation from the world evident (for instance) in the Johannine community at a comparable date, is persuasive. Imperial slaves based in Rome might advance to important posts, and the most successful became rich. As P. R. C. Weaver showed in his book *Familia Caesaris*, slaves with quite modest responsibilities would be freed at the legal minimum age of thirty; and epitaphs of the imperial household show that roughly two thirds of married male slaves and freedmen commemorated had freeborn wives. The husbands usually married in their twenties – before manumission (see Weaver 1972: 112–136). The fact that freeborn women and their families found marriages with imperial slaves desirable shows that these slaves' standard of living and future prospects were more than enough to compensate for their status.

An unusual arrest

After the Flavia Domitilla affair and the writings of Clement of Rome, the next evidence for Christianity in the *familia Caesaris* is in the *Martyrdom of Justin 4*. Euelpistus, one of Justin's followers, says in answer to questioning that he is an imperial slave. The sixty-year gap between this brief reference and the earlier clues about Christians in the imperial household reduces the confidence with which assertions can be made about Christianity as an abiding feature in the *familia*, but it is most economical to postulate that a Christian minority among imperial slaves and freedmen continued from Paul to Justin, rather than to think Euelpistus was an isolated case. The context fits Jeffers' model of the Clementine circle and Weaver's observations about the social position of imperial slaves.

Justin's Syrian pupil Tatian, in his *Address to the Greeks* 32, speaks of Christian teaching as an egalitarian intellectual enterprise ('Not only do the rich among us pursue our philosophy, but the poor enjoy instruction gratuitously'), but opponents seldom missed a chance to attack Christianity's pretensions. It was outside the acceptable canon of philosophical systems. But this was not necessarily a great hindrance to the progress of Christianity in the *familia Caesaris*. As Meeks observes (1983: 21–22, 63), slaves and freedmen of the emperor experienced an unusually high degree of status dissonance. They did complex work, from the next-to-top level in government downwards, and some gained influence via routine contact with the emperor. Yet although able to marry freeborn women, they could not gain esteem at high social levels. Tacitus, historian and Roman senator, records in his *Histories* (1.76.3) that Crescens, a freedman of Nero, gave a public dinner in Carthage to celebrate the accession of Vespasian, and comments: 'in troubled times these too make themselves part of the *res publica* [= Roman State]' (cf. Millar 1977: 69–70). He sneeringly categorizes an imperial freedman – one rich enough to give a free dinner to everyone in Carthage – as essentially *not* part of the *res publica*: the people who make government work are (in his view) non-participants in Roman statehood.[3]

Even if Euelpistus had done his best to comply with conventionally proper ways of studying philosophy or practising piety, nothing would

---

[3] A slave freed by a Roman citizen became a Roman citizen, so as the emperor's freedman Crescens *was* a citizen; but that technicality would not have impressed Tacitus.

have been enough to change the view taken of him by people like Tacitus. This limited his social horizon – snobbery was impregnable. But that very fact paradoxically opened up options. Euelpistus need not measure his choices against a standard set by the Roman élite.

Because he was found at a class in Justin's lodgings, Euelpistus was put to death for being a Christian. But he may have been unlucky to be punished. Membership of the imperial household ordinarily conferred some protection against government action. The basic Roman expectation was that punishing slaves was the business of their master; and freedmen continued to have strong obligations towards their former masters, becoming *clientes*, subordinates with legally defined duties to, and expectations of, their patrons. When the master or patron was the emperor, courts had reason to hesitate to impose punishments which might encroach on his prerogative.

Christians: a persistent presence in the palace

In the generation after Euelpistus, Christian literature provides three references to Christianity in the *familia Caesaris*. Hippolytus (*Refutation of all Heresies* 9.12.1) says that Callistus, later to be bishop of Rome, was the slave of Carpophorus, a Christian 'of the emperor's household' during the reign of Commodus (180–92) (cf. von Harnack 1905: II.199). Writing in the same reign, Irenaeus refers to 'those in the royal palace who are believers', without hinting at the scale of the group of Christians under discussion (*Against Heresies* 4.30.1). Then in the 190s Tertullian's *Apologeticum* (37.4) lists the palace along with other commanding heights of Roman life in which, he says, Christians have established a presence.

The principle that 'what I tell you three times is true' allows some confidence from this time on: it is clear that from the time of Commodus Christians formed a persistent minority among the emperor's slaves and freedmen. Tertullian, in a pamphlet aimed at inducing an incoming governor of Africa not to persecute Christians, actually claims that Septimius Severus (whose tour of Egypt and Africa in 202–3 brought a wave of persecution) knew of Christians within his household. He writes: 'Even Severus himself, the father of Antoninus [sc. Caracalla], was mindful of the Christians. For he sought out Proculus the Christian, also called Torpacion, the procurator of Euhodia, who had once cured him by means of oil, keeping him in his palace to the day of his death' (*To Scapula* 4; cf. von Harnack 1905: II.200).

Caracalla, he adds, knew Torpacion personally, as well as himself having been 'brought up on Christian milk' – i.e. nursed by a wet-nurse who was a Christian, and an imperial slave. Emperors knew what was happening – Severus received anointing with oil for healing – and chose not to punish their own slaves and freedmen for Christianity.

In the early third century, Christians in the imperial household began taking advantage of their untouchability by putting up grave-stones which noted, sometimes cryptically, that the deceased had been a Christian. This was a new departure. Christians who died before 200 were buried, and doubtless some had gravestones – but it was not possible to carve anything on the stone which would identify the deceased as a Christian. About 200 the bishop of Hierapolis in Phrygia, Avircius Marcellus,[4] had himself commemorated on his gravestone with a long Greek poem shot through with references to his Christianity. This stone,[5] which survives and is now in the Vatican Museum, is usually thought to be the earliest Christian inscription.

From a few years later, seven Christian inscriptions of the *familia Caesaris* survive – all in Latin; six from Rome and one from its port city, Ostia. Only one is from a catacomb, although use of catacombs at Rome for Christian burials goes back to the later second century: most were on display in above-ground cemeteries – cemeteries not exclu-sively for Christian use. They pre-date the Crypt of the Popes in the Catacomb of Callistus, where the earliest bishop to be buried was Pon-tianus (230–5) – and even there, discretion in the wording of grave markers was in order in the third century. The burial place of Bishop Fabian (236–50), who died in the Decian persecution, is marked ΦΑΒΙΑΝΟΣ ΕΠΙ Μ, and although it is easy today to supplement the abbreviations as *Phabianos epi[skopos] m[artyr]* ('Fabian, bishop and martyr'), they might not have been understood easily by non-Chris-tians who happened to come into the crypt.

Probably the oldest of the seven *familia Caesaris* inscriptions, and the oldest datable Christian inscription in Latin, is the gravestone of Marcus, a pupil of the Caput Africae school who had joined the pal-ace's tailoring department, before dying at the age of eighteen. His father, an imperial slave, put up the gravestone between 197 and 212 (McKechnie 1999: 431, 438). The most important texts in the series,

---

[4] I assume that the person memorialized in the inscription is the same as the Avircius Mar-cellus named by Eusebius (*Ecclesiastical History* 5.16.3) as writing against the Montanists: place and date both fit. There is a small divergence in the spelling of his name.

[5] Kearsley (1992) lists the literature about the inscription.

however, are those carved on the sarcophagus of Marcus Aurelius Prosenes, who died in 217. At the time of his death, Prosenes was *a cubi-
culo Augusti*, the emperor's chamberlain. This meant that he was in
charge of the emperor's bedchamber, responsible not only for having
the emperor's bed made and clothes ready, but also for regulating who
was allowed to greet him in the morning, and making other arrangements for his daily schedule. Under Commodus, successive chamberlains (Saoterus, Cleander, Eclectus) had been so powerful that they
were virtual deputy emperors. By Caracalla's day chamberlains were
not so much in the ascendant, but the post was always potentially
influential, because of the quantity of daily access the chamberlain had
to the emperor.

At the peak of a twenty-five-year career in the service by the time he
died, Prosenes had held two financial posts with procurator rank, after
being procurator of gladiator shows and procurator of wines. He was a
rich man, with slaves and freedmen of his own, and his freedmen
(wishing, like many Romans, to make funerary arrangements in
advance) got together and bought an ornate sarcophagus for his
remains to be deposited in when his time came. They had a record of
his achievements carved on it:

> For Marcus Aurelius Prosenes, freedman of the emperors, cham-
> berlain to the emperor, procurator of the treasury, procurator of
> the imperial estate, procurator of gladiator shows, procurator of
> wines, appointed to the service by the deified Commodus, and a
> most dutiful and well-deserving patron, his freedmen from their
> own money caused this sarcophagus to be adorned.

If this were all there was, no-one could tell that Prosenes had been a
Christian. But on the upper edge of the right-hand end of the sarco-
phagus a second text has been inscribed – probably after the first, when
Prosenes' remains came back to Rome:

> Prosenes, gathered to God on 3 May at S[ame in Cephalle?]nia
> in the consulship of Praesens and Extricatus for the second time,
> as he was travelling back to the city from the expedition. His
> freedman Ampelius wrote this.

Caracalla, the emperor, had died on 8 April of that year, campaign-
ing in Mesopotamia. Cephallenia lay on Prosenes' way home to Rome.

'Gathered to God' (*receptus ad deum*) is the key phrase. No-one was flaunting Prosenes' commitment, but it is explicit (McKechnie 1999: 430–431).

The little grouping of Christian gravestones goes down in date to the early 230s. The occupations of the deceased are mostly on the administrative side of the imperial household, rather than the domestic side. Administrative staff were better rewarded and could afford more, but another reason for the imbalance may be that like their first-century forebears, they experienced a status inconsistency which disposed them to be ready for Christianity when others were not. Eusebius (*Ecclesiastical History* 6.28) says that the household of Severus Alexander (222–35) 'consisted mostly of Christians', which must be an exaggeration; but with their high occupational status and their readiness to publicize their Christianity in an innovative way, it is perhaps not surprising that they made an impact. There is one solitary parallel to their inscriptions – a gravestone from the Cemetery of Hermes at Rome, dated to 234, not mentioning a connection with the palace, but decorated with a fish and an anchor (McKechnie 1999: 430 n. 10).

Third-century purges

The Christians in the palace could have been forgiven for thinking, in the early 230s, that a tide was running their way. The Emperor Severus Alexander allegedly had images of Abraham and Christ among other objects of his devotion (*Historia Augusta, Alexander* 29.2), and his mother Julia Mamaea invited Origen to visit her, when she was at Antioch (Eusebius, *Ecclesiastical History* 6.21.3–4). But unprecedented upheaval was to follow the end of his reign in 235. Previous changes of dynasty had apparently had little impact on the *familia Caesaris*. Rulers needed the people who put policy into action. Vespasian, on assuming control in 70 after the chaos which followed the end of Nero's reign, took over Nero's slaves and patronage of his freedmen, and left the machinery of the *familia Caesaris* working as normal. Others who won the throne by violence – Nerva (96–98), Septimius Severus (193–211) – adopted the same approach, moving into the palace and taking it over as a going concern (Weaver 1972: 45). The pattern was broken by Maximinus Thrax (235–38), who purged Severus Alexander's household.

Weaver (1972: 26) argues that the new palace officials, *Caesariani* (as they came to be called after 238), were freeborn. Such a radical change cannot have happened overnight, even if Maximinus from 235 acted ruthlessly to restructure the imperial household as he wanted it. There are, however, hints before Maximinus of a move away from a self-perpetuating internal system for recruitment and promotion. The last dated inscription of the school at Caput Africae comes from 214 (*CIL* 6.8986): the pattern of training slaves born in the household or bought at young ages seems to have ended. The *Historia Augusta* (*Heliogabalus* 6.2) claims that Elagabalus (218–22) *sold* governmental and military posts, including 'procuratorships and palace appoint-ments'. There is a chance that the charge is fictional – but if it had a basis in fact, it would fit in with an incipient practice of recruiting freeborn imperial servants, and might have given Maximinus a pre-cedent, if he felt he needed one, for a hands-on approach to selecting personnel.

Still, there is a straw in the wind which may point to a reversal after Maximinus of the reaction against Christianity in the imperial service: Gordian III (238–44), in a letter to Misitheus [Timesitheus] quoted (or fabricated) in the *Historia Augusta*, expresses regret that he did what his mother told him to do after she consulted Gaudianus, Rever-endus and Montanus.[6] The names, apparently Christian, may spring from the imagination of the novelist – but Montanus in particular is a plausible name for the period concerned, whereas by the time the *His-toria Augusta* was written, a century and a half later, it would have been an odd name for a Christian (the Montanists by then were only a tiny sect). A Montanus born around 190, at the high tide of the Mon-tanist movement, might have been discussing state business with Gordian III's mother in the early 240's.

Between the time of Maximinus and the Toleration Rescript issued by Gallienus in 261 the fortunes of Christian *Caesariani* were mixed. Early in Valerian's reign, Eusebius says,

... the emperor was friendly and favourable to the servants of

---

[6] *Scriptores Historiae Augustae, Tres Gordiani* 25. Syme (1968: 173–174) discusses these names: 'In truth, a choice company. Like "Gaudiosus" [*Scriptores Historiae Augustae, Probus* 22.3] "Gaudianus" conveys a Christian odour. Similarly "Reverendus", although not so easy to attest, so it happens. But one can adduce "Reverens" and "Reverentius". In "Montanus" resides a clear allusion to the notorious Phrygian sect which had votaries at Rome in the days of Theodosius, and even later.' The texts Syme quotes to attest 'Gaudianus' (*CIL* IV.2433 and 2456) are graffiti from the Corridoio de' Teatri at Pompeii, and hence date from before AD 79; but there is a Christian 'feel' in all three names.

God; none of the previous emperors, not even those who were said to be Christians, ever behaved with such kindness and favour to them as did Valerian. He treated them with quite undisguised friendliness and goodwill at the commencement of his reign; his whole court was full of pious people; it was a veritable church of God (*Ecclesiastical History* 7.10.3, quoting Dionysius of Alexandria).

Later, Valerian changed his mind. Exile and confiscation of property were to be the fate of Christian *Caesariani*, as Cyprian's quotation from Valerian's second rescript against the Christians shows:

.. those *Caesariani* who had previously confessed Christianity or who should now confess it should forfeit their property and be sent in chains as convicts to imperial estates (*Letters* 80, written between 6 August and 13 September 258).

The purged imperial household would not stay purged. Cyprian, reflecting on the period before the Decian persecution, says that a large number of bishops, 'scorning the divine procuratorship, became procurators of earthly kings' (*On the Lapsed* 6) – meaning that they took jobs in the palace. His point is to comment on lax conditions in the churches before the shock of 250. Angry as Cyprian is about bishops taking these jobs, their career moves were understandable. Bishops were likely to have the education and administrative experience required, and when the chance arose, they may have been less disposed to hold back out of Tacitus-style snobbery than members of the decurial (= town-councillor) class. Being highly esteemed by the Christian community but regarded officially as nothing more than leaders of an illegal sect, they had experience of the status inconsistency which high-ranking members of the *familia Caesaris* had been living with for centuries. The pay and fees were also attractive.

Perhaps it can be assumed that Decius purged the *Caesariani* as Maximinus had done fifteen years earlier, and as Valerian was to do eight years later. Von Harnack (1905: II.203) argues that he must have done, though unfortunately the direct evidence in favour of the proposition is confined to one martyr-act relating to one gardener from the imperial estate at Magydus in Phrygia – not near the heart of the Roman bureaucracy. There Conon, the gardener, like Euelpistus, was arrested by public officials (*Martyrdom of Conon* 1–2). Being owned by the emperor did not save him. While in earlier centuries membership of the *familia Caesaris* had provided partial shelter for Christians against persecution by magistrates, in the unstable conditions of the mid-third century the reorganized imperial household became an area of front-line confrontation between Christianity and the anti-Christian impulse. Pardons and reinstatements after Decius' death may account in part for the quick change which made Valerian's palace 'a church of God', but under Gallienus there was more substantive recognition of the realities of the situation, and for the first time toleration for Christianity was decreed.

Consequently under Diocletian (284–305) some high palace officials were Christians: Adauctus, a long-serving official, promoted from grade to grade, who was at the top of the ministry of finance when put to death in the Great Persecution (Eusebius, *Ecclesiastical History* 8.11); Dorotheus, a presbyter at Antioch, who knew Hebrew and read the Old Testament in its original language, and who joined the imperial service and was appointed manager of the dye-works at Tyre (another clergyman entering a palace career – Cyprian would have disapproved) (7.32.2–4); Philoromus, an Alexandria-based high official, executed in the Great Persecution (8.9.7); and Dorotheus and Gorgonius at Nicomedia (8.6.1, 5). Perhaps most importantly, Lactantius, later to write (among other books of Christian apologetic) *The Deaths of the Persecutors*, was serving as professor of Latin at Diocletian's court before the Great Persecution began (Frend 1965: 489).

Eusebius says that Constantius I, father of Constantine and in 303 senior Caesar (number three in Diocletian's team of four joint emperors), subverted the decree which had led to imperial servants being executed for Christianity. Constantius, he claims, set a trap:

> A choice was offered to all the imperial servants under him, from lowly domestics to those with commissions as governors: he proposed that either they sacrifice to the demons and be permitted to stay with him enjoying the customary advancement, or if they did not comply they should be excluded from all access to him and be removed and dismissed from his acquaintance and intimacy. When they had divided two ways, some to the latter group and some to the former, and the nature of the decision of each was clearly demonstrated, the amazing man then revealed his secret trick: he condemned the one group for cowardice and self-concern, and warmly commended the others for their sense of duty to God. Thereupon he declared those

who had betrayed God not worthy of imperial service either: how could they keep faith with the emperor if they were found to have no conscience about the Supreme? He therefore decreed that they were to be banished far from the palace, while those, he said, who for their truth had been attested worthy of God, would be the same where the emperor was concerned; he appointed them as bodyguards and watchmen for the imperial house, saying that he ought to employ such men among his chief and closest friends, and to prize them above stores of great treasure (*Life of Constantine* 1.16.1–2).

It is difficult to know what to make of this. Cameron and Hall (1999: 196) find the story 'hardly credible', and point out the parallel with the trap Jehu sets for worshippers of Baal at 2 Kings 10:18–25. Lactantius (*The Deaths of the Persecutors* 15.7) says that in response to Diocletian's order to persecute, Constantius destroyed church buildings, but did not harm Christian people.

Eusebius has assumed that imperial servants all claimed to be Christian (but some were weak or insincere), and it is hard to accept that reality measured up to this picture. But Cameron's and Hall's inference, based on nothing except this story, that Constantius *did* enforce sacrifice, takes scepticism too far. Killing people like Adauctus must have damaged the efficiency of government, and any emperor who was not actively anti-Christian might have thought it best to sideline the religious issue to keep the administration strong. Earlier emperors had sometimes exercised their powers to ensure that penalties against Christianity were not enforced against their households. It is possible that Constantius I felt that the loss the government would suffer, if he subjected his officials to persecution, outweighed the gains his colleagues hoped for.

The shape of things to come

The *de facto* privilege which allowed slaves and freedmen of the emperor through the first and second centuries to be Christians with apparently less risk of persecution than most Christians in Italy and the provinces faced made the *familia Caesaris* into a kind of weathervane, which showed in what direction society in general would move if the brakes of illegality, persecution, and élite disapproval were taken off. Lenient imperial attitudes to Christianity in the palace made it possible, in the last generation of the old-style *familia Caesaris*, to set up in and near Rome some of the earliest Christian grave inscriptions.

Like Christianity as a whole, the imperial household was cosmopolitan. Members of it were based everywhere. Third-century increases in the size of the civil service amplified the effect of church growth in the empire at large. Reactionary regimes in the middle of the century attempted to root Christianity out of it, and (under Decius and then Valerian) from the Roman world as a whole; but these measures were intermittent, and under the more fluid third-century entry conditions Christians were sure to be appointed, because attitudes to education and social life within the churches ensured that by that time a steady (and probably increasing) proportion of suitable candidates would be Christian.

By the time of the Great Persecution – as Constantius' decision shows – the disproportionately Christian Roman civil service constituted a great obstacle to the officially stated aim of wiping Christianity out. Chapter 10 will deal with how that conflict was played out. But first, more needs to be said about the poorly pruned bush which was Christianity, across the empire and beyond. In chapter 8, the reasons for Christianity's fissiparousness, and its consequences, will be examined.

8

Gnosticism and Christian diversity

'False teachers' in the New Testament

From the beginning the growth of Christianity was the growth of a community of communities – sometimes in contact, sometimes in conflict, always bushy. New Testament texts are full of warnings against false teachers – not meaning polytheists, nor (usually) teachers of Judaism. In early Pauline writings, 'false brothers' (Gal. 2:4, fn.) and 'false apostles' (2 Cor. 11:13) are mentioned, and all three Pastoral Epistles show concern at what false teachers do: making money from religion (1 Tim. 6:3–6; Titus 1:10–11; 2 Pet. 2:15), commending *gnōsis* (1 Tim. 6:20), saying our resurrection has already happened (2 Tim. 2:17–18), and gaining admission to homes, to 'captivate silly women' (2 Tim. 3:6–7). Colossians attacks ascetic teaching (2:16–23). In 2 Peter, false teachers are accused of bringing Christianity into disrepute (2:2) and loving 'the wages of doing wrong' (2:15). In Jude, the point of the letter is to warn against false teachers (Jude 4, 8–19). 1, 2 and 3 John also comment: attacking antichrists (1 John 2:18–19), speaking of 'many deceivers' who teach Docetism (2 John 7), and naming Diotrephes (3 John 9–10).

Not all the false teachers in Pauline, Petrine and Johannine texts have the ultra-conservative concern for Jewish ritual which Ellis (1999: 315–316) associates with his single 'fifth mission':[1] only the 'false brothers' in Galatians seem to fit that pattern. Elsewhere, New

---

[1] Cf. ch. 1 above.

Testament writers' objections to false teachers fall under three heads: they want to make money, they claim that majority Christianity is not rigorous enough,[2] or they interpret parts of the Christ-narrative in divergent senses – by saying that Jesus Christ did not come in the flesh, claiming that events of the eschaton have already happened, or speculating unacceptably about heavenly beings.[3]

Most of these objections are to things which were, at least sometimes, acceptable. Christian preachers could properly receive pay, as Paul argues (1 Cor. 9:3–18) – and the *Didache* confirms that a true prophet should receive generous payment.[4] There could be discussion over behaviour, as when James and the Jerusalem church decided on what terms Gentiles could be Christians (Acts 15:23–29). Even speculation on the heavenly world was not much restricted, with Revelation adding new ideas to the Christian repertoire.

The issues for the New Testament writers were subjective: did the ideas preached fit in with Christianity as they saw it, and was a given preacher one of us? 2 Peter 2:1–22 asserts at length the disloyalty and moral inadequacy of false prophets; 1 John 2:19 says of its 'many antichrists': 'They went out from us, but they did not belong to us; for if they had belonged to us, they would have remained with us. But by going out they made it plain that none of them belongs to us.'

These are ex-Johannine Christians; but Diotrephes in 3 John 9–10, who will have nothing to do with the writer and 'refuses to welcome the brothers' (mg.), appears to be from another background.

Both congregations and leading figures in the first century were weighing preachers up to decide if a given preacher was 'one of us' or not: warnings in the New Testament arise predominantly from instances when some (at least) in congregations found a particular teacher more persuasive than a writer did. The verdict in each case shaped what would happen next. Acceptance by a minority, or outright exclusion from Christian communities, formed the background to development of esoteric strands in Christian teaching. The churches were small minority organizations, and saw their members as 'chosen' (1 Pet. 1:2), those 'who are being saved' (1 Cor. 1:18), and 'the Israel

---

[2] As at Colossae, and in the case of the 'super-apostles' attacked by Paul in 2 Corinthians 11.

[3] Incarnation: 2 John 7; eschaton: 2 Tim. 2:18; 2 Thess. 2:1–4; Matt. 24:24; heavenly beings: 2 Pet. 2:10–11; Jude 8–9; also Col. 2:8–15.

[4] *Didache* 13.1–7; though elsewhere (11.6; 12.4–5) the *Didache* is cautious about people who want to be paid.

of God' (Gal. 6:16). Esoteric teachers circumscribed further. The 'antichrists' in 1 John teach that their followers have a chrism and knowledge which other Christians lack: the apostle reassures his readers that they, too, all have chrism and knowledge from the Holy One (1 John 2:20).

Status within the esoteric in-group was regularly expressed in terms of knowledge – the Greek term for which, *gnōsis*, denoted something which Christians, in the main stream of New Testament thought, ought to have (e.g. at Rom. 15:14 and John 17:3). Knowledge was part of Jesus' message. At Luke 11:52 he says, 'Woe to you lawyers! For you have taken away the key of knowledge (*gnōsis*); you did not enter yourselves, and you hindered those who were entering.' The parallel at Matthew 23:13 says, 'Woe to you scribes and Pharisees, hypocrites! For you lock people out of the kingdom of heaven. For you do not go in yourselves, and when others are going in, you stop them.' When Jesus spoke about 'knowledge', he was referring to the thing which he also called 'the kingdom of heaven' or 'kingdom of God'. This is the background to claims by Great Church writers including Clement of Alexandria that the Christian is the real Gnostic.[5] But the key term was contested from the Pauline period. In 1 Timothy (dated 55 by Robinson, 64 by Ellis)[6] the word is the subject of a warning (6:20–21: 'Avoid the profane chatter and contradictions of what is falsely called "knowledge" [= *gnōsis*]; by professing it some have missed the mark as regards the faith').

A second Gnostic key concept, the distinction between pneumatics (= spiritual Christians) and psychics (= other Christians), is referred to at Jude 19, which says that the false teachers 'who make the distinction are psychics, as they do not have the Spirit'.[7] The idea behind this, like the basic concept of gnosis, comes from ordinary Christian teaching: Paul says that 'the law is spiritual' (= pneumatic: Rom. 7:14), and addresses fellow-Christians as (lit.) 'you spiritual persons' (= 'pneumatics', *pneumatikoi*: Gal. 6:1), but takes his Corinthian readers to task for being 'infants in Christ', and needing to be spoken to as 'people of the flesh' (*sarkinoi*), instead of pneumatic (1 Cor. 3:1). A few years

---

[5] Clement, *Miscellanies* 1.44.2: 'our "man of many skills", our Christian Gnostic, is ... competent to distinguish sophistry from philosophy, cosmetics from athletics, cookery from pharmacy, rhetoric from dialectic, and then, in Christian thought, heresies from the actual truth'.

[6] See ch. 1 above.

[7] My translation (cf. ch. 1 above) of *Houtoi eisin hoi apodiorizontes, psychikoi, pneuma mē echontes*.

later, at the time of Jude (61/2 on Robinson's dating; Ellis, 55–65), instead of describing places people are at in their spiritual lives, the pneumatic/psychic framework (now expanded to three levels) is being used by Jude's opponents to differentiate between followers of their system and ordinary Christians: the self-styled pneumatics are a minority within the minority.

Key concepts in Gnosticism

So themes in Gnosticism are discernible in the New Testament. Some, indeed, had a track record before Jesus, as Moritz Friedländer argued as early as 1898. This fits in with Simon Magus having been a preacher and sect leader before he encountered Philip and Peter. As a result, some Gnostic theories introduce concepts foreign to most Christians' understanding of their religion – such as the theory of higher and lower gods – while others are differentiated by fine distinctions.

The *Gospel of Thomas* is a text whose distinctive features put it in the latter category. It is no long step, for example, from a Pauline view of predestined election to salvation, to *Thomas* 49, which says: 'Jesus said, "Fortunate are those who are alone and chosen, for you will find the kingdom. For you have come from it, and you will return there again."'

In the *Gospel of Thomas*, the vital part of the pneumatic's personality is pre-existent, which it is not in Paul; but in both systems a defined group of pneumatics is destined to ascend (back) to heaven.

These fine distinctions make the *Gospel of Thomas* important. It is esoteric, as the first verse implies: 'These are the hidden sayings that the living Jesus spoke and Judas Thomas the Twin recorded.' The readers of *Thomas* are meant to believe they are learning something extra. Later, the book elaborates on Thomas as a recipient of secrets, contrasting him with Simon Peter and Matthew:

Jesus said to his followers, 'Compare me to something and tell me what I am like.'

Simon Peter said to him, 'You are like a just messenger.'

Matthew said to him, 'You are like a wise philosopher.'

Thomas said to him, 'Teacher, my mouth is utterly unable to say what you are like.'

Jesus said, 'I am not your teacher. Because you have drunk, you have become intoxicated from the bubbling spring that I have tended.' And he took him, and withdrew, and spoke three sayings to him.

When Thomas came back to his friends, they asked him, 'What did Jesus say to you?'

Thomas said to them, 'If I tell you one of the sayings he spoke to me, you will pick up rocks and stone me, and fire will come from the rocks and consume you' (13).

Thomas's secret knowledge, he knows, would be unacceptable to his fellow-disciples. The reader is not meant to guess what Jesus said to Thomas, but to understand the exclusion of the writer (or of the Thomas group) by other Christians – and view it in terms of his/its possession of secrets hidden from the rest.

Other things in *Thomas* also fit the picture implied in New Testament warnings against false teachers. Like the writer's opponents at 2 Timothy 2:18, *Thomas* sees the eschaton as having happened already:

His followers said to him, 'When will the rest for the dead take place, and when will the new world come?'

He said to them, 'What you look for has come, but you do not know it' (51).

But reinterpretation of the parable of the lost sheep assures the minority that in the new world they are preferred to the ('ordinary' Christian) majority:

Jesus said, 'The kingdom is like a shepherd who had a hundred sheep. One of them, the largest, went astray. He left the ninety-nine and sought the one until he found it. After he had gone to this trouble, he said to the sheep, "I love you more than the ninety-nine"' (107).

In the synoptic parallels, the lost sheep is not the largest, nor does the shepherd love it more than the rest.

Divergent and convergent forces

Majorities as well as minorities felt a need to explain divisions and exclusions. Sect leaders might be accused of sexual immorality, or other bad behaviour. The story that Helen, companion of Simon Magus, started out as a prostitute in Tyre, has been mentioned;[8] but if there is substance in her story and that of Simon's sect, there seems to be none in the similar tale of Nicolas and the Nicolaitans. Irenaeus identifies the Nicolaitans in Revelation 2:14–15[9] as followers of Nicolas the deacon of Acts 6:5 – an identification which may be only an inference – and says, 'they teach that fornication is a matter of indifference and that one should eat meats sacrificed to idols' (*Against Heresies* 1.26.3). Irenaeus' claim is a spin-off in a literalistic direction from the Balaam analogy, whose original point in Revelation (as M. A. Williams [1996: 171] argues) was figurative: 'the Nicolaitans', he says, '... were probably Christians who took a stance towards the surrounding Greco-Roman culture that John considered to be far too open'.

Allegations might be thrown in either direction. Hippolytus' *Refutation of all Heresies* includes a section (9.12.24) against the Callistians – i.e. the Catholic Christians at Rome. The allegations against them include sexual impropriety:

> They hold Christ in contempt, and there is no sin which they forbid, since they say that he will forgive those who choose him; for he [Callistus] permitted women, if they were unmarried but of marriageable age and aflame with passion, if they did not want to compromise their own status by contracting a legal marriage, to have whatever one man they chose, whether slave or free, as their bedfellow, and reckon this man as their husband, without being lawfully married ...

Hippolytus attacks the Catholic practice of treating all marriages as marriages, including those not recognized in Roman law (as marriages between a free person and a slave were not). He goes on to claim that women living in such relationships habitually have abortions. 'Behold into how great sacrilege the lawless [Callistus] has advanced,' he says, 'teaching adultery and murder at the same time!'

Hippolytus spoke of something which was allowed (for practical reasons), and something else which penitents might be forgiven for, as if they were things his opponents actually favoured. He was attacking

---

[8] Irenaeus, *Against Heresies* 1.23.2–3: cf. ch. 2 above.

[9] 'But I have a few things against you [in Pergamum]: you have some there who hold to the teaching of Balaam, who taught Balak to put a stumbling-block before the people of Israel, so that they would eat food sacrificed to idols and practise fornication. So you also have some who hold to the teaching of the Nicolaitans. Repent then.' Cf. also Rev. 2:6 (to Ephesus): 'Yet this is to your credit: you hate the works of the Nicolaitans, which I also hate.'

the majority, but allegations against minorities worked the same way. So M. A. Williams is probably right to argue that allegations of immorality (and 'libertine Gnosticism') against the Nicolaitans are unfounded, arising from a standard vocabulary of controversy (1996: 170–171). Notice, too, that in Revelation the Nicolaitans are only partly excluded from the Christian mainstream: at Ephesus the church hates the practices of the Nicolaitans, but at Pergamum some in the church go along with their teachings.

Perhaps, after Revelation was distributed, the Pergamenes took action against their Nicolaitan minority, or perhaps not; but the situation whereby a Christian sect is part of acceptable Christianity in one place, but excluded somewhere else, is not unusual in later years. When Clement of Rome argues for set times for worship at Corinth (*1 Clement* 40.2–3), his aim is to tighten up on sub-groups with a distributed leadership.[10] Letter-writing between churches was a force in the convergent direction. But where control by Christian leadership in a particular city was loose, as in Corinth or Pergamum, sects excluded elsewhere might come within the pale.

Ignatius of Antioch

Like John and Clement, Ignatius of Antioch favoured tight control. In his letter to Magnesia, about 106, he says:

> It is right ... that we should be really Christians, and not merely have the name; even as there are some who recognise the bishop in their words, but disregard him in all their actions. Such people seem to me not to act in good faith, since they do not hold valid meetings according to the commandment (*Magnesians* 4).

The young bishop (3.1–2) of Magnesia is not in control of all Christian activities: Ignatius tells the flock to get behind him and his clergy:

> Be zealous to do all things in harmony with God, with the bishop presiding in the place of God and the presbyters in the place of the council of the Apostles, and the deacons (most dear to me) entrusted with the service of Jesus Christ ... (6.1).

[10] Cf. ch. 4 above.

Writing to Smyrna, Ignatius gives an argument against Docetics (who say that Christ only *seemed* to suffer; *Smyrnaeans* 2.1 – 7.2), casting it as a warning about teachers who might visit (4.1) – and following up, as in the Magnesian letter, with an exhortation to stay united and respect the bishop (8.1 – 9.2). At Ephesus, however, he says that the Christians 'stopped up their ears' when false teachers visited (*Ephesians* 9.1) – as might have been expected from the Ephesian record with the Nicolaitans, and the incident of Cerinthus' bath.[11] Instead of warning against meetings without the bishop's permission, Ignatius in his Ephesian letter speaks against one Christian who will not go to church:[12] the 'opposition' is already isolated.

Walter Bauer inferred from Ignatius' references to false teachers that orthodoxy was declining in Asia between the time Revelation was written and when Ignatius wrote. He argued that Gnosticism and Docetism were on the rise, accounting for a large proportion of Asian Christians (1971: 70–75). But, as Christine Trevett comments (1989: 315), not everything Ignatius disliked is to be regarded as heresy.[13] She argues that the Asian churches as reflected in Ignatius, especially the Philadelphian church, show tendencies which later formed the background to the growth of the New Prophecy/Montanism (1989: 313–318). At Philadelphia, close to Montanus' home village of Ardabau,[14] controversy over prophecy seems presupposed in the incident Ignatius describes, in which he prophesied that the congregation ought to 'pay attention to the bishop and the presbytery and the deacons'. Some of the Philadelphians thought he knew of their church's difficulties, and planned his 'prophecy' in advance (*Philadelphians* 7.1–2). This controversy, in Asian Catholic[15] communities, Trevett says, was behind the actual division later in the second century.

---

[11] Irenaeus, *Against Heresies* 3.3.4 (cf. ch. 5 above).

[12] 'Let no man be deceived: unless a man be within the sanctuary he lacks the bread of God ... he who does not join in the common assembly, is already haughty, and has separated himself. For it is written "God resists the proud": let us then be careful not to oppose the bishop, that we may be subject to God.' *Ephesians* 5.2–3.

[13] Trevett (1989: 315 n. 16) refers to earlier scholars' sceptical discussion of Bauer's idea.

[14] Eusebius, *Ecclesiastical History* 5.16.7.

[15] Ignatius, *Smyrnaeans* 8.2 is the first attested use of the term 'Catholic Church': 'Wherever the bishop appears, let the congregation be present; just as wherever Jesus Christ is, there is the Catholic Church. It is not lawful to baptize or to hold an *agapē* without the bishop, but whatever he approves, this is also pleasing to God, so that everything you do may be secure and valid.'

Who was a Gnostic?

Rivalry over leadership is a vital element in the way variant forms of Christianity arose in the second century and beyond. This book does not have space to list them all and record what made each one distinctive – and Riemer Roukema's *Gnosis and Faith in Early Christianity* (1999) is a sensible summary. Roukema traces the development and influence of Gnostic ideas, and the groups in which they were taught. Her argument is least persuasive at the boundaries between Great Church and sectarian Christianities. She records, for example, several features of Marcionite teaching which fit in with the usual Gnostic viewpoints (that the God who created the world [as in the Old Testament] is not the same as the unknown highest God of perfect love, that Jesus came to earth in a phantom body, and so on) – but she is ready in the end to conform with the convention of not regarding Marcionism as Gnostic: she defines it as 'an ascetic Christianity which was cut off from its Jewish roots' (1999: 137–138).

This is unsatisfactory because in a system as varied as Gnosticism, there is no feature of a particular sect which can be regarded as crucial to whether the sect is 'Gnostic' or not. M. A. Williams (1996: 26–27), mentioning the boundary problem posed by Marcionism, proceeds by distinguishing between typological and self-definitional categories: do modern scholars, he asks, use 'Gnosticism' as a category of social-traditional self-definition (so that people who think they are Gnostics *are* Gnostics), or a typological/phenomenological category (so that people who meet set criteria are Gnostics)? 'The answer', he says, 'seems to be: a bit of both, and not quite enough of either' (1996: 30).

More recently, Anne McGuire (1999: 258) has offered a new summary. Helpfully, she points out the importance of distinguishing between varieties of Gnosticism, and correctly foregrounds the role of modern scholars: 'Gnosticism' is our word; the thing it refers to was originally described from various viewpoints, none of which is the same as ours. McGuire's two 'essential features' of Gnosticism leave it very close indeed to ordinary Christianity: the first, 'emphasis on the salvific power of gnosis' is only inches from Jesus' reproach to lawyers for taking away the key of *gnōsis* (Luke 11:52), and the second, 'a worldview that distinguishes sharply between the superior realm of the divine and the inferior realm of the cosmos and its creator', might be a mainstream Christian worldview – except for the last three words, 'and its creator', stipulating higher and lower deities.

McGuire's formulation reflects the real world well. All heterodox theories of Christianity, in the centuries this book is concerned with, drew to a greater or lesser degree on the same pool of ideas. Even Tertullian, most often thought of as an essentially orthodox theologian who ended up in a schismatic (Montanist) church, used a quasi-Gnostic language of esoteric Christianity, placing his fellow-Montanists as pneumatics and the Catholics as psychics:[16] he, like all teachers in minority sects, was in the business of justifying to sectarians the fact of being the minority. So in his treatise on fasting, he shows his contempt for Catholics by contrasting his ideas with what is done 'among the (allegedly) "most glorious multitude" of the psychics' (*On Fasting* 11.1).

A sect might last if it included enough people, or people with enough surplus income, to support its teacher. Like their rivals and role-models the philosophers, Christian teachers (both Catholic and Gnostic) lived on what their students/sects gave. Therefore much more potential for peripheral Christian sects existed in large and rich cities than in small towns and the poverty-stricken countryside. Gnosticism prospered best in metropolitan areas. It is known where many sects were based. Some cannot be placed geographically – the Sethians, for example, who developed the 'Immovable Race' theology. In their case, M. A. Williams (1996: 186–209) can only infer that there were many groups rather than a single organization.[17] There is no reason, however, to think them special: the great cities of the empire are the most likely background to the development of Sethianism, as they were the background to Simonianism and to most of the peripheral Christianities. Exceptions include Ebionites, Montanists, and above all Elchasaites and Manichaeans; but to them I will return below.

Cosmopolitan theologizing

Antioch

The growing modern literature on Gnosticism, however, shows how deep the pool of ideas was – or how inventive teachers, differentiating

---

[16] McKechnie 1996: 427–428; cf. Tertullian, *On Fasting* 1.2 and *On Sexual Morality* 21.16.

[17] Scott 1995, followed by Logan 1996: 28–29, argues for Sethianism as an 'audience-cult' in which (in a way analogous to what is found in astrology, ancient or modern) believers read texts, or consult experts individually, but usually do not form congregations.

their sects from the Great Church and from other sects, could be. Simon Magus, exceptional because he was a sect leader before his contact with Christianity, seems to have been influential in the formative stages.[18] Although the Simonian sect itself had a worldwide membership of fewer than thirty by Origen's time (*Against Celsus* 1.57), Celsus, two generations before, knew of a derivative sect, 'who are Simonians, who reverence as teacher Helena or Helenus and are called Helenians' (5.62). Simon's theories lived on, then – and eventually in multiple reformulated shapes. In his myth (see figure 8.1, overleaf, combining information from Acts and Hippolytus' *Refutation of all Heresies*), Helen features as the First Concept of Simon (the Great Power of God) – and so takes a role rather like the biblical role of Wisdom, God's first creature (Prov. 8:22), present with him while he created the world and humankind (Prov. 8:27–31). Some later Gnostic creation theories also feature a female heavenly being (Sophia [= Wisdom], Barbelo, or whoever) with a comparable role in creation of subordinate deities and/or the world: these ideas derive from a reading of Proverbs mediated through an outlook like Simon's.

Simon's ideas moved into metropolitan circles when his pupil Menander based himself at Antioch; and, if Justin (*First Apologia* 26) is right, followers of the Simon sect went on describing themselves as Christians. Then Satornil/Saturninus, a pupil of Menander, according to Irenaeus, took over in the third generation. Again Syrian-based, he originally came from Antioch-by-Daphne (Irenaeus, *Against Heresies* 1.24.1), and he taught, in *the* Antioch, 'opinions akin to whatever Menander [advanced]' (Hippolytus, *Refutation of all Heresies* 7.16). But changes had come since Simon's day. While Thought is a creative sub-deity in Menander's system, there is no mention of Helen as Thought.[19] A divergence had occurred, although it is impossible to say when there first came to be more than one Simonian group. There were other changes. In Antioch, where the Great Church was a success (and Christians had first been called Christians), there was a gravitational pull on the sects towards mainstream ideas. Three heresiologists[20] say Saturninus taught that Christ came to destroy the God of the Jews –

---

[18] See ch. 2 above.

[19] *Pace* McGuire (1999: 260), who argues that 'second-century followers of Simon looked back to the relations of Simon and Helena as earthly manifestations of a familiar mythic pattern'. In fact Helen (at least) dropped out of the myth, as it was taught by Menander and Saturninus.

[20] Irenaeus, *Against Heresies* 1.24.2; Hippolytus, *Refutation of all Heresies* 7.16; Epiphanius, *Medicine Box* 2.6.

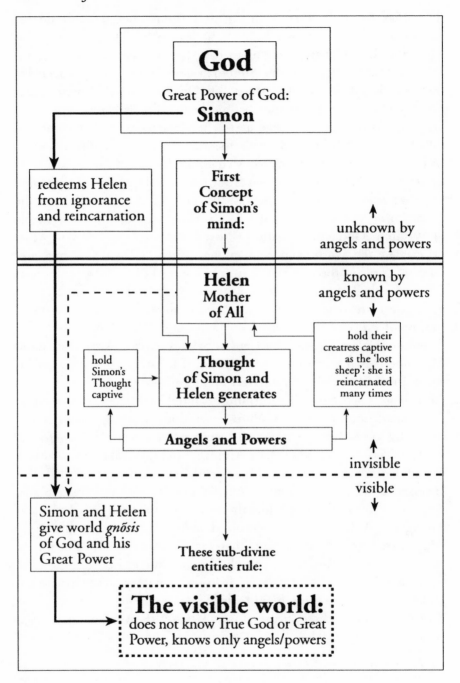

Figure 8.1. Simonians/Helenians: *gnōsis* and the invisible and visible worlds.
Sources: Acts 8:9–12 and Hippolytus, *Refutation of all Heresies* 15.

visiting the earth docetically, 'in human shape and appearance only'.[21] But in Simon's original teaching Christ has no known place, while in Menander's system, *Menander* was the Redeemer.[22]

The Docetic view of Christ worried Ignatius in his Asian letters. Even if Epiphanius had not attributed it to Saturninus, it would have been natural to think that it was around in Antioch as well as the cities Ignatius wrote to. Saturninus, two generations after Simon (who met Peter in the 30s), may have taught in Antioch in the 90's/100's, while Ignatius was bishop. This would account for Ignatius' concern. At Ephesus, destination of one of the letters, Cerinthus had his own version of Docetism, in which Jesus was born of Joseph and Mary (no virgin birth), died on the cross and was raised; but *Christ* came down on Jesus at his baptism in the form of a dove, and left him again before the crucifixion – Christ being spiritual (= pneumatic), and thus unable to suffer.[23]

Alexandria

At Alexandria, about the turn of the first and second centuries, Carpocrates set up a sect, and his son Epiphanes, according to Clement, wrote a book of moral theory called *On Righteousness* before his death at the early age of seventeen.[24] In Alexandria, too, a still more important early second-century figure, Basilides, a pupil of Simon's successor Menander, taught a system in which the God of the Jews, chief of the angels who possess the lowest heaven, tried to subject other nations to the Jews. But the Father, the highest Deity, sent Christ, his firstborn Mind, to the world to free those who believe in him from the power of the lower-heaven angels who made the world. Christ did not die on the cross – Simon of Cyrene did, while Christ stood by laughing at the angels who thought the Mind of the Father could be put to death.[25]

Basilides' system had points of resonance at Alexandria in the period (about 120–40) when he was teaching: hearers after the Second Jewish War (115–17) might respond to the idea of danger from the Jews, with their God trying to make them rulers of the world. This war had

[21] Epiphanius, *Medicine Box* 1.10.

[22] Irenaeus, *Against Heresies* 1.23.5.

[23] Irenaeus, *Against Heresies* 1.26.1; Hippolytus, *Refutation of all Heresies* 7.21.

[24] Clement, *Miscellanies* 3.5.1 – 6.1. On Carpocrates and Epiphanes see M. A. Williams 1996: 184–187.

[25] Irenaeus, *Against Heresies* 1.24.3–4.

featured fighting all over Egypt, and ended with the destruction of the
Jewish community of Alexandria. Afterwards, any drop-off in the
popularity of anti-Jewish preaching was held at bay by the Third
Jewish War (132–35). Isidore, Basilides' son, carried his teaching on
after his father.[26]

Did Christians in Alexandria see Basilides as an outsider? Perhaps
not: Löhr (1996), not accepting anything except actual fragments of
Basilides as valid evidence for his ideas, views him as a moderate re-
interpreter of the Christian message. Löhr has in his favour the fact
that the heresiologists do not say that Basilides was excluded from the
church at Alexandria. Roelof van den Broek (1996: 197) argues that in
the second century there was no authorized Christian 'School' in Alexandria (as Eusebius later thought) – just individual Christian
teachers.[27] If this is true, there may have been no-one in the Alexandrian church whose business it was to clamp down on variant theories of Christianity. But even if there was no regulation, there was
controversy: Eusebius quotes Agrippa Castor, who wrote (in Eusebius'
opinion) 'a most powerful refutation of Basilides' (*Ecclesiastical History*
4.7.6–8).

Agrippa Castor says Basilides wrote twenty-four books about the
Gospel. Their content was not to Agrippa Castor's satisfaction, but the
decision to *comment* rather than to compose a new gospel, as the
Gospel of Thomas writer(s) had done twenty-five years or so before,
shows that Basilides accepted the New Testament and Christian tradition in a way some earlier Gnostic writers had not. He interpreted
mainstream texts rather than composing parallel 'primary' material.
M. A. Williams (1996: 166–167) argues that liberal views on remarriage and eating idol meat suggest that Basilides' teaching shows an
impulse to reduce tension between the Christian community and the
outside world.

Rome

Rome was a still stronger magnet for Gnostic teachers than Antioch or
Alexandria. Bigger, richer and more cosmopolitan, the career possibilities it offered were unrivalled.

[26] Hippolytus, *Refutation of all Heresies* 7.20.1.
[27] Van den Broek takes his theory to extremes when he speculates (1996: 199) that Origen
may not have been taught by Clement.

Valentinus

Valentinus' career in the second century at Rome offers additional reason not to assume that Basilides was excluded from the church at Alexandria. Sources do not make Valentinus Basilides' student (Hippolytus [*Refutation of all Heresies* 6.16] identifies Pythagoreanism and Platonism as his influences), but he was from Egypt. Epiphanius (*Medicine Box* 31.2.2) says he was 'born a Phrebonite, on the coast of Egypt, and received the sort of education which the Greeks do in Alexandria'. Arriving in Rome, he started out within the Great Church: Tertullian claims (possibly unfairly) that he expected his talent as a preacher to gain him the job of bishop – which went to someone else, with a stronger claim based on having been imprisoned for Christianity. Valentinus set out on his own, and, Tertullian adds, at that point had to find a distinctive theory:

> Just like those restless spirits which, when roused by ambition, are usually inflamed with the desire for revenge, he applied himself with all his might to exterminate the truth: and finding the byway of a certain old opinion, he marked out a highway for himself with the subtlety of a serpent. Ptolemy afterwards entered on the same highway, by distinguishing the names and the numbers of the Aeons into personal substances, which, however, he kept apart from God. Valentinus had included these in the very essence of the Deity, as senses and affections of motion. Sundry lanes were then struck off therefrom, by Heracleon and Secundus and the magician Marcus (*Against the Valentinians* 4.1).[28]

Tertullian then (4.2–4) takes a swipe at Valentinus' pupils, who (he says) nearly all taught theories different from their teacher's. Only Axionicus of Antioch, as Tertullian saw it, kept to authentic Valentinianism.[29] Progressive adaptation of a system of thought within one Gnostic tradition has been seen above in the Simonian case, where in the second generation (Menander) Helen is less important, and in the third generation (Saturninus) a place for Christ is needed to give the

---

[28] Cf. *Ruling out of Court the Heretics* 30, where Tertullian says that Marcion and Valentinus 'at first were believers in the doctrine of the Catholic Church'.

[29] This is why so many different Gnostic sects are named by the heresiologists: a sect was not a denomination – it was normally *one* group of people loyal to one teacher.

sect credibility in competition with successful Great Church Christianity at Antioch.

Valentinian theology was equally adaptable. It developed an esotericism 'writ large' because it built on the pneumatic/psychic/hylic distinction by adding the belief that the *spirits* of pneumatics, growing from seeds sown by Achamoth (Hebrew *ḥokmâ*, wisdom) in just souls, and disciplined and nurtured in the material world, achieve blessedness in the next world by being given in marriage to the angels of the Saviour, while *souls* after death (both of psychics and of pneumatics who leave them behind to advance to the spiritual realm) remain in an intermediate region.[30] As a consequence of this theory, each Valentinian subsect could claim that it offered the best nurture for the spirit, while implying that (even) Valentinians in alternative Valentinian sects might be destined for a middling-grade afterlife, no better than that of a psychic.

Cerdo

Just as Valentinus had moved from Alexandria, Cerdo, pupil of Saturninus, moved from Antioch to the capital during the bishopric of Hyginus (150–4). Although Irenaeus places Cerdo in the Simonian tradition, he, like Valentinus, was part of the Great Church, at least when he first arrived in Rome. Irenaeus (*Against Heresies* 1.7.5), later quoted by Eusebius (*Ecclesiastical History* 4.11.1), says that he

> ... joined the Roman church and declared his faith publicly, in the time of Hyginus, the ninth bishop, then he went on in this way: at one time he taught in secret, at another he again declared his faith publicly, at another he was convicted of mischievous teaching and expelled from the assembly of the brethren.

He operated through unofficial classes ('taught in secret'), presumably getting students via church contacts; when confronted about his teaching activities he reaffirmed his loyalty to Christianity, but did not stop teaching, or amend his ideas: a second inquiry led to his exclusion. Irenaeus and Eusebius do not say whether by then he had enough of a following to go on as leader of a self-sustaining sect, but he had bought time to give his career at Rome a start.

---

[30] Irenaeus, *Against Heresies* 1.7.5.

Marcion

Like John the Baptist, Cerdo was followed by one greater than himself: his pupil Marcion.[31] Marcion was the son of a bishop and came from Sinope in Pontus, the province where Pliny persecuted the Christians about twenty-five years before. After he arrived in Rome he not only joined the church but made it a large gift of money: 200,000 sesterces, half the value of the property qualification of a Roman knight. Even if this was his whole wealth, he was a rich man – all the more so if he had also kept something for himself. Things went wrong, and, along with Valentinus (Tertullian says; *Ruling out of Court of the Heretics* 30), Marcion was more than once expelled from the Roman church, eventually on a permanent basis – at which point the church repaid his money. At the end of his life, Tertullian continues, Marcion repented and was told he could be brought back into the Great Church 'if he restored to the church all the others whom he had been training for perdition': but he died before this condition could be met.

As a sect leader, Marcion made two moves which separate him from the herd of Gnostic teachers, whose practical ambitions extended only to securing an income by getting a sufficient following. He understood the potential of mission, as the son of a small-town bishop well might – and encouraged his followers to spread his message quickly: they were (as W. Bauer [1971: 2–17] showed) the first Christians at Edessa.[32] Justin in the 150s, in Marcion's lifetime, said that Marcionism had spread 'to every human nation' (*First Apologia* 1.26), and fifty years later it was still growing: 'Marcion's heresy', said Tertullian, 'has filled the whole world' (*Ruling out of Court of the Heretics* 5.19). Confirmation of a serious truth behind Justin's and Tertullian's view comes a century and a half later in advice given by Cyril of Jerusalem to Christians: when you go to a strange town, he says, do not just ask where the church is – check that the one they send you to is Orthodox, because Marcionites (and other heretics) 'try to call their caves "churches"' (*Catechisms* 18.26).

Marcion's other key move, anticipated by Basilides, was to tap into anti-Jewish sentiment caused by the Third Jewish War. Werner Eck (1999) has recently shown how dangerous the Romans thought this war was – and how lavish the monuments they built to celebrate their

---

[31] Irenaeus, *Against Heresies* 1.25.1; Epiphanius, *Medicine Box* 41.1.9
[32] Cf. chs. 2 and 4 above.

eventual victory were. Marcion, teaching in Rome from the 130s and probably parting company for the last time with the Great Church about 144,[33] not only made the Jewish God subordinate to the highest Deity (as many Gnostic theorists did), but completely abolished the Old Testament from his version of Christian Scripture. Since the New Testament quotes the Old Testament in hundreds of places, abolition of the Old Testament required consequential editing of the New. The Marcionite Bible consisted of one Gospel (a shortened Luke, the one most closely associated with the Pauline mission) and ten Pauline Epistles (no Pastorals). Marcion's good God, the God of the New Testament, was not the ruler of this world, and was not known to the subordinate god who created it until he appeared (but not with a body of flesh and blood) in Christ. He is not a judge who punishes the wicked (though on the Last Day he will separate believers in himself from worshippers of the creator-god). The creator-god, on the other hand, is the ruler of this world – his promises refer to this world, were made to the Jews, and are valid only for them: the Old Testament is his book, and does not refer to or prophesy about Christ (cf. Blackman 1948: 48).

Although it grew quickly, Marcion's church does not deserve Lüdemann's (1996: 215) description of it as 'the great motive power in second-century church history'.[34] Its success came from Marcion's energy and his knack for combining ideas whose time had come. Gnostic thought was attractive (and had potential to spread beyond metropolitan settings), hatred of the Jews was in fashion,[35] and a shortened Bible offered Marcionite preachers the chance to simplify.

Seen through a modern filter, Marcion can seem more important than he was. His preoccupation with Paul and his dislike of the Old Testament have seemed to some scholars to make him a sort of Protestant. August Neander in the first half of the nineteenth century said that 'we recognise in Marcion a Protestant spirit though mixed with error' (1878: 87). Later, part of the impulse behind von Harnack's

---

[33] Stevenson 1988: 93.

[34] Cf. Introduction above.

[35] Hill argues that Cerinthus' (late first-century) views about the Jews and their sacred texts influenced Marcion's attitude to the Old Testament (2000: 162), and that Marcion's teaching advanced quickly in Asia because the ground had been prepared for it there by Cerinthus (2000: 170). But Hill's assumption that Cerinthus' teachings would have been known as far away from Ephesus as Sinope is questionable. His theory as a whole is not satisfactory, because he posits that a long-dead theologian had more influence than the recent war in forming anti-Jewish feelings.

book on Marcion was his own liking for the idea that only the New Testament (and not the Old) should be the Christian sacred text. Next, E. C. Blackman, a century after Neander, claimed that 'this was the first "protestant" schism' (1948: 74, where Neander and von Harnack are quoted). And the theme of protest and Protestants persists, still winning Marcion admirers. Recently, Alastair H. B. Logan (1999: 29) has called Marcionism 'a protest movement within Christianity harking back to the pure message of Jesus and his Father, the God of Love, and to Paul's understanding of the faith'. Logan's is a sentimental view,[36] sidelining the importance of monotheism and the Old Testament, both to Jesus and Paul. The Marcionite/Protestant analogy is misleading if taken too far.

So Valentinus', Cerdo's and Marcion's dissatisfactions with things in the Roman church prompted them to lead their own sects: Novatian and Hippolytus, also in the capital, and Tertullian in Carthage, later took the same route, though their post-schism theological teachings were arguably less divergent. These cases show that the Great Church was the motive force in Christian growth: it had the numbers fringe teachers needed to draw on to get their enterprises established. Sects might look back to the Great Church and amend their theories, as Saturninus did in Antioch, to improve their appeal to the Christians who were their prime targets for recruitment. Even Marcion did this, late in life, when he tried to bring about a reconciliation between his church and the Catholics.

Non-metropolitan sects

Ebionites

In Christian congregations outside large cities, the situation was different: the potential payoff from leading a minority within a minority was small or non-existent. Non-metropolitan sects, therefore, were usually local (majority) Christian groups. The Ebionites are a good example. A Jewish-Christian sect, they were based in northern Judea/Palestine and southern Syria. Epiphanius in his *Medicine Box*, asserting mistakenly that the Ebionite sect was established by a person called Ebion, connects the Ebionites with the Nazarenes:

---

[36] He continues, 'No wonder Marcion was excommunicated and expelled from the Church.'

Ebion, the founder of the Ebionites ... held doctrines like those of the Nazarenes ... being from their sect ... (30.1.1).

[The Ebionite] sect began after the capture of Jerusalem. For when all those who believed in Christ settled at that time for the most part in Peraea, in a city called Pella belonging to the Decapolis mentioned in the Gospel, which is next to Batanea and the land of Bashan, then they moved there and stayed, and that provided an opportunity for Ebion. He took up residence in a village called Kokaba by the region of Karnaim, which is also called Ashteroth, in the land of Bashan, as the report which we received has it (2.7).

Kokaba has been mentioned before, as one of the villages where Jesus' relatives settled. Epiphanius reflects part of the reality of Jewish Christianity in the earliest generations. Bauckham (1990: 62–63), canvassing modern places which might correspond to Epiphanius' Kokaba, notes that the name was common – but argues that Epiphanius' identification of it as an Ebionite centre is confirmed by Eusebius, who in his list of Palestinian place-names (*Word-List* 172) refers to an Ebionite village called Khoba: 'Khoba, which is to the left of Damascus. There is also a village of Khoba in the same district, in which there are Hebrews who believe in Christ, called Ebionites.'

The Ebionites, whose name really derives from Hebrew *'ebyôn*, meaning 'poor', are described by the heresiologists as believing that Christians must be circumcised, venerating Jerusalem as the house of God, and not accepting the virgin birth of Jesus. They believed that he was conceived in the normal way, and then (unlike other humans) kept the law perfectly,[37] so being named the Christ of God – with the result that 'they themselves also, when in like manner they fulfil [the law], are able to become Christs'.[38] The only Gospel they read was Matthew (probably the original Matthew in Hebrew or Aramaic), and they did not read Paul.[39] Their belief in a human Christ was unlike the Docetic/Gnostic view shared by many sects, and the practice which an Ebionite splinter group followed of worshipping on both Saturdays and

---

[37] Eusebius, *Ecclesiastical History* 3.27, 6.17.
[38] Hippolytus, *Refutation of all Heresies* 7.22.
[39] Circumcision, Jerusalem, Matthew, rejection of Paul: Irenaeus, *Against Heresies* 1.26.2.

Sundays[40] implies that most Ebionites had always maintained Saturday worship. They were a one-off case: a Jewish group which was not ready to face the changes implied by growth of Gentile churches and the destruction of the temple, and hung on in a few Palestinian and Syrian villages until Eusebius' time. Unwilling to go with people in the cities who did not think it necessary to be Jewish in order to be Christian, they were as dissimilar from second-century Gnostics as any Christian could be.[41]

Montanists

Another rural background, this time in Asia Minor, was the setting for the growth of Montanism from the middle of the second century. Montanus, together with two prophetesses, Priscilla and Maximilla, started a movement in Phrygia which called itself the New Prophecy. Stressing that the days of prophecy and the Holy Spirit's intervention in the lives of believers were not over, they experienced what they saw as a fresh outpouring of the Spirit. Trevett (1996: 40–41) describes what happened next:

> The women abandoned their husbands and became part of the circle which included Montanus ... prophesying in ecstasy and at what seemed to the catholics to be inappropriate moments. What seems to have started as revivalist outpourings with demands and promises attached – challenging the lives of listeners, condemning some and praising others ... turned to condemnation of unreconstructed catholics and the tradition of which they remained uncritical.

Increased moral rigour went with the Montanists' attention to the Holy Spirit. Extra fasting was recommended, and remarriage after the death of a wife or husband discouraged. In Asia, by the 170's, a dispute began, with books written against the Montanists.

Montanists' attempts to defend themselves in their dispute in Asia were behind an incident in which Eleutherus, bishop of Rome 174–89, first endorsed the New Prophecy, then withdrew his approval. He had

---

[40] Most Ebionites worshipped on Saturday; the splinter group's point of difference was *adding* Sunday worship. Eusebius, *Ecclesiastical History* 3.27: 'like the others, they observed the Sabbath and the whole Jewish system; yet on the Lord's Day they celebrated rites similar to our own in memory of the Saviour's resurrection'.

[41] Ebionites are a boundary case for M. A. Williams (1996: 38–39), who points out that while almost no-one in the modern world counts them as part of 'Gnosticism', Hippolytus in the *Refutation of all Heresies* could lump them in with Cerinthus.

received letters from the martyrs who were put to death in Gaul in 177
– and they in turn, Trevett argues (1996: 41, 56), had probably heard
from Asia Minor about the dissension surrounding Montanism. A
decision at Rome, however, had only persuasive force in other cities'
churches, and international contacts the Montanists made did not lead
to reconciliation in Asia. From probably the late 170s, Montanism was
unacceptable there as part of Great Church Christianity. But it was not
banned everywhere: so Perpetua and the other martyrs put to death in
Carthage in 203 were Montanist-influenced (this is clear from the
tenor of references to the work of the Holy Spirit in the *Martyrdom of
Perpetua*), but, once martyred, they were celebrated as Catholic saints
(McKechnie 1996: 426–427).

Rather like Marcionism, Montanism gained popularity. But unlike
Marcionism, it started its growth from an area with little urban settle-
ment, and was first preached and practised in villages. Eusebius intro-
duces his section on Montanism by saying:

> In Phrygian Mysia there is said to be a village called Ardabau.
> There they say that a recent convert called Montanus, when
> Gratus was proconsul of Asia, in the unbounded lust of his soul
> for leadership gave access to himself to the Adversary, and sud-
> denly fell into frenzy and convulsions. He began to be ecstatic
> and to speak and to talk strangely, prophesying contrary to the
> custom which belongs to the tradition and succession of the
> Church from the beginning (*Ecclesiastical History* 5.16.7).

It is unfortunately not known when Gratus was proconsul of Asia.
The claim that Montanus was a recent convert may be correct, or a
slander spread by his opponents. His aspirations for leadership fit the
pattern observed among the metropolitan Gnostic teachers, but possibly he was not moving against existing leaders, but had a place in the
established leadership of the church in his local area. After Montanus'
prophecies began, his followers were based at the villages of Pepuza
and Tymion, which, Montanus taught them, were destined to be the
new Jerusalem.[42]

---

[42] These villages were to the east of Philadelphia. Trevett (1996: 24) draws attention to the
probable relevance of Rev. 3:12 (directed to the church at Philadelphia): 'I will write on you
the name of my God, and the name of the city of my God, the new Jerusalem that comes
down from my God out of heaven ...' On one reading, this might be taken as implying that
the new Jerusalem was to descend out of heaven in the Philadelphian region.

Montanism's heart was in Phrygia, where it became, or always had been, the majority form of Christianity. Montanists could be called simply 'Phrygians' by the heresiologists.[43] By the fourth century distinctive gravestones using the phrase 'Christians for Christians' in epitaphs were being put up, only in Phrygia: these belong to the Montanist community and show that long after Montanism had ceased to be a large-scale movement in Christianity, the Phrygian churches held on to it. In urban centres, Philadelphia, Hierapolis and Ancyra, there was debate, and eventually rejection of the Montanist message; but in the rural area where it originated the Montanist church *was* the church. The Montanists did not cross the road and build new chapels – they were the people in charge. But from the 170s the followers of their preachers in the Asian cities were excluded from Catholic churches, while in the remote rural areas their churches were cut off from the organizational contact they used to have with Christian churches empire-wide.

The story of the New Prophecy is a story of what could happen when a local movement tried to spread beyond its roots (which Ebionism never would have wished to do). Churches were diverse, and people in them knew little about what was done and said in other areas. This could minimize conflict, but when differences became known, they were hard to resolve. So it was with the Quartodeciman controversy in the late second century. Roman Christians, who celebrated Easter on the Sunday following the fourteenth day of the lunar month of Nisan, came face to face with the fact that Asian Christians celebrated it on the fourteenth day itself (the day of the Passover): as they saw it, Easter Day did not have to be a Sunday. Letters flew back and forth. Victor, the first native Latin-speaking bishop of Rome (189–99) (previous bishops having been Greek-speakers), moved to excommunicate all the Asian churches over the dispute. Others, including Irenaeus, urged moderation:

> Irenaeus ... wrote in the name of the brethren in Gaul, whose leader he was; and, while holding that the mystery of the Lord's resurrection should be celebrated on the Lord's day and on that alone, he nevertheless gave Victor much suitable counsel besides, not to cut off whole churches of God for observing an ancient

---

[43] Hippolytus, *Refutation of all Heresies* 8.12, 10.21–22; Eusebius, *Ecclesiastical History* 5.16.1 and elsewhere.

custom handed down to them. Then he goes on to add, in these very words:

'Not only is there a controversy about the day, but also about the very manner of the [pre-Easter] fast. For some think they ought to fast a single day, but others two, others again even more. And in the opinion of others, the 'day' amounts to forty continuous hours. This variety of observance did not originate in our time, but much further back, in the times of those before us, who (no doubt mistakenly) held closely, in their simplicity and ignorance, to this custom, and have transmitted it to posterity. Yet none the less they all lived in peace, and we live in peace, with one another; and the difference concerning the fast enhances the unanimity of our faith' (Eusebius, *Ecclesiastical History* 5.24.11–13).

Brought up and educated in Asia, but bishop of a western city, Irenaeus knew more about both sides than most. But the Quartodeciman problem proved less serious than the problem raised by Montanism, because no-one exploited it to the full in struggles over leadership – except in Rome, where perhaps Victor feared Greeks might unite against him around the issue.

By contrast, in Carthage Montanism was used to polarize allegiances. Tertullian, an intellectual with high qualifications, was converted to Christianity about 190. He was not ordained, but it seems certain that he became a catechism teacher. By the time of the martyrdom of Perpetua (203) there was a rift between the bishop of Carthage and a catechism teacher called Aspasius, who was a colleague of Tertullian's and probably saw things his way. Saturus, about to be martyred with Perpetua and the rest, dreamt that he and Perpetua went to heaven; when they came out of the Lord's presence, says Saturus in the *Martyrdom of Perpetua* (13.1–6),

we ... saw outside the gates Bishop Optatus on the right and Aspasius the presbyter and teacher on the left, separated and sorrowing. And they threw themselves down at our feet and said, 'Mediate between us, for you have passed away and left us like this!' And we said to them, 'Are you not our father? And are you not our presbyter? So how is it that you are throwing yourselves down at our feet?' And we were moved with emotion and we embraced them. Perpetua began to talk with them in

Greek, and we took them aside into the garden beneath a rose tree.

While we were talking with them, the angels said to them, 'Let them take their ease, and if you have any disagreements between you, settle them between yourselves.' And they put them to confusion. They said to Optatus, 'Correct your people, since they gather to you just as if they were coming back from the racetrack arguing about the teams.'

The dream is about a church facing a deepening rift. Perpetua might have been a suitable reconciler (Saturus' unconscious mind tells him), but she is destined for heavenly joys which (the angels decree) shall not be disturbed by earthly worries. Those left alive must take responsibility for their worldly concerns.

Three years later, in 206, Tertullian and a Montanist-influenced group who came to be called 'Tertullianists' split from the Carthaginian church.[44] Trevett (1996: 67–76) comments on how different African Montanism seems from the Asian version: but difference is what one would expect. Tertullian, a strong character who had not been (or had not allowed himself to be) fully co-opted by the leadership of the church, used the Montanist model of church life as a template on which to construct a sect based around himself. Montanism, as an international movement, was something he could draw on as a source of legitimacy.

Manichaeans

The Marcionites, then, started in Rome and succeeded in growing through mission, while the New Prophecy's attempt to spread revival into bigger churches from its rural base proved controversial – catching on best in Africa, where (and because) Tertullian pressed it into the service of his own bid for leadership. At the eastern end of the Roman empire, however, a small and very early Christian movement gave birth in the third century to a Christian-based new cult which was to develop into the broadest-based religion, in geographical terms, in the ancient and medieval worlds.

There was a man called Elchasai: 'Hidden Power'. Hippolytus says that in his (Hippolytus') time a man called Alcibiades of Apamea came

---

[44] Dating and detail argued at McKechnie 1996: 427.

to Rome and described how Elchasai came into possession of a book revealed by an angel:

> It is said that Elchasai, a righteous man, had received a book from the Seres in Parthia [= northern Iran] and had transmitted it to certain baptists. It had been communicated by an angel, whose height was 24 schoinoi, which is 96 miles, his breadth 4 schoinoi, and from shoulder to shoulder 6 schoinoi, and the tracks of his feet in length 3½ schoinoi, and in height half a schoinos. And with him was also a female figure, whose measurements Alcibiades says were commensurate with those mentioned; and the male figure was the Son of God, and the female was called Holy Spirit ...
>
> He [Elchasai] affirms the following: that the gospel of a new forgiveness of sins was preached to men in the third year of Trajan's reign. And he appoints a baptism ... of which he says that through it anyone who is defiled by any licentiousness and pollution and lawlessness receives forgiveness of sins ... if he is converted and listens to the book and believes in it (*Refutation of all Heresies* 9.13.1–2).

The third year of Trajan (98–117) was 100; Samuel N. C. Lieu (1992: 40–41) argues, however, that the third year of the *reign* may be confused here with the third year after Trajan conquered Parthia (116/ 17). In either case, thirty to fifty years before the Marcionites first reached Edessa, on the eastern border of the Roman empire, Elchasai's version of Christianity was revealed (according to Alcibiades, whom Hippolytus disbelieves) well outside Roman territory, in Parthia – and not even revealed to him, but to 'Seres', perhaps silk-merchants,[45] from whom he got his book. The special characteristic of the Elchasaite sect was its use of baptism. Sometimes called 'hemerobaptists' (= 'daily-baptizers'), the Elchasaites believed they should be rebaptized regularly – both when they repented of their sins, and when they suffered accidental defilement:

> If ... any man or woman or youth or maid is bitten, torn or touched by a mad and raving dog, in which is a spirit of

---

[45] *Sēres* is the Greek word for Chinese people, whom Romans mostly met on the silk route.

destruction, let him run in the same hour with all he wears, and go down to a river or a spring, wherever there may be a deep place, and let him baptize himself with all he wears, and pray to the great and most high God with a faithful heart. Then let him call to witness the seven witnesses written in this book: 'Behold, I call to witness the heaven and water and the holy spirits, and the angels of prayer and oil and salt and earth. These seven witnesses do I call to witness, that I will no more sin, nor commit adultery, nor steal, nor claim more than is due, nor hate, nor transgress, nor take pleasure in any wickedness' (Hippolytus, *Refutation of all Heresies* 9.15.4–6).

The outlook of Elchasai's sect was unexceptional: it forbade marriage, which the Marcionites did, and believed, as many sects did, that worshipping idols when forced to was not a sin. They were never numerous, but in the early third century they gained a convert called Patik, in Seleucia/Ctesiphon, the twin cities on the Tigris river at the heart of the Parthian empire. He joined the Elchasaites after responding to an experience he had in a pagan temple: a voice commanded him not to eat meat, drink wine, or be married. He, his wife Maryam (whom he later left for the sake of the celibacy the voice demanded), and their son Mani (born 216) went east and joined an Elchasaite community in Dastumisan, near Basra in what is now Iraq (Welburn 1998: 67; Lieu 1992: 36).

Brought up in the sect, Mani ended up dissatisfied with it. The *Cologne Mani Codex* speaks of his feeling of not fitting in, and his confidence in angelic protection:

> ... with wisdom and skill I was going about, keeping the Rest. Neither doing wrong nor inflicting pain, nor following the law of the Elchasaites though I was in their midst, nor speaking the way they did (5).
> ... Then I, Mani, gained entrance to the teachings of the [Elchasaite] Baptists in which I was reared, while my body was young, being guarded by the might of the light-angels and the exceedingly strong powers, who had a command from Jesus the Splendour for my safekeeping (11).

The tension of living among Elchasaites while feeling he could not follow their lifestyle brought Mani, in 240, to the turning-point of his life. He had a vision of his heavenly Twin, bringing him instructions from God:

> When I was twenty-four years old, in the year in which Ard-ashir, the King of Persia, subdued the city of Hatra, and also in which his son Shapur, the King, crowned himself with the grand diadem, in the month of Pharmouthi, on the eighth day of the lunar month, the most blessed Lord was greatly moved with compassion for me, called me into his grace, and immediately sent to me from there my Twin, appearing in great glory ... When my Father was pleased and had mercy and compassion on me, to ransom me from the error of the Sectarians, he took consideration of me through his very many revelations, and he sent to me my Twin ... (18–19).

Soon afterwards, his differences with his fellow-sectarians came into the open. Washing food before eating, he believed, and washing the body after sinning, were worthless:

> I said to them ... 'There is [no value] in [this] ritual washing with which you cleanse your food. For this body is defiled and is formed by a defiled moulding. Consider how, when someone purifies his food and partakes of it after it has been ritually washed, it is apparent that from it come blood, bile, belches and shameful excrement and the foulness of the body ... And the way you ritually wash yourselves in water every day, this also has no value. For if you have once been cleansed and purified, why do you ritually wash yourselves again every day? ... it is clearly very plain that all defilement is from the body. Behold, you yourselves are clothed in it' (80–83).

This outspoken attack on everything they stood for provoked the sect members to seize Mani and beat him. His father's intervention prevented them from killing him. Reflecting on his escape, Mani received further encouragement from the heavenly Twin:

> You were not sent only to this creed, but to every people and [school] of learning and to every city and region; for [this] Hope will be made manifest and preached by you in every clime and [zone] of the world and many [people] will receive your word.

Go from here and travel about. For I will be with you as your helper and protector at every place where you will preach everything which I have revealed to you (104–105).

He went to Ctesiphon, where he was initially joined by two El-chasaites, who believed that he was a reincarnation of the True Prophet, previously incarnate in Adam, Christ and Elchasai (106). Then Mani's father Patik came on board, and slowly his sect began to grow. A complex system of doctrine was contained in seven canonical texts, written in Aramaic by Mani,[46] and a middle Persian summary of Manichaean teaching, also written by Mani, for Shapur I, called the *Sabuhragan*. Manichaean writers elaborated and proclaimed Mani's ideas over the following centuries in books written in languages from every region between western Europe and China. The *Cologne Mani Codex* is in Greek, Augustine of Hippo before his reconversion to Catholicism learnt Manichaean doctrine in Latin, and Manichaean manuscripts in Uighur and Chinese were discovered in 1905 by Aurel Stein in the Temple of the Thousand Buddhas in Tun-huang (Lieu 1992: 8).

The missionary impulse evident in the experience Mani had of the heavenly Twin was behind this diffusion of his sect. Mani lived to be sixty before being tortured to death in Vahram I's prison at Bet Laphat/Gundashapur in Khuzistan in 276 (Lieu 1985: 106–109): by that time he had both travelled extensively himself making converts, and sent missionaries in all directions. Adda and another Patik (not Mani's father) were sent into Roman territory, where they held debates with religious leaders, wrote books, made converts and generally promoted Manichaeism. Known in the west by the lengthened name of Adimantus, Adda wrote a book about Manichaeism, called the *Modius* (= 'Bushel'),[47] and was important enough for Augustine of Hippo, nearly two centuries later, to think it worth writing a book against him.

Mani's ideas were capable of being popularized. There were two categories of Manichaean: not all had to follow the celibacy and poverty embraced by the Elect. Hearers, Manichaeans of the lower grade, were free to marry (or live with an unmarried partner, as Augustine did in his Manichaean days) and own property, but adopted a vegetarian diet. The souls of the Elect, Manichaeans believed, would

---

[46] The *Living Gospel*, the *Treasure of Life*; the *Pragmateia*; the *Book of Mysteries*; the *Book of the Giants*; the *Letters*; *Psalms and Prayers* (Lieu 1992: 8).

[47] Lieu (1985: 91–92) considers possible backgrounds to the unusual title of this lost book.

attain the Kingdom of Light after death, while Hearers would undergo reincarnations on earth until, by eventually being reincarnated as a Manichaean Elect, each gained liberation (Lieu 1985: 29). Prospects of being reincarnated as an Elect were influenced by how devotedly a Hearer served the Elect in the present life – for instance by preparing food, which it was not lawful for the Elect to do for themselves.

Adda's mission and others brought converts in many parts of the Roman empire. Back in Persia, Mani's Elchasaite critics accused him of having 'eaten Greek bread'[48] – by which they probably meant that he was influenced by Pauline Christianity. When it was preached, his system was far from strange to western ears. Eusebius was later to refer to the influence of second-century Gnosticism:

> [Mani] ... stitched together false and godless doctrines that he had collected from the countless long-extinct godless heresies, and infected our empire with, as it were, a deadly poison that came from the land of the Persians; and from him the profane name of Manichaean is still commonly on men's lips to this day (*Ecclesiastical History* 7.31.2).

Eusebius' phrase about 'countless long-extinct godless heresies' may underestimate the liveliness of Gnostic sects in Mani's time. But it would be fair comment about Gnosticism in Eusebius' day. Mani re-invigorated Gnostic thought, and the boost he gave it drove some competitors out of business. Marcion in the mid-second century had delivered a stripped-down missionary Christianity with an anti-Jewish streak, exactly when anti-Semitism was at a premium; now Mani's followers combined Gnostic theorizing with missionary zeal and church organization – so that individualistic Gnostic teachers, like Valentinus' seven variously minded disciples, found it hard to keep up.

Sectarianism in the development of Christianity

Sects which existed only to earn their teachers income were prone to collapse. Purely local strands of Christianity, like those of the Ebionites and the Elchasaites, lacked growth potential. But more co-operative, broader-based Christian enterprises made gains. Most modern scholars agree that initiatives like Hegesippus' tour of the empire show that the

---

[48] *Cologne Mani Codex* 87 and Lieu 1985: 51.

Great Church was giving ever greater attention to interlocal organizational connections before 200, even though troubles like the Quartodeciman dispute could put a damper on moves towards unity. Marcion made his sect a success by going for mission in all directions from Rome, and Mani did the same thing, working from a different starting-point. They both acted under the influence of Paul – the 'Greek bread' Mani was accused of eating, and, in Marcion's system, the person who sat at the left hand of the Father while Jesus occupied the seat on the right.

M. A. Williams (1996: 109–110), drawing on Stark and Bainbridge (1985) (and on Max Weber and Ernst Troeltsch), argues that successful religious movements 'drift' towards accommodation with their sociocultural environment: as the movement succeeds and brings a larger percentage of the whole society into membership of it, the points of conflict between the movement and the surrounding world lessen, because the movement's distinctiveness becomes harder to maintain with a larger membership.

Accordingly, Christianity started as a sect, not only in the sense of being a renewal movement within first-century Judaism (like Pharisaism, the Qumran sect, the House of Hillel), but also, once there were Gentile Christians, in that they lived in a state of high tension with the Greco-Roman cultural environment. Socially powerful members of a sect tend, Stark and Bainbridge argue, to desire to reduce the tension between the sect and its environment – and usually have the power to cause the reduction they want. This accounts for a drift in Christianity from (in Stark and Bainbridge's terms) 'sect' to 'church'. In Christianity, even while it remained illegal, it is possible to see cultural accommodation: Aristides, Peregrinus, Justin and the rest identifying as Greek philosophers and also Christians; and sect leaders, including those in the Elchasaite sect, deciding that worshipping polytheistic gods, under duress, was not sinful.

Williams in his discussion distinguishes usefully between 'sect movements' within Christianity, which split off in order to maintain a higher level of tension with the social environment, and what he calls 'church movements', whose aim was to reduce tension. He quotes Stark and Bainbridge, who say that there is

... a powerful motive for upwardly mobile members of a deviant religious group to seek to lower their group's tension. But if these members are too marginal to the group, if they are not in fact its most powerful members, they may be unable to cause a reduction in tension. In such a predicament, these persons may form a new religious organization that is in lower tension with the world than is the parent body (Stark & Bainbridge 1985: 123).

Valentinian Christians, they add, suit this description. So do many followers of metropolitan Gnostic groups. Williams sums up the situation in a useful diagram (given as figure 8.2), which shows sect movements reacting against Christianity's overall 'tendency to low-tension sociocultural accommodation', while church movements 'break off the front end' by moving faster towards acceptability in the world. Thus on the left-hand side of Williams' diagram come the Marcionites, who forbade marriage, and the Montanists, who were stricter about fasting than the Catholics, and the Ebionites, who persisted in having nothing to do with Greek Christianity at all. On the right-hand side are the Valentinians, who, Irenaeus says, took a scornful attitude to Christian martyrs and martyrdom, and the followers of Basilides, who were allegedly prepared to deny Christ to avoid suffering.[49] The two Theodoti and Natalius, also listed on the right, were behind a short-lived split in the Roman church around the first decade of the third century.[50]

The sect-movement/church-movement distinction adds an analytical tool to the observation that divisions within urban Christianity were about leadership. Urban leaders were more likely to succeed by leading in the front-end direction; high-tension sect movements, however, prospered away from the great metropolitan areas: thus Marcionism, though begun in Rome, took off because it turned to empire-wide mission; Montanism, begun in the Phrygian countryside, provoked opposition as soon as it reached Ancyra. In Manichaeism the country came to town: *vis-à-vis* the Elchasaites,[51] Mani's was a front-end break,

[49] The opponents at Irenaeus, *Against Heresies* 3.18.5, are usually identified as Valentinians (e.g. M. A. Williams 1996: 103); on the Basilideans, *Against Heresies* 1.24.6.

[50] Eusebius, *Ecclesiastical History* 5.28.3–19. M. A. Williams (1996: 111–112) identifies theirs as a movement which 'broke off the front end', but scepticism may be in order: the enterprise began when Theodotus the cobbler was excommunicated by Bishop Victor – and he, as the Quartodeciman dispute shows, may have been inclined to be hasty about excommunicating Greeks.

[51] Logan (1999: 30) makes the point that in Stark and Bainbridge's terms Manichaeism should count as a *cult*, i.e. a new religion, rather than (as Stark and Bainbridge describe it) a sect. This comment is perceptive, but does not allow for the fact that Mani's movement split off not from the Great Church but from the Elchasaites, a small sect who practised a high-tension version of Christianity.

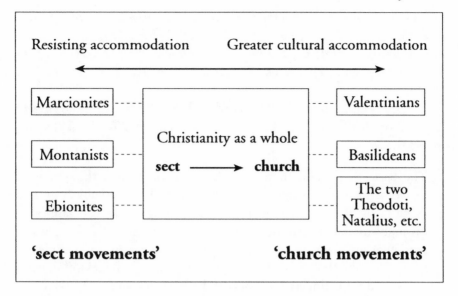

Figure 8.2. Select Christian demiurgical movements and other groups compared in terms of tendency towards high-tension sociocultural resistance versus tendency towards low-tension sociocultural accommodation. From M. A. Williams 1996: 111.

ending daily baptismal washing, modifying dietary rules and (metaphorically) 'eating Greek bread': the Manichaean religion gained from its founder some of the features it needed to make it appeal, in the next century, to a young, high-powered urbanite called Augustine.

The Great Church and doctrinal development

I have argued, contrary to Lüdemann, that the Great Church, not Marcionism or any of the other outcrops of the bush, was where the energy came from in second- (and third-)century Christianity – and yet I have used more pages sketching sectarian beliefs than describing the beliefs of the majority. This does not mean to imply that majority ideas were less interesting; still less that they remained static while the fringe teachers innovated. Part of the reason this book does not explore the doctrinal issues with which Great Church authors were most concerned (including soteriology, Scripture and tradition, morality, martyrdom, forgiveness versus unforgivable sin) is that almost any theologian could do the job better than I could – and many have:

important books include Henry Chadwick's *Early Christian Thought and the Classical Tradition* (1966), Meeks' *The Origins of Christian Morality* (1993), Eric Osborn's *Tertullian, First Theologian of the West* (1997) and Theissen's *The Religion of the Earliest Churches* (1999).

But I am also persuaded by Maurice Wiles's baby against trying to be a historian of pre-Constantine dogma. Wiles (1967: 18–19) comments that

> The basic distinction in the whole realm of human thought is between the self and the not-self. It is here that the baby begins as he takes his first steps in human reasoning ... In the case of distinguishing between the self and the not-self the baby pays particular attention to those things which appear to stand somewhere on the borderland between the two – the extremities of his body, his fingers and toes, and the gloves and socks which he finds so closely associated with them. So also with the Church ...

Thus (Wiles argues) it was the heretic, 'the would-be Christian whom she was unwilling to recognise', who provoked the church to articulate Christian beliefs more precisely. Like Wiles, I see the principled exploration of 'toe-or-sock' issues as happening at the moment when 'the sock falls off'. The events leading to separation have their own causes – and *those* are what this book is about. M. A. Williams' observation about Christianity's drift to lower tension with society adds to Wiles's picture (using different imagery), but the two views are not at all irreconcilable.

A case where 'no sock fell off': Origen

This chapter closes with an example on the 'self' side of the 'self versus not-self' question. The development of normative Christianity was only secondarily about competition between systems of theological thought. In some arenas, such as Alexandria, this competition may have gone on in a less fettered form than in Rome, where bishops imposed a sanction of exclusion against some teachers from as early as the first half of the second century; but the acceptability to bishops of particular theories was not the heart of the issue. The teacher who proves that proposition is Origen.

Born in 185, Origen was a child prodigy as a literature student. He began earning his and his family's living by teaching Greek literature at the age of sixteen, after his father, a centurion, suffered martyrdom in Alexandria (Eusebius, *Ecclesiastical History* 6.1.1 – 2.15). Before the end of the Severan persecution he was teaching Christianity to cat-echumens in Alexandria, because the other Christian teachers had fled (6.3.1–3). Eusebius claims that Origen in his childhood was already asking the allegorical meanings of the Bible passages his father made him learn – the literal meaning was never enough (6.2.9).

His sophisticated understanding of the Bible, inherited from the style of interpretation practised by Philo and in the *Epistle of Barnabas*, made Origen's outlook on the Christian thought-world very different from that of those he called 'the simpler ones of the church'. At the same time, it gave him a framework within which to understand why 'the hard-hearted and ignorant members of the circumcision' (Jews) and 'heretical sects' (Gnostics) misinterpreted Scripture (Origen, *Principles* 4.2.1; cf. Dechow 1988: 338). The heart of the trouble, as he saw it, was literalism – to him, it was basic that 'Scripture is not understood in its literal sense' (4.2.2). It said things which 'did not happen ... could not happen, and ... might have happened but in fact did not' (4.2.9). Energetic commentary on the beginning of Genesis shows how vital he thought non-literal hermeneutic was:

> What person of intelligence will believe that the first, second and third days, and the evening and the morning, existed without the sun and moon and stars? And that the first day (if we can call it that) was even without a heaven? And who is so silly as to believe that God, after the manner of a farmer, 'planted a paradise eastward in Eden', and set in it a visible and palpable 'tree of life', of such a sort that anyone who tasted its fruit with his bodily teeth would gain life? And again, that one could partake of 'good and evil' by masticating the fruit taken from the tree of that name? And when God himself is said to 'walk in the paradise in the cool of the day', and Adam to hide himself behind a tree, I do not think anyone will doubt that these are figurative expressions which indicate certain mysteries through a semblance of history, and not through actual events (4.3.1).

As early as 215, when he began writing books, Origen was well enough known for the governor of Roman Arabia to write to Bishop

Demetrius of Alexandria and the prefect of Egypt, asking for Origen to be sent to him – presumably, to discuss Christianity (Eusebius, *Ecclesiastical History* 6.19.15; cf. Crouzel 1989: 14). Afterwards, during Caracalla's persecution at Alexandria, Origen went to Palestine, where he was asked to preach in church – a request which caused a stir at home, since he had not been ordained (6.19.16–17; cf. Crouzel 1989: 15–16). In the 220s, Origen attracted the notice of Julia Mamaea, mother of the Emperor Severus Alexander (222–35): she asked him to Antioch to explain Christianity to her. This marked him out as a star in the cultural firmament of the Roman world, and not only of the church: but, Eusebius says, he 'went back to his accustomed duties' (6.21.3–4), teaching beginners in Alexandria, after his visit to court.

The situation was full of potential for conflict. Status dissonance applied to Origen in multiple measure. He was born an Egyptian (and not a Roman citizen) because his mother was Egyptian and his father, as a soldier, could not contract a legal marriage. He received an élite education, unusual for a person of his low civic status. He started in a highly valued profession – which he then gave up to teach an illegal religion. A fashionable intellectual, invited to discuss his ideas with people from ever more powerful circles, he remained a layman in Alexandria. He was a prophet without honour in his own country. Tertullian, a high-powered intellectual like Origen, remained out of the ordained ministry in his home church at Carthage, then finally split off as leader of a sect. Origen, too, seems an obvious candidate as a sect leader. Certainly he could have found followers.

Eventually the explosive mixture detonated – but with only a muffled bang. No new sect was created. In Caesarea, in the course of a journey in 231/2, Origen, by now in his forties, was ordained presbyter by Bishop Theoctistus, with the support of Alexander, the bishop of Jerusalem (Crouzel 1989: 18–24). When the Council of Nicaea in 325 made a rule on such cases, it provided that if someone from diocese *A* were ordained by the bishop of *B*, and then returned to *A* and presented his bishop with a *fait accompli*, the ordination was invalid. At Origen's time there was no rule, but Theoctistus and Alexander must have realized that Demetrius, bishop of Alexandria, had some reason for not having ordained a theologian of Origen's stature: by that date, he must have been known to everybody in the Alexandrian church, and remembered as their catechism teacher by almost all the adults under fifty. The Palestinian bishops must have known they would create a worse dispute than they had created in 215 by merely asking him to preach.

Back at Alexandria, Origen was asked to leave town: he went to Caesarea, where the last two decades of his life were spent (Crouzel 1989: 22–34). Perhaps Theoctistus was devious enough to have this outcome in mind when he made Origen a presbyter. Origen himself was shocked, although later he could find a hidden meaning even in his expulsion – as he explains in his *Commentary on John* (6.2.8–9):

As far as volume 5, even though the storm at Alexandria appeared to oppose me, I dictated what was given to me, since Jesus rebuked the winds and the waves of the sea. After making some progress with volume 6, I was rescued from Egypt, for God, who led out his people from that land, saved me. As my opponent warred against me most bitterly by his subsequent letters (which are truly in opposition to the gospel), and stirred up all the winds of wickedness that are in Egypt against me, the Word exhorted me to stand to the contest and guard the supreme part of my soul, lest mistaken arguments should prevail to bring the storm even upon my soul, before my understanding gained tranquillity, rather than continue with the rest of my writing. Moreover, the absence of my usual shorthand-writers prevented me from continuing my dictation . . .

New shorthand-writers became available, and until the end of his life the Caesarean church protected him against Christian enemies who alleged that his views were incorrect. It could not protect him against the civil authorities. Arrested in the Decian persecution, Origen was tortured, but released after Decius' death. He lived into the mid-250's and died aged sixty-nine (Crouzel 1989: 33–36).

Why did Origen stay with the Great Church? He was sure of the rightness of the kind of Christianity he taught – and knew that he was in serious disagreement with the literal understanding of Scripture which simpler believers preferred (Crouzel 1989: 155–156). Sometimes irritable and vain, he was not kept in the majority fold by an unusually saintly disposition. But there seem to have been two reasons for his loyalty. First, he accepted (and echoed) Hegesippus' claim that apostolic succession guaranteed that the Great Church's teaching was Christ's teaching:

... because there are many who think that they hold the doctrine of Christ, and some of them differ in their beliefs from the
Christians of earlier times, and yet the proclamation (*kērygma*)
of the church is preserved unaltered handed down in apostolic
succession from the apostles and existing to this day in the
churches, I maintain that *that only* is to be believed as the truth
which in no way conflicts with the tradition of the church and
the apostles (*Principles* 1 preface 2).

Second, and crucially, Origen really was uninterested in leadership.
He was one of the most prolific writers in the ancient world. Much of
his work is lost, but enough remains to prove that he lived to communicate, and found writing his best medium. He knew that chances for
advancement existed, but disliked the unattractive side of ecclesiastical
careerism. In his *Commentary on Matthew* (16.8) he wrote: 'In many
so-called churches, especially those in large cities, one can see rulers of
the people of God who do not allow anyone, sometimes not even the
noblest of Jesus' disciples, to speak with them on equal terms.'

He had identified something near the heart of Christianity's tendency to be fissiparous. Changes in the theory of Christianity did not
necessarily cause splits – Origen was a great innovator in theology, but
stayed inside the majority organization. Competition over leadership
was the central difficulty, and, especially in the big cities, there were
opportunities for Christian leaders to form their own sects.

Examining diversity shows up the adventures of churchmen, and
sectarians, on the make. But it is also about lively local traditions.
Sometimes churches were ready to accept advice from fellow-Christians
hundreds of miles away; sometimes they just did things their own way.
In a few cases, too, minorities dedicated themselves to mission. Marcionites and Manichaeans were the sects which did the most in this
direction. Rejection of marriage put Marcion's sect at a disadvantage
which its expansion by conversion was too slow to overcome. The
Manichaeans, however, had a great future. In Roman territory, the
Catholics over time had more momentum and vigour: other Manichaeans besides Augustine must have been absorbed by the Great
Church. But beyond the eastern border of the empire, through Asia as
far as China, Manichaeism was to be the most widespread form (or
derivative) of Christianity preached in antiquity and the Middle Ages.

The pressures which produced sectarianism existed everywhere in
the churches. They did not always lead to division, but change could

not be avoided as Christianity continued to grow and have a wider engagement with the secular world. As churches became less like extended families and more like smaller versions of the communities they were in, issues of Christian distinctiveness presented themselves in different forms. The place of women in the churches was an important area of praxis and debate as this process advanced, and to that place chapter 9 will turn.

9

Women and Christianity

Feminist readings of the early church

A new impulse to understand the role of women in early Christianity began making its impact from the late 1970's onward. At the (Catholic) Detroit Ordination Conference, Elisabeth Schüssler Fiorenza (1976: 96) spoke up for the idea that Junia (Rom. 16:7) was a woman apostle.[1] Then Bernadette Brooten (1977: 141–142) showed that the name was understood as Junia (feminine), not Junias (masculine), in ancient and medieval liturgy and Bible commentary until Aegidius of Rome (1245–1316) (cf. Eisen 2000: 47–48). In 1982, Brooten's book *Women Leaders in the Ancient Synagogue* drew important Jewish material together.

Next, in 1983, Schüssler Fiorenza's *In Memory of Her: A Feminist Theological Reconstruction of Christian Origins* had the effect of strengthening the bases of second-wave feminist Christian theologizing, and posing feminist questions about where study of the past ought to be centred. If *In Memory of Her* has a limitation, though, it is that the author restricts herself so tightly to the New Testament period: at times, the book threatens to become just another volume of commentary. This is not accidental: as Sawicki (2000: 69–70, 222–224) points out, Schüssler Fiorenza has no sympathy for positivist history – interpretation of texts is what she has to offer.

[1] A succession of earlier twentieth-century scholars had discussed the possibility that 'Junias' might actually be 'Junia'.

Schüssler Fiorenza's influential book set an agenda through which feminist scholars are still working. Some have been sceptical: Susanne Heine in *Women and Early Christianity: Are the Feminist Scholars Right?* (1987) argues against (what she sees as) naïve exegesis and counterfactual suppositions. But if there are tares in the field, there is wheat too. During the nineties the trend towards 'feminist theological reconstruction of Christian origins' has expressed itself in more books and articles, and prompted some, among them Ross Shepard Kraemer (1992: 128), to say that the connection between early Christianity and women has 'only recently received serious and critical attention'. This is no great exaggeration. Stark sums the situation up by positing that women enjoyed higher status in the Christian subculture than in the Greco-Roman world as a whole, but adds that 'if historians have long noted this fact, they have made no serious efforts to explain it' (1996: 95).

Schüssler Fiorenza's book delivers what its subtitle announces. She discusses the transition from Jesus movement to early church, focusing on Pauline evidence. Her premise is that missions and house churches allowed, even facilitated, exercise of leading roles by women as missionaries, prophetesses and house-church patronesses. Paul was not comfortable with this – a fact which Schüssler Fiorenza believes motivated him and deutero-Pauline writers to produce the 'household codes' in some Pauline Epistles. The house church, she argues, 'by virtue of its location provided equal opportunities for women, because traditionally the house was considered the woman's proper sphere' (1983: 176). And yet a thread of struggle ran through Christian history, with patriarchy eroding egalitarian elements: 'Patriarchalization of the early Christian movement and ascendancy of the monarchical episcopacy not only made marginal or excluded women leaders in the early church but also segregated and restricted them to women's spheres, which gradually come under the control of the bishop' (1983: 309–310).

Most nineties scholars who have followed Schüssler Fiorenza have kept her theological dimension central. So Luise Schottroff gives *Lydia's Impatient Sisters* (1995) the subtitle *A Feminist Social History of Early Christianity*, and devotes most space to feminist New Testament exegesis, giving just enough background to support the claim that her book is about social history. Historical method, however, comes second after selection of compelling illustrations – so that Paul's and his companions' apparent reluctance (1995: 109–110) to accept hospitality at Lydia's house in Philippi (Acts 16:15) is read by Schottroff in the light of Paul's reluctance in *Paul and Thecla* to do everything Thecla's way.

Schüssler Fiorenza was also inclined to accord *Paul and Thecla* some factual standing. She says that 'since Paul does not stand in the foreground of the narrative, the author ... appears to have incorporated independent traditions about Thecla' (83: 173). This might be right, if it were also true to say that 'since Washington Irving does not stand in the foreground of *Catch-22*, Joseph Heller must have incorporated independent traditions about Yossarian'. But Thecla is as fictional as Yossarian. Schüssler Fiorenza wanted to use her because, as she says, 'the image of Thecla retains reminiscences of the power and authority of women missionaries at the beginning of the Christian movement' (1983: 174). Schottroff, writing later, presents the argument for factual material in the story less sophisticatedly.[2] The move to make Thecla historical continues: Francine Cardman (1999: 302) has recently argued that 'it is likely that Thecla represents not one historical woman, but many women of the first and second centuries who publicly preached and baptized, claiming the authority of Paul for their ministries'.

Kraemer in *Her Share of the Blessings* (1994) takes a different cross-section through Greco-Roman society. She examines women's religions as they existed among polytheists, Jews and Christians. The issue in her book is how women's religious experience interacted in the ancient world with the expectations of society. To analyse it, Kraemer uses the conceptions of 'grid' and 'group', defined and argued for by Mary Douglas (1978; 1982). Douglas's idea is that social experience is governed by a combination of factors operating on the one hand at the macro level in society (the grid dimension), and on the other hand at the level of the people by whom an individual is surrounded. The latter factor, the group dimension, is measured by 'how much of the individual's life is absorbed in and sustained by group membership ... the strongest effects of group are found where it incorporates a person with the rest by implicating them together in common residence, shared work, shared resources and recreation, and by exerting control over marriage and kinship' (1978: 16).

---

[2] See Schottroff 1995: 108: 'Even though it reads like a novel, it is clear that this text presupposes these or similar events.'

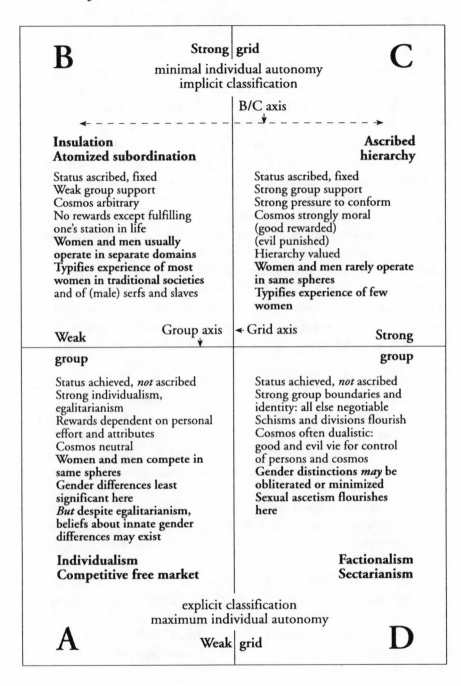

Figure 9.1. Grid, group and gender. From Kraemer 1994: 15 (based on the work of Mary Douglas).

The grid dimension relates to the regulation individuals experience: 'for this the possibilities ... run from maximum regulation to maximum freedom, the military regiment with its prescribed behaviour and rigid timetabling, contrasted at the other end with the free life, uncommitted, unregulated' (1983: 3).

Kraemer's table showing the four major combinations arising from grid and group is reproduced as figure 9.1. A position defined by co-ordinates would describe the factors operative in an individual's life. Twenty-first-century western lives, for example, would usually fall into the weak-group, weak-grid quadrant. Kraemer argues that the experiences of early Christian communities moved within a few decades of the death of Jesus from the strong-group/weak-grid quadrant into the strong-grid sector. Some, especially the male leadership, she sees as experiencing strong group and strong grid: strong support, fixed status, strong pressure to conform. This situation, she argues, encourages hierarchies to develop. But others, especially women, children and slaves, experienced 'the constraints of relatively weak group and strong grid' (1994: 156): less support, less reward for goodness, less reason to believe that evil is punished.

Like others, Kraemer sees a corner turned by the time of the Pastoral Epistles (which, however, she puts unusually late, in the mid-second century),[3] at which point a male hierarchy is pushing to control the behaviour of Christian women both in church and at home. Kraemer finds a crucial struggle, enacted in a prolonged Pauline period, between a strong-group/weak-grid egalitarian Christianity, drawing on the ideals of the Jesus movement, and a (strong-group/strong-grid) emerging male clergy whose success in taking control of the churches led to suppression of traditions of equality, and leadership by women. But while other participants in the debate continue to work on how Paul himself fits in, Kraemer moves on from the equality/hierarchy struggle, which became unwinnable for women (as she sees it) around the time of the Pastorals, to argue for a strong nexus between women's religion and heretical versions of Christianity – cemented from the mid-second century onward. To this second element in her model I will return later.

Anne Jensen's *God's Self-Confident Daughters* (1996) starts the quest for the role of women in the early churches from a different angle. She

---

[3] Kraemer 1994: 140. This is an unreconstructed F. C. Baur viewpoint: cf. Neill & Wright 1988: 57.

	Court	Others	Named	Anonymous
Eusebius	7	55	26	29
S, S and T together	22	43	13	30
Socrates	19	14	4	10
Sozomen	14	33	10	23
Theodoret	7	15	3	12

Individuals mentioned by more than one of Socrates, Sozomen and Theodoret count only once in the overall total for the three authors.

Figure 9.2. Mention of women in the church histories.
From Jensen 1996: 7.

notes that the second wave of church historians, after Eusebius, mentioned women less often. Despite Eusebius' having given no great prominence to women, his successors Socrates of Constantinople, Sozomen and Theodoret thought it better, or perhaps just found it natural, to mention between the three of them only as many women as Eusebius had (1996: 6–9; see Jensen's table, reproduced as figure 9.2). And where a woman comes in, the later writers are more likely to mention her without giving her name.

There are two possible explanations for the diminished prominence of women: either that writers played down the part they took in events, or that they actually took less part. Jensen follows up traces of the activities undertaken by women and the institutional roles open to them through to the fifth century, concluding that the balance of evidence points to the first explanation. One instance centres on a statue in Caesarea, which Eusebius describes – as well he might, since it was in the city of which he was bishop. He says this statue was outside the house where the woman cured of a haemorrhage by Jesus (Matt. 9:20–22) lived:

> For ... on a tall stone base at the gates of her house stood a bronze statue of a woman, resting on one knee and resembling a suppliant with arms outstretched. Facing this was another of the same material, an upright figure of a man with a double cloak neatly draped over his shoulders and his hand stretched out to the woman. Near his feet on the stone slab grew an exotic plant, which climbed up to the hem of the bronze cloak and served as a remedy for illnesses of every kind. This statue, they said, bore

the likeness of Jesus: and it was in existence even in my day, so that I saw it with my own eyes when I was based in that city ... (*Ecclesiastical History* 7.18.1–3).

Forty or fifty years later, this healing site was destroyed. Sozomen tells the story:

After Julian heard that in Caesarea Philippi ... there was a famous statue of Christ which was erected by the woman healed from haemorrhages, he had it torn down and a statue of himself erected. Yet fire fell from heaven ... (etc.) (*Ecclesiastical History* 5.21.1).

Sozomen had read Eusebius, and refers to his account, but eliminates the reference to there being a statue of the woman as well as one of Christ – and he omits to say where the statues were. His idea of an appropriate retelling included playing down what the site was, and how it recalled the life and faith of the healed woman, as well as the healing act of Jesus. Jensen (1996: 30) calls Sozomen's spin on the story 'a typical example of how women's traditions were suppressed in the consciousness of Christendom'.

Jensen goes down to the fifth century, giving more detail on the Christian side than Kraemer's comparative angle allows. She approaches the emblematic figure of Thecla cautiously: she has no high opinion of Vatican II's decision to remove her from the Catholic calendar of saints (1996: 80), but says that the picture of her in *Paul and Thecla* 'is already fancifully drawn, and thus it is hardly possible to expose the historical core' (1996: 79).[4] It is all the more interesting to note that she identifies a similar overall shape in events to that argued for by those with more radical methods: she sees the church starting out as an egalitarian organization, with comparatively little gender-based differentiation of function, and moving towards being a religion run on the lines expected in society.

On the Stark and Bainbridge model of progression towards lower tension, this would be expected. Jensen's account, which shows significant elements of autonomy for women and leadership undertaken by women still there in the fourth century (and then suppressed by the

[4] Another who is cautious about Thecla is Eisen (2000: 40): she dates *Paul and Thecla* later than many (185–95), and describes Thecla as 'the type of the preaching, baptizing and teaching Christian woman'. Note that she says 'the type', not 'an example'.

male hierarchy), is backed up by Eisen's document collection, and is preferable to the story told by the Schüssler Fiorenza camp – because on their timescale, even in Kraemer's stretched-out version, Christianity comes into conformity with its surroundings on gender issues so early. Why would persecuted churches in the mid-second century want to start doing things the world's way?

Stark's *The Rise of Christianity*: a bullish view?

There is, however, another way of telling the story of women in the early churches: less pessimistic, but not irreconcilable with the idea of early churches as weak-grid, strong-group communities, which over time brought in more gender differentiation, putting a lower valuation on the things women did. Stark, in a vigorously argued chapter (1996: 95–128), claims that women, and the position of women in the churches, were an important cause of Christian growth in the early centuries. He gives less attention than some feminist writers to the importance of sexual continence, and the chances it may have given to women to live without the control of their lives which the patriarchal household imposed on married women.

He is not the only scholar to be sceptical on women's asceticism having been their key to freedom from men. Kate Cooper in *The Virgin and the Bride* (1996) brings powerful arguments to bear against the idea that the chance of swapping married love and children (with the subordination they brought in the household and society) for continence (with the freedom of action a woman without a husband could claim) was a factor which influenced many women in the direction of Christianity.

Stark does, however, see Christianity's effect on women's lives as a factor in its growth. Adopting Christianity extended to Greeks and Romans the Jewish prohibition against abortion and infanticide. Female infanticide was widespread in the Greco-Roman world – so much so that it skewed the sex ratio throughout the population. Stark exaggerates only a little in saying that exposure of unwanted infants was 'legal, morally accepted, and widely practiced by all classes': disapproval was mild (1996: 97, 118).[5] In a church, provided that there was a good rate of compliance among Christians with their leaders'

[5] On what criticism there was of infanticide see Pomeroy 1983: 209. On the general issue see Harris 1994.

teachings, the prohibition on infanticide would over time make the male:female ratio in Christian families approximate to 1:1.

At the same time, and as with other religious movements, there is reason to think that more women than men were attracted to Christianity, especially via 'primary conversion' – which Stark defines as occurring in cases where 'the convert takes an active role in his or her own conversion, becoming a committed adherent based on positive evaluations of the particular faith'. A 'secondary convert' Stark defines as going along with the choice made by a spouse or another primary convert. He instances modern cases in which most primary converts are women (1996: 100–101). Guessing, in line with some recent experience, at a sex ratio in primary conversions of two women to one man, he calculates that a Christian population starting out with a 1:1 sex ratio and not growing by natural increase, but growing by conversions at 30% per decade, would comprise 64% women within fifty years (1996: 101).

These inferences are persuasive. Stark is also probably right to say that the Christian population was more fertile than the non-Christian (and non-Jewish) population. His inference (1996: 122) that the population of the Roman empire was in decline because of infanticide may not be right: marriage laws brought in by Augustus during Jesus' lifetime were aimed at correcting the low fertility of the senatorial aristocracy of Rome, rather than at increasing the population density of the Roman world. Recent estimates assume a static population empire-wide. In the Christian case, it is realistic to suppose that the effects of ascetic behaviour towards limiting population growth were more than counterbalanced by broad affirmation of marriage and discouragement of divorce, coupled with the higher proportion of females in the Christian population. The biggest sect which banned marriage was Marcionism – a movement which grew quickly in the second century, but did not subsequently become an important minority in the way Manichaeism did.

Stark outlines advantages Christianity had for women – and here his outlook is open to more question. He uses Hopkins' 1965 article on the age of Roman girls at marriage to suggest that Roman girls married very early – and pagan girls on average earlier than Christians: 20% under thirteen (but only 7% of Christian girls married under thirteen), and 24% at thirteen to fourteen (Christians 13%). The beneficial effects of delaying marriage to the late teens, he argues, constituted an advantage for Christian girls (1996: 105–107).

Unfortunately he seems not to have known of an article by Brent D. Shaw (1987), which pointed out flaws in Hopkins' use of statistics. Hopkins' ages come from gravestones of women 'which mention age at death, and length of time married (allowing calculation of age at marriage). So far, so good. But a large proportion come from near Rome, and the deceased are of the freedman class – ex-slaves of the aristocracy of Rome. Preference for very early marriage, Shaw argues, was a quirk of the aristocracy, picked up by their ex-slaves, who aspired to their way of life. When the data are sliced another way, they tell a different story: aristocrats and their dependants in the Roman region married their girls off very young, but in the provinces and outside senatorial-influenced circles, women were more often married at eighteen to twenty. Religion, as Shaw reads it, was not a factor in age at marriage.

In his section on roles played by women in the churches (1996: 108–109), Stark focuses on the fact that women 'could become deacons (Rom. 16:1–2; 1 Tim. 3:11). He has less to say about widows and virgins. Jensen, however, deals with them, making sensible distinctions: widows, she argues from 1 Timothy 5:3[6] and elsewhere, received support as workers in the churches (rather than because they needed relief from poverty).[7] As well as bishops, presbyters and deacons, she notes, there was 'a multiplicity of different orders' in the early churches – subdeacons, readers, acolytes, healers and so on. Widows and virgins counted as members of 'orders' in that sense, but by the time of Hippolytus' third-century *Apostolic Tradition*, distinctions were being drawn between who was *ordained* (bishops, priests, deacons) and who was merely appointed – while for a virgin, the (inner) intention to live as a consecrated virgin was enough. Jensen (1996: 23–25) draws attention to the way the framework described in the *Apostolic Tradition* imposes more regulation and tighter role restriction on widows than on other (and male) church workers.[8]

[6] Jensen 1996: 22, reading 'honour' in this verse as meaning 'pay an honorarium to', which is consistent with 5.17–18, prescribing double pay for well-performed elders/presbyters.

[7] Note also Diehl 1925: I: no. 1581, the fourth/fifth-century gravestone of Regina, who 'sat as a widow' for sixty years in the church in Rome and 'never burdened the church', i.e. did not receive charitable support. See discussion at Eisen 2000: 145–146.

[8] Widows are expected to be celibate, which other clergy are not: this may account in part for the caution expressed in the regulation for widows – but its tone justifies Jensen's reference to 'vicious insinuations in matters of sexuality': 'a widow ... is to be appointed only when her husband has already been dead a long time; if her husband has not been dead long, she is not to be trusted. But even if she is already old, she is to be tested for a period of time. for even the passions can grow old when one gives them free rein.' Hippolytus, *Apostolic Tradition* 19.

It is not easy to gauge how large an element in the clerical work-force women deacons, widows and virgins were. Eisen warns that restrictions on women's activities which are preserved in written sources – church orders, canons of synods, theological works – must not always be read as showing that the things they forbade were never done. More the reverse: they reacted against things which *were* (at least sometimes) happening, and so 'must be interpreted as refractions' (not reflections) 'of desire and reality' (2000: 3). The gravestone of Theo-dora, a woman deacon who died in Gaul in 539, illustrates the point (2000: 184–185): the Synods of Nîmes (396), Orange (441), Epaon (517) and Orléans (533) had all forbidden ordination of women deacons – evidently without *preventing* it.

Stark's upbeat view of leadership opportunities for women in 'the period covering approximately the first five centuries' (1996: 107), and Eisen's demonstration that there continued to be women clergy, ought not to be treated as evidence that hardly anyone except male clergy opposed leadership by women. Egyptian monasticism in the fourth century was almost wholly a lay movement, but still Mother Sarah, who lived a life of prayer in the desert, found people who thought badly of her: 'If I prayed God that all men should approve of my conduct, I should find myself a penitent at the door of each one; but I shall rather pray that my heart may be pure towards all' (Ward 1975: Sarah 5). This when the Desert Fathers were the great popular heroes of Christianity. Her problem was that many Christians thought she had taken up an improper life *for a woman*. Not all: some, including some men, would visit to pay their respects and receive guidance, and some of her sayings were collected and anthologized.[9] But her feelings about how she was regarded are revealing: her chosen path was hard, and not only physically.

Feminists adapt the New Consensus

As Schüssler Fiorenza and others point out, the New Testament, including the Pauline letters, shows a Christian movement in which leadership has not gelled into hierarchy – or (in Max Weber's terms) in which charisma has not yet been routinized. Individuals with impressive qualities or closeness to God get noticed: Prisca is men-

---

[9] Ward 1975: Sarah 8: 'Some monks of Scetis came one day to visit Amma Sarah. She offered them a small basket of fruit. They left the good fruit and ate the bad. So she said to them, "You are true monks of Scetis."'

tioned in front of Aquila (Acts 18:18, 26; Rom. 16:3; Aquila gets in first at 1 Cor. 16:19), Junia is called an apostle (Rom. 16:7), and Lydia not only entertains Paul, Silas and Timothy, but also has a meeting of the Philippian Christians in her house to send them off after their release from jail (Acts 16:15, 40) – which makes her a house-church patroness.

Reflection on this evidence for women in leadership of churches has led to questioning of the New Consensus view of Christian development. Theissen argued that there were three social forms of Christianity: 'itinerant radicalism', 'love patriarchalism' and 'gnostic radicalism'. The second of these is seen by New Consensus scholars as the type of Christianity practised in house churches, while itinerant radicals including Paul adapted Jesus' method of travelling ministry – and left their converts in house churches, to be made into communities under the leadership of figures whose social profile fitted Paul's observation that 'not many of you were wise by human standards, not many were powerful, not many were of noble birth' (1 Cor. 1:26).

This, as read by Schüssler Fiorenza, implies assimilation of Christianity from the beginning to the pattern of relationships usual in the patriarchal Greco-Roman household. 'To state it crudely,' she says, 'the church is not built on prophets and apostles, who as charismatics belong to the "radical" tradition, but on love patriarchalism, that is, on the backs of women, slaves and the lower classes' (1983: 79).

Perhaps 'love patriarchalism' is a provocative phrase – but the essential New Consensus observation, that co-operation between itinerant preachers and house-church patrons contributed vitally to the success of the earliest churches, cannot be overturned by outraged rhetoric. Meeks' *The First Urban Christians*, published in 1983 and not available to Schüssler Fiorenza, laid a more broadly persuasive foundation than Theissen had articulated for understanding the social groups in which first-century Christianity spread. It is quoted with approval by Kraemer (1994: 135–136), who comments that the women in Meeks' list of eighty people mentioned in the Pauline Epistles and Acts, though fewer in number, are of similar social status to the men. Phrases defining these women by their relation to men are comparatively uncommon: 'derivative identity' is not foregrounded.

More recently Schottroff, admirer of Schüssler Fiorenza though she is, has elaborated a framework for bringing the New Consensus into the feminist fold. The patriarchal household in Christian churches, she argues, was in important respects different from the patriarchal household as figured by Greco-Roman élites. Having laid out a picture of the ideal of the household described by Cicero, a Roman politician, lawyer and philosophical writer of the first century BC, she contrasts it with what Christians had:

> ... the thinking of all New Testament documents is patriarchal. The father–son relationship occupies so central a place that no further evidence is needed. In contrast, a fundamental difference can be found in the function of the family, of the *oikos* [household]. The *oikos* is not the bearer of the patriarchal family's possessions and therefore of its material basis of existence. The majority of Christian families would not be counted by Cicero among those who own property. Neither marriage nor *oikos* has any ideological significance comparable to that found in his system ... But the *oikos* had an important place in Christianity: it was a private space in which Christians carried out activities identified with the public sphere. Rome's patriarchal system did not infringe on that space ... households provided the free space for 'strangers' that travelling female and male apostles required ... (1995: 30).

Households, then, Schottroff acknowledges, were both a key to the development of Christianity and themselves part of the patriarchal discourse of the early church. But élite ideals which made the household a vital part of the mechanism of transfer of wealth between generations in rich families were not important in Christians' more modest households. Not everything in the churches was the same as in the secular world:

> On the one hand, the situation of women is comparable to that in Cicero's patriarchy: women are subordinated to men, at least according to the household codes (and 1 Corinthians 11). On the other hand, they are not spoken of exclusively as being part of the patriarch's sphere of power. There are women without men in the New Testament, and they obviously lack nothing. Not everything revolves around virginity, modesty, and having babies. In my view, then, the portraits of patriarchy found in Cicero and the New Testament have decisive differences: the image of God and the practical significance of the *oikos* (1995: 31).

Against this background, Origen's rebuttal (in the third century) of Celsus' claim that the churches were made up of ignorant people from the lower classes, trying to subvert the legitimate teachings given by fathers and schoolteachers,[10] comes to seem to Schottroff like a betrayal of the best features of Christianity. Origen answered in terms of Christianity's mission to offer teaching for no fee, to anyone who was ready to learn. Schottroff would have preferred something which did more to affirm the dignity of lower-class Christians:

> There seem to have been frictions between the Christians of different classes, for Origen concedes that there are communities which 'defend their own ignorance' (3.44; cf. 5.16); nor do they want to admit people of the upper classes. He believes this is contrary to the teachings of Jesus. The church Origen has in mind is one that is guided by the leading elite, which seeks to instruct and improve the lower-class people (3.49, 51, 59). 'We keep women from unchastity and marital infidelity and seek to convert them from all morbid passion for theater and dancing and heresy' (3.56) ... In Origen the church appears as a great rehabilitation center for women, children, criminals, workers, the uneducated, and the poor, all under the leadership of an upper-class elite. Origen's contempt for women and the lower classes is congruent with that of his own class – the upper class – *and* that of Celsus (1995: 147).

Simplifying Origen into a member of the upper class sidelines the status inconsistency in his background. I would attribute more to his being a teacher (since teachers tend to suppose education will improve their pupils' welfare). In other respects, however, Schottroff's comment is fair. Origen as an apologist was leading towards making the churches less different from the world around them: he wanted to play down egalitarian elements.

Leadership given by women

Beyond the first two or three Christian generations, Eisen's *Women Officeholders in Early Christianity* (2000) is the most comprehensive examination of the roles women took. At the heart of the book is a

[10] See ch. 6 above.

series of discussions of inscriptions (usually epitaphs) naming women who held leading Christian roles. Eisen's main argument is that epigraphical evidence for what really happened can raise important questions about the literary tradition which has been used over the centuries to inform views of the history of the church. 'To write the history of Christian women', she says, 'is to seek for those women's hidden, forgotten and suppressed heritage' (2000: 223).

She gives instances of women undertaking nearly all the leadership roles known to have existed in Christianity. But here and there alarm bells ring. Eisen's prime example of a woman bishop is Theodora, mother of the ninth-century Pope Paschal I (2000: 200–205). Having argued that a *venerabilis femina episcopa* ('venerable lady bishop'), whose gravestone was set up about 500 in Umbria, was a bishop in her own right, rather than the wife of a bishop (2000: 199–200), Eisen goes on to argue that *episcopa* (Theodora's title in mosaics in the church of Santa Prassede at Rome) was not a courtesy title for Theodora as mother of the bishop. Scepticism is in order. *Augustus*, for example, meant 'Roman emperor', while *Augusta* was an honorific title which might belong to his wife or mother. Eisen uses Canon 14 of the Council of Tours (567) to argue for Theodora as bishop in her own right. This text directs that a bishop who has no *episcopia* shall not have a retinue of women. She says that this *episcopia* must be a female colleague, not the bishop's wife. But the canon makes best sense as a measure to protect unmarried bishops from sexual temptation, to which married bishops were (assumed to be) less susceptible.

Clerical leadership

Eisen's case for women bishops is stronger when she argues that in the first generations in the churches a house-church patron, man or woman, must *ipso facto* have been the leading figure in the church which met at his or her house, and so must have been (in Paul's vocabulary) a bishop (*episkopos*; 2000: 206–207). But in the examples she then mentions, Eisen may have overplayed her hand. She refers to Nympha (Col. 4:15), who had a church at her house, but also to Tavia and the widow of Epitropus (or 'of the procurator') – both from Ignatius. Ignatius extends greetings (*Smyrneans* 13.2), but apparently only to Tavia, and Epitropus' widow, and their own children/relatives/servants – not to house churches. By Ignatius' time, as argued above, bishops and presbyters were getting to be differentiated from each other, and from owners of houses at which churches met.

In the period when 'bishop' and 'presbyter' were no longer alternative words for the same job, Eisen finds some more explicit source material for women clergy at presbyter level. Her first example is Ammion, a third-century woman presbyter from Phrygia (2000: 116–118). Eisen is reluctant to agree that Ammion was a Montanist, despite the fact that her gravestone was found in an area where Montanism was widespread; but her reluctance is based on doubtful premises.

The background to the case is that in Montanism there were women clergy, in the grades of deacon, presbyter and bishop – as Epiphanius and others knew.[11] Modern scholars have sought to understand why. Klawiter (1980: 254) argued that the importance of martyrdom in Montanism was behind the existence of women clergy. At least in Rome, confessors, after being imprisoned and put on trial for being Christians, could not (if they survived) be ordained presbyters – *because they already held that rank* by virtue of their ordeal. In Asia, persecution was also prevalent – with the result, Klawiter argued, that Montanist zeal produced women who were presbyters because they were confessors – they, he says, are behind the observation that the Montanists had women clergy.

Trevett points out difficulties with Klawiter's theory, preferring an earlier idea of his about the importance of the Montanist prophetesses Prisca and Maximilla to the formative stages of Montanist thinking: the high status of the prophetesses (and the generally high civic status of women in Phrygia, compared to other areas), he had suggested, led to evolutionary change in the Montanist movement which ended up with women ordained as clergy. This Trevett herself develops into a fuller theological explanation of why Christians in the Montanist movement decided to make women into clergy as well as men (1996: 194–195).

But Eisen's wish to see Ammion as representative of mainstream Christianity may be close to the mark, in that Montanists may not have *decided* to ordain women. It may be that in Phrygia (and hardly anywhere else) there were women clergy in the churches as soon as there were clergy at all. Trevett assumes consistently that clericalization of women in Montanism was a change from a Catholic pattern (1996:

---

[11] Epiphanius, *Medicine Box* 49.2.5. Trevett (1996: 185–186) discusses this and other primary sources on the issue.

188–196); but I suggest[12] that there just was no 'non-Montanist' church in Phrygia, at least until after the division. Women clergy were probably an original feature of Christian ministry in Phrygia – unusual by non-Phrygian standards, but not a matter for discussion at home.

No controversy was necessary about this local practice until the larger dispute, over the New Prophecy, flared up. It had most probably begun the way local variations do: to Phrygian Christians at the beginning, making women part of the leadership structure of their church was the obvious thing; in other parts of the Roman world, it seemed equally obvious that presbyters/bishops had to be men. Misunderstandings can arise from this sort of difference, but they need not become really difficult unless someone tries to enforce uniformity. In the Phrygian case, the women clergy were eventually a point detractors could use against Montanism.

Eisen's collection records some other women presbyters. The picture is complicated by Epiphanius' assertion that older widows used to be called 'eldresses' (*presbytides*), 'but were never assigned the rank of "presbyteresses" (*presbyterides*) or "priestesses"' (*hierissai*; *Medicine Box* 79.4.1, cf. Eisen 2000: 119). He seems to be wrong: the Synod of Laodicea, between 341 and 381, banned women presbyters (*presbytides*) from being installed in churches in Asia Minor. Probably, as Eisen says (2000: 121–123), this indicates that the banned practice had been going on. But even granted that Epiphanius is mistaken to deny that women were ever presbyters, it remains hard to know which of those who are commemorated should be seen as having a widow's ministry, and which a ministry equivalent to that of a male presbyter.

Eisen has examples whose ministry probably was like a male presbyter's: she includes the fourth/fifth-century gravestones of Kale, from Sicily, and of Leta, from Bruttium, and notes that Pope Gelasius I in 494 said in a letter to southern Italian/Sicilian bishops, 'We have heard to Our annoyance that divine affairs have come to such a low state that women are encouraged to officiate at the sacred altars, and to take part in all matters imputed to the offices of the male sex, which they are not suited to discharging' (*Letters* 14.26). The story he has heard is of women officiating in church because suitable men are not available: Kale and Leta come into the category he is referring to.

There is a comparative wealth of references to women deacons in inscriptions (Eisen 2000: 158–159). Not until the fourth century did the

[12] Cf. ch. 8 above.

word 'deaconess' (*diakonissa*) come into use, and then it was a synonym for 'deacon' (*diakonos*) (2000: 14), not indicating a separate role. Eisen's exploration concludes that making women into deacons came to be regarded as problematic only during the fourth century (2000: 185). In the period covered by this book, women deacons (like the *ministrae* tortured by Pliny) were a widespread feature in Christianity.

House churches

The importance of the issue of women as patrons of house churches turns on how house churches worked. Campbell (1994: 241–243) underlines the importance of family structure, since churches came into existence within households or extended families, and goes on to posit an early move to describe a representative leadership consisting of several heads of households as 'the elders' (= 'presbyters'). If he is right, and if (as argued in ch. 3 above) Christianity had a 'flying start' which resulted in multiple house churches (not just one) in medium-sized and large cities, then growth in particular cities from single-household (quasi-private) to multiple-household (quasi-public) churches may account for a fast change away from the initial situation, in which women who were heads of their own households were likely to figure as Christian leaders by virtue of that position.

There is not much evidence against which to test this supposition. A little can be learnt from the Dura-Europos house church[13] about how Christians organized the space at their disposal. The house was adapted, with a partition removed to form a large room for meetings, a dais added in that room, and another room converted into a baptistery, with a pool. There is no living space downstairs, but there was an upper storey, which may have been where the owner lived. No-one can tell if this house church was typical. Many houses may not have been re-modelled or repainted for church use. Particular houses may not have been used by churches for long. Reliant on owners' continued goodwill and prosperity, congregations may have expected to move from time to time.

It is not clear, for instance, whereabouts in Rome third-century Christians worshipped. St Peter's Basilica is the only one of the 'titular churches', established at Constantine's time, with clearly identified Christian remains of pre-Constantine date beneath it. Church-owned

---

[13] Cf. ch. 1 above.

buildings were confiscated empire-wide in 303–5, and even though they were handed back a decade later, Christians must have made new arrangements in the meantime. Possibly very few fourth-century Christian sites had been used for church purposes earlier.

There is, however, a snippet of information preserved about churches in Alexandria. Epiphanius, writing about 375, records the names of churches there:[14] the Caesareum church (mid-fourth century), the churches of Dionysius, of Theonas, of Pierius, of Serapion, of Persaea, of Dizya, of Mendidius (or better 'Mendidion church'), of Annianus and of Baukalis.

A couple of these names (Mendidion, Annianus) are familiar from the *Acts of Mark* – and it is not known whether most celebrate great names of the Christian past (as the name of Annianus seems to do, since Annianus is Mark's successor in the *Acts of Mark* story – but a later Alexandrian Christian might have been named after him), or whether they are names of owners of the houses. Three of them (Persaea, Dizya and Baukalis) are women's names, as against five names of men and two of places/monuments (Caesareum, Mendidion). This shows a higher proportion of women as church house owners than one might expect. If, over the first three centuries, a large minority of house-church patrons were women, then the moment in the fourth century when churches began to be able to build premises at public cost can be seen not just as a step to institutionalize Christianity, but also as another step restricting the direct influence women had.

Prophesying and teaching

Teachers, too, exercised leadership – and might not always be bishops or presbyters, as Tertullian's and Origen's cases show. New Testament evidence for women as teachers in churches is disputable, turning on issues like how Prisca's role should be construed, or what, as an apostle, Junia (Rom. 16:7) must have done. Some scholars who put the Pastorals late would posit women teachers working for a matter of decades before the words 'I permit no woman to teach or to have authority over a man' (1 Tim. 2:12) were written. I have argued that the Pastorals are early,[15] and accordingly I think the supposition that

[14] Epiphanius, *Medicine Box* 69.2.2 (Caesareum church) and 2.4 (the rest of the list). On Arius (presbyter at the Baukalis church) Epiphanius (*Medicine Box* 68.4.2), says 'one presbyter is assigned to each church (for there were many churches, and now there are more), and the church was entrusted to him, although there was someone else with him'.
[15] Cf. ch. 1 above.

there was a period with numerous women Christian teachers is probably not accurate. Eisen's examples of women teachers of theology are
late, from the fourth and later centuries (2000: 89–115). As most early
Christians (but not in Phrygia) assumed that bishops and presbyters
had to be men, so most would have expected teachers to be men.

Christians had prophets as well as preachers and teachers, and there
might be a crossover between teaching and prophetic roles. Women
might be prophets (as Philip's four daughters were: Acts 21:9). Apelles,
cast in Eusebius (whose source was Rhodo) as a Marcionite who failed
to argue for his sect's position with any consistency, had, Eusebius
says, been influenced in his theological thinking by 'the utterances of a
demon-possessed virgin called Philumene' (*Ecclesiastical History* 5.13.1–
2). A complex case: where is the line between prophecy and teaching,
when a theologian changes his mind because of a prophecy? The same
thing happened to Tertullian, who as a Montanist quoted in his books
from the prophecies of Prisca and Maximilla.

Philumene, Jensen argues by drawing sources together (1996: 194–
222), had a theological theory. Tertullian, in his *Ruling out of Court of
the Heretics* (6.5–6), makes her Apelles' evil genius:

> If an angel from heaven proclaimed a different gospel, he would
> be accursed by us [cf. Gal. 1:8]. For the Holy Spirit already
> foresaw at that time that an angel of seduction would appear in
> a certain virgin, Philumene, changed into an angel of light; in-
> stigated by his signs and magic tricks, Apelles introduced a new
> heresy.

Philumene was influential at the fringe of Marcionism, as Tertullian
says: 'That virgin Philumene persuaded Apelles and other opponents of
Marcion ... that Christ assumed flesh, yet not through birth but
through the union of the elements' (*Against Marcion* 3.11.2).

In terms of emphasis, at least, Tertullian contradicts himself: at one
moment, he is ready to put the blame for Apelles' version of Marcionism on the woman he got it from, but at another he manoeuvres to
avoid implying that a woman has taken the leading role. When it suits
him, he will refer to 'the Apellian virgin Philumene' (*On the Flesh of
Christ* 24.2) – but actually, Apelles followed Philumene's theory.

In sect-formation terms, perhaps Tertullian was right to call Philumene an Apellian. Sect leaders were men, and in the context of second-
century Christianity in Rome, it is hard to think that a woman acting

on her own would have been able to establish a sect. Even in Phrygia, where the most influential prophetic figures were Prisca and Maximilla, their sect ended up called by Montanus' name. It is common ground among Schüssler Fiorenza (1983: 300), Jensen (1996: 227–228) and Trevett (1996: 159) that Montanus (in Jensen's phrase) 'placed his organizational talents at the service of a movement that owes its character to two women'. As Trevett observes, 'catholicism thought in terms of heresies with a nameable and male head'. This was so with the Apellians – even though Apelles was no uncompromising advocate of Apellian theory:

> When old Apelles met with us, he was shown that he had presented many things badly, but he said, 'One should not talk a conviction to death. Those who put their hope in the Crucified One will attain salvation if they contrive to do good works.' He commented that the God question was for him the most difficult of all questions ... (Eusebius, *Ecclesiastical History* 5.13.5)

Martyrdom

The presence of women as actors at a high level of symbolic word and action is even more marked in the case of women martyrs. No-one needed permission to be a martyr, and the selection process was controlled by non-Christians. Sabina, martyred with Pionius at Smyrna,[16] took his advice and gave a false name when she was questioned,[17] to avoid falling into the hands of Politta, the mistress she had run away from – but it was sensible advice, and Pionius had established himself as the controlling figure on the Christian side. Elsewhere, a woman would sometimes take the leading role.

At Lyons in 177, persecution followed an unusual course, with the governor not allowing those who abandoned Christianity under the pressure of arrest and imprisonment to go free (Eusebius, *Ecclesiastical History* 5.1.11, 25–26, 33, 45–48). Most of the martyrs were tortured and then strangled in the prison (5.1.27), but (as Bowersock [1995: 50] notes) spectacle was an important part of martyrdom – important to both sides.[18] Blandina, a slave woman (and not of robust physique,

---

[16] See ch. 6 above.

[17] *Martyrdom of Pionius* 9.3, calling herself Theodote ('God-given').

[18] Bowersock is not right, however, to add that 'no early martyr was taken aside discreetly

5.1.18) survived two appearances in the amphitheatre and died in the third, on the last day of the games (5.1.18–19, 41–42, 53–56). The writer of the martyr-act speaks of how unarrested fellow-Christians found inspiration in her sufferings. In the second show,

> Blandina was hung on a stake and offered as a prey to the wild beasts that were let in. She seemed to be hanging in the shape of a cross, and by her continuous prayer gave great zeal to the combatants, while they looked on during the contest, and with their outward eyes saw in the form of their sister him who was crucified for them, to persuade those who believe on him that all who suffer for the glory of Christ have fellowship for ever with the living God.

The animals did not attack her. In the third show,

> Blandina, last of all, like a noble mother who had encouraged her children and sent them forth triumphant to the king, having herself endured all the tortures of her children, hastened to them, rejoicing and glad at her departure as though invited to a marriage feast rather than cast to the beasts. And after scourging, after the beasts, after the gridiron, she was at last put in a net and thrown to a bull. She was tossed about a long time by the beast, having no more feeling for what happened to her, through her hope and hold on what had been entrusted to her and her converse with Christ. So she too was sacrificed, and the Gentiles themselves confessed that never before among them had a woman suffered so much and so long.

Things had changed since Polycarp died in Smyrna twenty or so years before. Then, the bishop had been brought into the arena and allowed to engage in a dialogue with the governor, in which Polycarp got the best lines, including 'Death to the atheists!' But in Lyons,

---

and executed out of sight'. (To these deaths in prison, and the Roman citizens examined in private and beheaded at Eusebius, *Ecclesiastical History* 5.1.47–48, add the *Martyrdom of the Scillitans*, in which the martyrs are tried in the governor's palace [not the forum], and executed immediately after sentence.) He is also mistaken in saying that 'no interrogations were conducted in small towns' (note the *Martyrdom of Conon*, set at Magydus in Phrygia, or the *Martyrdom of Apaioule and Pteleme*, in Reymond & Barns 1973, set at 'a village called Psoutoumet').

Bishop Pothinus was severely beaten at his trial, and died of his injuries two days later in prison (5.1.31). In Smyrna, the Christians were allowed to gather up Polycarp's charred bones; in Lyons, the remains of the martyrs who died in jail and in the arena were put out under guard and unburied for six days, then burnt to ashes and scattered on the river Rhône (5.1.57–63). These measures were directed against ways Christians turned persecutions to their advantage. So with leading figures eliminated from the public show, Blandina's actions became the focus of Christian interpretation of the conflict.

The situation was different again in Carthage in 203, when Perpetua was martyred. The Lyons writer said that through Blandina 'Christ showed that things which are mean and obscure and contemptible among people are counted worthy of great glory with God'. That text would not have fitted Perpetua. She was 'nobly born, liberally educated, respectably married' (*Martyrdom of Perpetua* 2.2), and herself wrote most of her story while in prison before being killed in a gladiator show put on for the army. Her non-Christian father, begging her not to confess Christianity at her trial, reminds her of the effect her being put to death will have:

'Take pity on my grey hairs, my daughter; take pity on your father – if I am worthy to be called father by you. If I brought you up to this prime of your life with these hands of mine, if I preferred you above all your brothers, do not give me over to disgrace before men! Look at your brothers! Look at your mother and your aunt! Look at your son, who will not be able to live after you are gone! Put aside your pride. Do not bring us all to ruin! For none of us will be able to speak freely again, if anything has happened to you.'

He said these things as my father, out of his sense of what was right, all the while kissing my hands and casting himself down at my feet and weeping. Then he began to call me not 'daughter' but 'my lady'. And I was sad at my father's misfortune, because he was the only one out of my whole family who would not be rejoicing at my martyrdom (*Martyrdom of Perpetua* 5.2–6).

Perpetua's family had a social position to maintain. Having a family member executed would stop former equals taking them seriously ('none of us will be able to speak freely again'). Her father would go from Roman patriarch to loser swamped in shame.

A catechumen when she was arrested, Perpetua had probably married recently. Tertullian, active in the Carthaginian church at the same date, recommends in his book *On Baptism* (18.6) that Christians should not be baptized until they are either married or committed long-term to celibacy (cf. McKechnie 1996: 426). If the church was taking this advice, the time of marriage would be the time to start receiving instruction. At twenty-two, Perpetua was one of a mixed-sex class arrested during the persecution associated with the Emperor Septimius Severus' tour of Africa in 202–3 (*Martyrdom of Perpetua* 2.1).[19] The dreams she records tie in with her waking life: she dreams first of being taken to heaven and joining the martyrs, then of her late brother Dinocrates (at first, undergoing punishment in the next life, but in a later dream, after she has prayed for him, enjoying a happy existence), and finally of her victory over a fearsome Egyptian opponent in a dream amphitheatre – prefiguring, she says, her contest with the Devil in the amphitheatre of the waking world (4.1 – 10.15).

The leadership role she took on comes through. When her brother suggests she has the right to ask God for a vision, she tells him simply that she will report it to him tomorrow (4.1–2). She is the one who tackles the military tribune about harsh treatment of her and her fellow-prisoners, and embarrasses him into keeping them under better conditions (16.2–4). When fellow-prisoner Saturus has a dream, Perpetua is not only in it – she figures as the person the bishop and the priest ask to mediate in their dispute (11.1 – 13.8). No-one in the group in the jail hesitates to structure the conflict against the secular authorities around Perpetua. The Montanist connection[20] may have made it easier to go in this direction – or just raised the stakes: Patricia Cox Miller (1994: 175) argues that the account at the heart of the *Martyrdom of Perpetua* is crucially about the debate between revivalism and patriarchy at Carthage:

> As opposed to … strategies that deflect a reading of Perpetua's diary as a *woman's* testimony, I suggest that, when it is so read, it expresses the plight of a woman caught in the cross-currents of a theological debate in which sexual politics played a prominent role. Although the evidence is not conclusive, it is certainly strong enough to indicate that there was a debate about the

---

[19] On the Severan persecution see Frend 1974: 340.
[20] See ch. 7 above.

status of women's leadership and authority in the Carthaginian church. It appears that in Perpetua's religious context femaleness was affirmed by the views and practices of a revivalist movement, but finally subjected to the dictates of the patriarchal metanarrative of the larger institution.

Cox Miller's verdict catches the atmosphere, although it perhaps goes too far to downplay the fact that the threatening feature in Perpetua's situation was the prospect of execution: ecclesiastical politics came a long way behind.

The pull of gravity

New Testament narratives in which women were prominent gave place as time went on to church narratives in which their position was structured more on the model of Greco-Roman secular society. It has sometimes been argued – for instance, by Kraemer – that the move within the Great Church in the churchward direction provoked women to find homes in minority sects, in which they were able to take a more positive role than in Catholic Christianity. The difficulty with this theory is the lack of evidence for it. Kraemer herself essentially finds only the Montanist movement pointing in the direction she wants (1994: 167–171; cf. McKechnie 1996: 426). The Montanists had their founding prophetesses, and in Phrygia there were women clergy; but Eisen's work shows that it was not only at the fringe that such things were done.

Elsewhere, there were plenty of high-tension sects – but few whose programme included leadership from women. Many favoured avoiding marriage, or sex, or both: the Marcionites, for example, and the El-chasaites. While individuals might find themselves freed for prayer by turning to celibacy, it is not clear that ascetic sects opened possibilities up for women in general. In most cases, they were more likely to negate some of the advantages the Christian community as a whole derived from discouraging divorce, abortion and infanticide. When in the 270s Antony, the founder of monasticism, sold the farm he had inherited from his parents and went to take up a solitary life, he put his sister in the care of a community of virgins,[21] which was a responsible action – but is it certain that men who decided against family life

---

[21] Athanasius, *Life of Antony* 3.

always made provision for the women and children they left behind? What happened to Mani's mother when Patik divorced her, or Augustine's girlfriend when he became celibate? If celibacy liberated women from men, it could also liberate men from women.

Much of this chapter is premised on a perspective which takes access to positions of leadership as an index of how the social structure of churches was developing. Examining Christianity from that perspective leads to the conclusion that as it grew and made greater numerical inroads into its society, so it moved (not always without provoking protest from Christian women) to become a less egalitarian organization in gender terms. Stark's overarching argument, however, should not be discounted, even if it seems paradoxical: evidence suggests that women, for their own reasons, went on coming into the Christian churches in disproportionate numbers throughout the early centuries – and sometimes bringing their men with them.

10
The Great Persecution and Constantine

The calm before the storm

In the third century, until Decius, Christianity had been advancing in a promising way. Origen saw expansion beyond the urban environment: Christians had 'done the work of going round not only cities but even villages and country cottages to make others pious towards God' (*Against Celsus* 3.9). Even after the great setback of 250, Cyprian, recently back from hiding out, spoke in expansive terms:

> The church is ... one, though she be spread abroad, and multiplies with the increase of her progeny, even as the sun has many rays, but one light ... thus the church, flooded with the light of the Lord, puts forth her rays through the whole world, with yet one light which is spread upon all places ... She stretches forth her branches over the universal earth, in her riches of plenty, and pours abroad her bountiful and onward streams; yet there is one head, one source, one mother, abundant in the results of her fruitfulness (*Unity of the Catholic Church* 5).

It is hard to gauge what this enthusiasm reflects in numbers. But, also around 250, Bishop Cornelius of Rome was moved to write a letter asserting that he was bishop of the true Christian congregation, and no attention should be paid to Novatian. He points out that Novatian does not have the resources of Roman Christianity behind him:

This 'vindicator of the Gospel' did not know that there should be one bishop in the Catholic church, in which he was not ignorant (for how could he be?) that there are forty-six presbyters, seven deacons, seven sub-deacons, forty-two acolytes, fifty-two exorcists, readers and door-keepers, and above fifteen hundred widows and persons in distress, all of whom are supported by the grace and loving kindness of the Lord. But not even this great multitude, so necessary in the Church, that number who by God's providence were rich and multiplying, nor an immense and countless laity, could turn him from such a desperate failure and recall him to the Church (Eusebius, *Ecclesiastical History* 6.43.11–12).

Cornelius enumerates 155 paid officials, counting the bishop – but lumps widows together with recipients of charity. With forty-two presbyters, the Roman church was a sizeable organization. If they were distributed at two per house church, as Epiphanius says they were at Alexandria, there might have been twenty-one or so congregations[1] – a total proportional to Alexandria's ten in Epiphanius, since Rome was about twice the size of Alexandria. Not much later, under Bishop Dionysius (259–68), the Roman church sent envoys to Cappadocia to negotiate the ransom of prisoners captured by the Goths – they took the Cappadocian churches gifts lavish enough to be remembered a hundred years later (Basil of Caesarea, *Letters* 70; cf. Frend 1965: 446). This was a church with the means to make its influence felt.

Once an emperor had intervened, as Gallienus did in 261, to order restoration of buildings to the churches, the door was open for church affairs to take another step towards the public sphere. In Antioch in the 260s, Paul of Samosata, the bishop, went further in this direction than any Christian leader had yet managed to. He was a flamboyant man with a talent for publicity. When Antioch, outside Roman control, formed part of Zenobia's Palmyrene empire, Paul – while concurrently bishop – acted for Zenobia's government as the city's chief financial officer. Church councils at Antioch discussed his behaviour in 264, 265 and 268 (Eusebius, *Ecclesiastical History* 7.30.3–4; cf. Frend 1965: 441). On the last occasion sixteen presbyters and deacons,

---

[1] Sixty or so years later, in 314, after Christianity became legal, there were forty (Optatus of Milevis, *On the Donatist Schism* 2.4).

including Malchion, presbyter and headmaster of a secular school (7.29.1–2), joined in writing a letter to gather support against him. They accused him of making himself rich 'as a result of lawless deeds and sacrilegious plunderings and extortions exacted from the brethren by threats', adding that he accepted bribes to make inconvenient lawsuits go away (7.30.7). In passing, they described him acting the part of a high official:

> ... clothing himself with worldly honours and wishing to be called *ducenarius* instead of bishop, strutting in the marketplaces, reading and dictating letters as he walks in public, attended by a bodyguard, some of whom walk in front of him, and some behind – so that the faith is ill thought of and hated because of his conceit and the pride of his heart (7.30.8).

A *ducenarius* was an equestrian official paid 200,000 sesterces a year. Paul was perhaps not much grander than the bishops whose haughtiness Origen had attacked – but the Antioch clergy thought he had gone too far. Such a conflict was not unique. Cyprian, at Carthage, had been made bishop over the heads of local clergy – to the delight of the laity. Some difficult relations resulted. But Cyprian was following a normal Roman pattern. He, and Paul, cared for their congregations the way patrons cared for clients. Cyprian, owner of valuable inner-city real estate, already *was* a local Roman patron, before he was a bishop. A patron dealt with legal problems, and sometimes represented clients in court: this may be behind the Antioch clergy's claims about legal cases. They assert that Paul was acting corruptly, but he may only have been looking out for his clients in the approved (secular) way.

After further complaints, the Antioch clergy inform their readers that they have deposed Paul in favour of Domnus son of Demetrianus. Their complaints about his theology arouse scepticism: Paul had asserted that the Son was 'of one substance' with the Father. This unusual pronouncement was used successfully to impugn his orthodoxy – embarrassingly for Athanasius, as defender of the Council of Nicaea's adoption of 'of one substance' in 325 (Athanasius, *On the Councils of Ariminum and Seleucia* 45). The clergy's insinuations about Paul's and his supporters' relations with women (Eusebius, *Ecclesiastical History* 7.30.11–15) are routine invective. Perhaps the worst affront, as the clergy saw it, was the *secretum*, Paul's committee of advisers (7.30.9) – another part of the normal apparatus of a Roman ruler. Apparently they were not asked to join.

The churches and Roman society

The coup against Paul of Samosata illustrates how Christianity in the mid-third century was becoming part of the fabric of Roman society – and choosing bishops who could become public figures, adopting roles familiar from secular life. Cyprian combined the confidence the upper classes felt in the exercise of leadership in society with a sense that divine revelation made a difference in deciding who should be appointed to positions in the church (Robeck 1992: 156–165). But Paul, seemingly treating foundational values less sensitively, had cut hymns to Christ out of the church service on Easter Day and (the clergy said) replaced them with hymns 'to himself', sung by a choir of women (Eusebius, *Ecclesiastical History* 7.30.10).

The sequel to the coup shows still more clearly the way the wind was blowing. In 272 Aurelian, the Roman emperor, recaptured Antioch. In the city, he received a complaint that Paul was still occupying the church's house, years after being deposed (Frend 1965: 443–444). He was glad to rule against an important supporter of the rebel government. Eusebius describes the incident:

> ... when Paul had fallen from the episcopate, as well as from his orthodoxy in the faith, Domnus, as has been said, succeeded to the ministry of the church at Antioch. But because Paul completely refused to move out of the church's house, the Emperor Aurelian, on being petitioned, gave an extremely just decision on what was to be done, ordering that the house should be assigned to those with whom the bishops of the [Christian] teaching in Italy and the City of Rome should communicate with by letter. Thus, indeed, the aforesaid man was driven out of the Church, in the utmost disgrace, by the empire of this world (7.30.18–19).

Not many years earlier, this lawsuit would have been unthinkable. It marks another step towards mainstream Roman life for the Great Church. Having just reasserted Roman power in Antioch, Aurelian acted consistently by stipulating that the house should go to the side which the leaders of Roman and Italian Christianity preferred.

Persecution was not over, but from the 260s until 303 it lived on only in scattered incidents (Frend 1965: 442–445). In some provinces, the swing in Christianity's favour was such that emperors turned a blind eye to failure of high officials to sacrifice – even though governors were supposed to take a leading role in the cult of the emperors. Eusebius, who was growing up in Palestine in those years, comments:

> It is beyond my powers worthily to describe the measure and nature of the honour and freedom which was accorded by all people, Greeks and barbarians, before the persecution in my day, to that word of piety towards the God of the universe which had been proclaimed through Christ to the world. But proofs might be forthcoming in the favours granted by the rulers to our people – to whom they would even entrust the government of the provinces, freeing them from agony of mind as regards sacrificing, because of the great friendliness they used to entertain for their doctrine (8.1.1).

North Africa, Egypt, Syria and Asia Minor were showing signs of advancing christianization (Frend 1965: 446–447).

The crisis of empire and anti-Christian propaganda

While Christianity grew, the Roman empire in the mid-third century went through its worst crisis. Between 235 and 284 emperor followed short-lived emperor bewilderingly fast. For about thirty years from 240, economic difficulties were so severe that there was an almost complete cessation, empire-wide, of the practice of carving and displaying inscriptions on stone – at other times a characteristic habit of Greeks and Romans. After Claudius II's victory over a Gothic invasion at the battle of Naissus in 269, however, things began to improve. For the next fourteen years the empire was competently governed under Aurelian (270–5), Tacitus (275–6), Probus (276–82) and Carus (282–4). Then Diocletian came to the throne. He had ideas, and reigned long enough (284–305) to implement them. He made big changes to tax collection, and split the Roman provinces into smaller territories to make them easier to administer. He doubled the size of the civil service, to improve his control of the state. To strengthen top-level leadership and reduce the chance of successful rebellions, he brought in a system of four emperors, with himself first, Maximian sharing his title of Augustus, and two junior emperors (Constantius I and Galerius) each holding the title of Caesar.

As well as tightening up military, political, fiscal and legal operations, Diocletian made up his mind to reassert traditional morality and religion. A new law on marriage, issued in 295, specified in detail which relatives were distant enough to marry each other and which were not (Frend 1987: 3). Legal loopholes were no excuse for misbehaviour, as the emperor explained: 'We have chastity so much at heart, as to remove the obscurity of previous law ... for it is not proper that legal cunning and trickery should prevent retribution for violated chastity' (*Justinian Code* 9.9.27; cf. Corcoran 1996: 70).

In religion, too, excuses were not encouraged. On 31 March 302, replying to Julianus, proconsul of Africa, who had informed him about the prevalence of Manichaeism in his province, Diocletian decreed that Manichaean books should be burnt, along with the leaders of the sect. Other Manichaeans were also to be put to death – except those of higher social station (*honestiores*), who were condemned to the mines (Frend 1965: 488). 'It is the greatest crime', the emperor thundered, 'to wish to undo what once has been fixed and established by antiquity' (*Fontes Iuris Romani Anteiustiniani* II.580; cf. Frend 1965: 478). The argument against new religions could be applied equally well against the Great Church.

The establishment of Diocletian's successful regime coincided with an intensification of the propaganda war between defenders of Greco-Roman polytheism and Christian apologists. Frend (1987: 8–14) traces how Porphyry of Tyre (c. 232–c. 304) went from restrained criticism of Christianity in his early works *On the Return of the Soul* and *Philosophy from Oracles* to more vigorous opposition in his (mostly lost) fifteen-volume book *Against the Christians*, written perhaps about 290. This book asked tough questions. Why did Jesus let the demons take control of the Gadarene swine? Why did he exclude the rich from the kingdom of heaven? Why did he not find something to say when he was on trial in front of the high priest? And along with the debate went the threat of violence. 'What punishments', Porphyry asked, 'are too severe to inflict on individuals who desert the laws of their fathers?' (*Against the Christians* fragment 1, lines 14–15).

It is hard to know how much influence intellectuals like Porphyry had on government. The propaganda traffic was not all in one direction. About 293 Arnobius of Sicca, a literature teacher and an opponent of Christianity, was converted – and about 295/6 he began his *Against the Gentiles*, whose title mirrored Porphyry's (except that Arnobius wrote in Latin, Porphyry in Greek). When he started this project, he seems not to have known much about Christianity. Michael Bland Simmons asks:

> How can books 1–2 be called an apology when Arnobius betrays very little knowledge of that which modern historians impose upon him to defend? One hears nothing about the organization, liturgy, sacraments, or polity of the North African Church. He is apparently ignorant of the Old Testament, and there are only two possible allusions to the New Testament … There is not a reference made to the virgin Birth, the Holy Spirit, and only one Christian predecessor is named. Also, he twice mentions his recent conversion … (1995: 126).

Jerome, late in the fourth century,[2] wrote that Arnobius had been converted as a result of dreams, and wrote his books to convince a reluctant bishop to accept him into the church. Simmons (1995: 130) suggests that the bishop may actually have set Arnobius to write the books, as a recantation of his former views.

Arnobius was swimming against the tide. He was a vigorous writer with some interesting ideas, but not a first-rate thinker, and no expert on Christian doctrine. His most important legacy was not his written work, but his student Lactantius, who in the early fourth century made more impact as a Christian apologist. So, because in his first few years as a writer Arnobius was so much a lone voice on the Christian side against Porphyry's arguments, it is hard to disagree with Frend's view (1987: 5) that 'until the arrival of Eusebius of Caesarea on the scene *circa* 300, the advantages in the debate lay with the Neo-Platonist defenders of the gods'. If Simmons is right about Arnobius' bishop asking him to write *Against the Gentiles* as a spiritual exercise, then it would seem that the clergy did not think it urgent to counter Porphyry and the Neoplatonists in the bookshops.

The Great Persecution

Before Arnobius had written the last of his seven volumes, the Great Persecution was on. The lead-up started when army authorities

---

[2] Jerome, *Chronicon* for the year 326/7 (Jerome's year is wrong).

stopped turning a blind eye to soldiers who did not participate in sacrificing. At first, most who would not comply were allowed to leave the army. A few were put to death. Eusebius says: 'as yet the instigator of the plot [= Galerius] was working with a certain moderation and daring to proceed to blood only in some instances; fearing, presumably, the multitude of believers, and hesitating to plunge into the war against us all at once' (*Ecclesiastical History* 8.4.4).

Then, at a public sacrifice with Diocletian and Galerius present, probably at Antioch, in 302, some imperial servants crossed themselves. When repeated sacrifices failed to produce acceptable results, the chief of the *haruspices* (inspectors of entrails of sacrificed animals) told the emperors that the gods refused to give an answer because profane persons were in attendance.[3] Angry, Diocletian ordered that everyone in his palace must offer sacrifice, and be whipped if they refused.

On 23 February 303 in Nicomedia, residence of Diocletian and effective eastern capital, the Praetorian prefect and other officers searched the church, burnt its copies of the Scriptures, and then (warned by Diocletian not to start a fire which might burn the city down) had the Praetorian Guard demolish the building (Lactantius, *The Deaths of the Persecutors* 12.2–5). The next day, Diocletian's first Persecution Edict was posted on a public notice-board: churches throughout the empire were to be destroyed and sacred books burnt; Christian *Caesariani* were to be purged;[4] Christian *honestiores* were to lose their social privileges; no Christian could be the accuser in a case of personal injury, adultery or theft; and Christian slaves could not be freed. There was no death penalty for Christianity under this edict, although a Christian who pulled the notice down and tore it to pieces was arrested and executed (Eusebius, *Ecclesiastical History* 8.5).

A fire started in the imperial palace. Lactantius (*The Deaths of the Persecutors* 14.2.5) alleges that Galerius was responsible, but the explanation he refuses to countenance – that Christians did it – struck Diocletian as obvious, and he had some Christians burnt, although judges set to investigate the case found out nothing about it because (perhaps prudently) they would not torture members of the emperor's household.

Implementation of the edict varied in differing parts of the empire (Corcoran 1996: 180–181), but at Nicomedia resistance continued.

---

[3] Lactantius, *The Deaths of the Persecutors* 10; cf. Frend 1965: 489.
[4] Frend (1965: 491) argues that they were fired from their posts; Corcoran (1996: 180) that they were re-enslaved – but many *Caesariani* at this date were of free birth.

Eusebius' suggestion that Diocletian might have hesitated to persecute out of fear of 'the multitude of believers' is not unrealistic: the non-violent response of Christians to earlier persecutions had been easier to maintain because a small minority had no chance of defending itself. Plotinus, Porphyry's teacher, had said that failure to resist violent attack ran against a universal law ('the law says that those who fight bravely, not those who pray, are to come safe out of wars...', *Enneads* 3.2.8) – and he may have had Christians' response to the Decian persecution in mind – but conditions in his time had restricted available options. For what was now a large, not a small, minority, vigorous direct action had something in its favour – and the moral line between tearing up an edict and burning down the palace might not seem clear-cut.

There was a second fire at the palace.[5] Afterwards, the (apparently pro-Christian) Empress Prisca and her daughter Valeria were required to sacrifice (Lactantius, *The Deaths of the Persecutors* 15.1), and further action was taken against palace staff. There was also a roundup of Nicomedian Christians, from presbyters down (Bishop Anthimus seems to have escaped). On 28 April, 268 were martyred (Frend 1965: 492).

Elsewhere, prospects for success in violent resistance looked better. Short-lived revolts began in Armenia Minor and Syria – areas where Christianity was strong. A second edict, in summer 303, provoked by the revolts, ordered that clergy should be arrested, with the result that 'the prisons were filled with bishops, presbyters, deacons, readers and exorcists, so that there was no room left there for those convicted of crimes' (Eusebius, *Ecclesiastical History* 8.6.9). A third edict, dated 20 November 303, the twentieth anniversary of Diocletian's accession, required the arrested clergy to sacrifice and be released. Some officials saw this as a chance to get rid of an embarrassment:

> ... in the case of one man, others held him fast by both hands, brought him to the altar, and let fall on it out of his right hand the polluted and accursed sacrifice: then he was dismissed as if he had sacrificed ... When yet another cried out and testified that he was not yielding, he was struck on the mouth and silenced by a large body of persons appointed for that purpose, and forcibly driven away, even though he had not sacrificed. So

[5] Lactantius, *The Deaths of the Persecutors* 14.6 (alleging that Galerius caused it).

much store did they set by seeming to have accomplished their purpose (Eusebius, *Martyrs of Palestine* 1.4).

Ill-health, lovingly described by Lactantius (*The Deaths of the Persecutors* 17), hampered Diocletian through 304. With him out of action, Galerius had more scope to do things his way, and raised the stakes with a fourth edict, commanding that everyone should sacrifice. It took time for enforcement to gather momentum, and in western parts of the empire less was done than in the east. Even outside Gaul and Britain (Constantius' area, where anti-Christian action was limited to destruction of church buildings), there was little zeal for persecution: Frend (1965: 500) says of local officials that 'in modern police terminology, they were "correct"'. In Roman Africa after the Great Persecution the hot issue in the churches was how individuals had behaved when it was demanded that they hand over copies of the Scriptures. Many had been reluctant, and some had tried to find ways out (like Mensurius, bishop of Carthage, who handed heretical books over instead of Bibles), but few went as far as Felix, bishop of Thibiuca, who preferred to be martyred rather than give up the books (Frend 1965: 500). It is not clear if a general requirement to sacrifice was implemented in any of the western provinces, but at Ammaedara (in modern Tunisia) a stone balustrade and a mosaic are preserved from a church's martyr shrine, and record the names of thirty-four people who 'suffered persecution under ... Diocletian and Maximian' (Frend 1984: 461).

While persecution was proceeding, on 1 May 305, Diocletian and Maximian retired. Lactantius (*The Deaths of the Persecutors* 18.1 – 19.1) describes Galerius browbeating an old and tired Diocletian to step down, but Diocletian had built a great palace at Spalato (Split) on the Dalmatian coast, and lived there for eight years after his retirement, in 308 refusing an invitation to return and sort out the mess his successors were making. He probably chose freely to retire. Constantius, now advanced to the rank of joint Augustus, was still in Britain; Galerius, the other Augustus, controlled central government. He tried to strengthen his position by bringing in Severus, a senior general, and Maximinus Daia, his own nephew, as Caesars. This caused more problems than it solved: Maxentius, son of Maximian, had expected promotion on his father's retirement, and Constantine, son of Constantius, had also expected to become a Caesar.

The Great Persecution in the west lasted just under two years, but in the eastern half of the empire governmental efforts to stamp Christianity out went on until 313. Actual moves to arrest and punish Christians were still intermittent. During 307 and 308 Maximinus changed the standard punishment from death to condemnation to the quarries. In Palestine in 309, libations (drink offerings to the gods) and blood of sacrificial animals were sprinkled over food offered for sale in markets, and soldiers were stationed at public baths to make bathers comply with the requirement for sacrifice.[6] But the normal procedure for enforcement was that officials went looking for someone to punish. There was no way of making pressure consistent from month to month. The Coptic *Martyrdom of Apaioule and Pteleme* reflects the situation. In the martyr-act, Diocletian gives his edict to Count Sebastianus to take to Egypt:

> He came south through all Egypt; and when he came to Alexandria, he gave the dispatches to Culcianus the governor of Alexandria. Straightway as soon as he received the dispatches, he saluted them; and he ordered all those of his entourage to be assembled, and he had the epistle of the emperor read to them, and they all sacrificed. Thereupon Sebastianus took the ordinance, and came south through all Egypt with a large force of soldiers attendant upon him, until he reached the nome of Hnes [= Heracleopolis]. He came up to a village called Psoutoumet, and commanded the tribunal to be set up beside the river, and he ordered all his soldiers to be assembled round him, and had the ordinance of the emperor read out to them. They all cast themselves down and worshipped it, crying out and saying, 'There is no god save Apollo and Zeus and Artemis and Athena.'
>
> But there was among them a young soldier of gentle birth, wise and righteous, whose name was Pteleme; he was thirty-three years old, and the whole host of soldiers loved him; for he was a man of God, attentive to both small and great; and the youth was a Phoenician of Antioch. The count said to him, 'Do thou also come and worship the ordinance of the emperor.' The noble man said to him, 'I will not worship idols made with hands, and one who is but a man like myself; for it is written in the prophet Jeremiah: "Woe to a man whose hope is in man; but blessed is a man whose hope is in the God of heaven"' (in Raymond & Barnes 1973).

[6] Eusebius, *Martyrs of Palestine* 9.2–4; cf. Frend 1965: 509 and Corcoran 1996: 185–186.

Pteleme was tortured over a period of days, and eventually beheaded.

Apaioule, a monk who came to visit and support him, was also tortured and executed. Monks were a new feature in the Christian landscape. About 270, Antony, a young man who had inherited from his parents a farm of about 300 acres in the nome of Heracleopolis Magna, decided to seek perfection by selling his property, giving to the poor, and leading a solitary life. He went for help to an old man in the next village who had 'lived a solitary life from his youth' (Athanasius, *Life of Antony* 2–3). For twenty years before the Great Persecution Antony lived in an abandoned fort in the Eastern Desert, but in the time of Maximinus Daia he came to Alexandria – partly to support arrested Christians, partly in the hope of being martyred himself:

> ... but as he did not wish to give himself up, he ministered to the confessors in the mines and in the prisons. He was busy in the courtroom, stimulating the zeal of the contestants as they were called up, and receiving and escorting them as they went to their martyrdom and remaining with them until they had expired. So the judge, seeing his fearlessness and that of his companions and their zeal in this matter, gave orders that no monk was to appear in court or to stay in the city at all. All the others thought it well to remain in hiding that day, but Antony thought so little of it that he washed his clothes, and on the following day posted himself at a prominent place in front, in plain view of the Prefect (*Life of Antony* 46).

The prefect did not respond to this provocation, which Antony had modelled on Revelation 7:14 ('These are they who have come out of the great ordeal; they have washed their robes and made them white in the blood of the Lamb'). It is uncertain whether the *Life of Antony* is anachronistic in saying that the prefect banned 'monks': Antony was not the only Christian dedicating himself to solitude and prayer (as his mentor in the next village, and Apaioule in the same nome, show), and he and the people who accompanied him may have appeared distinctive enough for the prefect to learn a term describing them.

Constantine's rise to power

While Galerius and Maximinus Daia were working at reducing the east to religious conformity, difficulties grew in the west. Constantius I died at York on 25 July 306, and his son Constantine, with his legions behind him, proclaimed himself Augustus in his place. The best Galerius could do to preserve the Tetrarchy was to recognize him with the lower title of Caesar – which Constantine accepted. Worse was to come for Galerius. On 26 October 306 Maxentius, Maximian's son, had himself proclaimed emperor in Rome. His chance had come when Severus, in charge of Italy and north Africa, started taking a census. Everyone knew he intended to begin collecting tax in Italy, which had been tax-free for three centuries. Maximian's legions supported Maxentius, and in 307 they captured Severus and forced him to commit suicide (Lactantius, *The Deaths of the Persecutors* 26.1–11). Maxentius ended persecution in the territory he controlled (Eusebius, *Ecclesiastical History* 8.14.1; cf. Corcoran 1996: 185). Galerius promoted Licinius, an old friend, to replace Severus – this time angering Maximinus Daia by passing him over. Licinius made slow progress with his attempts to regain Italy, and so gave Constantine an opening. In 310 the Spanish provinces transferred their allegiance to him, and he began preparing for a push on Rome.

So, by 310, Galerius' policy of promoting personal friends had produced poor results. A serious illness (expounded with the usual enthusiasm by Lactantius, *The Deaths of the Persecutors* 33.1–11) may have influenced his next move – or perhaps he calculated that eight years of persecuting Christians had not led to the religious unity he wanted. Either way, at Nicomedia on 30 April 311 he published a decree ending persecution and legalizing Christianity:

Among other steps which We are always taking for the profit and advantage of the State, We had formerly sought to set all things right according to the ancient laws and public order of the Romans, and further, to provide that the Christians, who had abandoned the religion of their own ancestors, should return to sanity. For the said Christians had somehow become possessed by such an impulse, and such stupidity had taken hold of them, that instead of following the traditional practices of the ancients (the practices which perhaps their very own ancestors had originally established), they made laws at their own will and pleasure and for their own observance, and held meetings of various ethnic groups in various places. Eventually, when We issued a command to the effect that they should bring themselves back to the traditions of the ancients, many of them were subjected to danger, and many even completely overthrown.

Since most of them persevered in their purpose, and We saw that they were neither giving worship and due reverence to the gods nor practising the worship of the god of the Christians, We are giving consideration to Our most gentle clemency and Our immemorial practice of extending pardon to all people, and We have judged it right to extend Our speediest indulgence to them also, so that they may again be Christians and hold their meetings, provided always that they do nothing contrary to public order.

Further, by another letter We will inform governors of provinces what conditions Christians must observe. Under the terms of this Our indulgence it shall be their duty to pray to their god for Our well-being, and that of the State, and their own: to the end that the State may be kept unharmed on every side, and they may be able to live securely in their own habitations (Lactantius, *The Deaths of the Persecutors* 34.1–5; cf. Corcoran 1996: 186–187).

Issued in his own name and those of Constantine, Licinius and Maximinus Daia, this toleration edict was Galerius' last move. On 5 May he died.

Afterwards, Maximinus moved faster than Licinius and took control of most of the east, including Nicomedia, Diocletian's capital. With a brief pause, he pushed ahead with the persecution policy which Galerius had abandoned. On 25 November 311 Peter of Alexandria and 'many other bishops with him' were put to death at Alexandria; and Lucian of Antioch, who taught theology to some of the clergy who were to be key voices in the Council of Nicaea and the 'of one substance' dispute, was put to death at Nicomedia on 7 January 312. Eusebius, who visited upper Egypt in 311/12, describes what persecution there was like:

I myself also saw, when I was in those places, many people executed in a single day – some by beheading, some by burning – so that the murderous axe was blunted, and the executioners were worn out with fatigue and had to give one another rest-breaks. And that was when I observed a most marvellous eagerness and a truly divine power and zeal in those who had trusted in the Christ of God: for during the sentencing of earlier ones, others would leap up from one direction after another to the tribunal in front of the judge and confess themselves Christians, paying no attention to the dread consequences and the many and varied kinds of torture, but speaking freely and without fear about reverence towards the God of all things, and receiving their sentence of death with joy and laughter and gladness – so that they sang psalms and hymns and gave thanks to the God of all things until their last breath (*Ecclesiastical History* 8.9.4–5).

Roman officials had not usually allowed situations like this to develop – Antony had sat in his clean clothes in the front row and been ignored, Origen had visited his catechism students in jail and not been arrested, and back in 185 Arrius Antoninus had told would-be martyrs to find themselves ropes or cliffs. Frend (1965: 516) calls Eusebius' story 'a terrible picture ... of desperation encountering fanaticism' – and both sides would have to continue to share the province afterwards; and yet, as Frend goes on to add, 'this was a revolution on the point of success'. In the *Martyrdom of Apaioule and Pteleme*, Count Sebastianus moves south into Egypt with an army to enforce obedience – then finds that even his soldiers are not unanimously behind the decree. The Coptic story may have improved in the telling, but the brittle loyalty of provincials when faraway rulers demanded anti-Christian violence is clear. Persecution may have united communities in the days of Polycarp, but in 311 it was divisive.

Maximinus' aggressive moves after Galerius' death pushed Constantine and Licinius into alliance against him. Constantine defeated a Frankish invasion in 311, then in 312 marched south and attacked Maxentius on behalf of the official emperors. With strong support in Rome, whose walls had been rebuilt by Aurelian, Maxentius might have settled in for a siege. But he consulted the Sibylline Books, a conventional source of advice at times of national crisis, and found that the entry for 28 October said, 'on this day, the enemy of Rome shall perish'. With that in mind, as well as the danger that someone might let Constantine into the city one dark night, he advanced across the Milvian Bridge on the auspicious day and attacked his enemy's position.

Constantine's conversion

Constantine later told Eusebius about a dream which had prompted him to adopt a Christian sign for his army. His father had been a monotheist, and Constantine (at some point between his father's death and the battle of the Milvian Bridge) made the decision to pray to only one God – his father's. He prayed, Eusebius says, for revelation and aid:

> As he made these prayers and earnest supplications there appeared to the emperor a most remarkable divine sign. If someone else had reported it, it would perhaps not be easy to accept; but since the victorious emperor himself told the story to me a long while after, when I was privileged with his acquaintance and company, and confirmed it with oaths, who could hesitate to believe the account, especially when the time which followed provided evidence for the truth of what he said?
>
> About the time of the midday sun, when day was just turning, he said he saw with his own eyes, up in the sky and resting over the sun, a cross-shaped trophy formed from light, and a text attached to it which said, 'By this conquer'. Amazement at the spectacle seized both him and the whole company of soldiers which was then accompanying him on a campaign he was conducting somewhere, and witnessed the miracle.
>
> He was, he said, wondering to himself what the manifestation might mean; then, while he meditated, and thought long and hard, night overtook him. Thereupon, as he slept, the Christ of God appeared to him with the sign which had appeared in the sky, and urged him to make himself a copy of the sign which had appeared in the sky, and to use this as a protection against the attacks of his enemy. When day came, he arose and recounted the mysterious communication to his friends. Then he summoned goldsmiths and jewellers, sat down among them, and explained the shape of the sign, and gave them instructions about copying it in gold and precious stones (*Life of Constantine* 28–30).

Lactantius shortens the story and puts Constantine's dream right before the battle, and adds that he ordered his soldiers to mark the chi-rho monogram on their shields – which Eusebius does not mention. Maxentius' army was larger, but Constantine's men got the upper hand, and as Maxentius tried to retreat across the river, his bridge of boats gave way. Maxentius was drowned, his army decisively defeated, and Constantine made a ceremonial entry into Rome the next day.[7]

---

[7] Lactantius, *The Deaths of the Persecutors* 44.1–12; Eusebius, *Life of Constantine* 38 and *Ecclesiastical History* 9.9.1–11.

Christianity becomes the official religion

News of Constantine's victory was unwelcome at the eastern court. Maximinus Daia manoeuvred to manage the consequences. Already he had adopted measures to make less clear the association between his wishes and the persecution, and to gloss over the legal difficulties of acting contrary to Galerius' Toleration Edict (Corcoran 1996: 148–152). Now, at the end of 312, he directed Sabinus, his Praetorian prefect, to put an end to persecution:

> Jovius Maximinus Augustus to Sabinus.
> I am persuaded that it is manifest both to Your Gravity and to all people that our masters Diocletian and Maximian, Our fathers, when they perceived that almost all people had abandoned the worship of the gods and associated themselves with the nation of the Christians, rightly gave orders that all who deserted the worship of the immortal gods, their own gods, should be recalled to the worship of the gods by open chastisement and punishment ...
>
> Therefore, although letters have been sent to Your Devotion before this time, and likewise it has been laid down by ordinances that no harsh measures should be adopted against provincials who are determined to persevere in such a custom, but that people should treat them in a long-suffering and adaptable spirit, nevertheless, in order that they may not suffer insults or extortions at the hands of *beneficiarii* or any others whatsoever, I have judged it right to advise Your Gravity, by this letter also, that you should rather cause Our provincials to recognise their duty to the gods by persuasive words and exhortations. Therefore if any of them shall choose of his own free will to acknowledge the worship of the gods, it shall be correct to welcome such persons; but if some desire to follow their own worship, you should leave that in their own power ... (Eusebius, *Ecclesiastical History* 9.9a.1, 7–8; cf. Corcoran 1996: 188).

This measure was unsatisfactory. It was distrusted because of Maximinus' past record, and it did not specifically legalize holding of meetings, or building of churches, by Christians. 'None of our people, therefore,' Eusebius says, 'dared to convene an assembly or even show himself in public' (9.9a.11). But in the west, Licinius and Constantine met at Milan in June 313 and issued the edict which definitively made Christianity a legal and privileged religion:

> Already long ago, when We were watching that liberty of religion should not be denied, but that to each one's thought and desire authority should be given to practise divine things according to each individual preference, We ordered that both to Christians ... and to non-Christians should be conceded the freedom to maintain the faith of their own sect and religion. Since, however, many and various conditions seem to have been added to the rescript in which such authority was granted to the said persons, perhaps some of them have been deterred from the maintenance of such faith.
>
> When I, Constantine Augustus, and I, Licinius Augustus, had met happily at Milan and were conferring about all matters advantageous and related to public security, among the matters which We saw would benefit most people – or rather, first and foremost – we believed that ordinances should be issued on matters involving reverence for the Deity; that is, that We should concede, both to Christians and to all, an unrestricted possibility of following whichever religion each person wishes, so that whatever Deity exists in its celestial abode may be placated, and may be propitious to Us and to all who are placed under Our authority.
>
> Accordingly We have believed with sound and most correct reasoning that We should follow this course of action: that freedom of worship should be denied to no one at all who has given his mind either to the religion of the Christians, or to that religion which he himself thinks most suited to himself; in order that the Supreme Deity, whose worship with free conscience We follow, may vouchsafe to Us in all things his accustomed favour and benevolence.
>
> Wherefore it is proper that Your Excellency should know that it has pleased Us that all the conditions which were contained in letters previously sent to Your Devotion concerning the name of Christians have been completely abolished. Thus those things which seemed truly unfavourable and alien from Our Clemency may be removed, and now each one who shows the said purpose to observe the religion of the Christians may freely and simply

exert himself in such observation without any inquietude or molestation to himself. And We have believed that these things should be made known to Your Diligence in the fullest manner, that you may know that We have granted to the said Christians free and unconditional facility to practise their religion. When you perceive that We have made this grant to the said persons, Your Excellency will understand that similarly open and free authority has been granted to others too for their own religion or observance, in keeping with the peacefulness of Our times, so that each one may have free facility in practising what he has chosen. We have done this in order that We may not appear to have detracted anything from any rite or any religion.

Further, We have resolved that the following ordinance shall be established in relation to the persons of the Christians: if any appear at an earlier period to have purchased, whether from Our fiscus or from any source whatever, the places at which they were formerly accustomed to assemble, and about which a definite formulary was established in a letter previously sent to Your Devotion, such places shall be restored to the Christians, without money and without any demand for payment, disregarding all deception and doubtfulness. Any person who has obtained these by gift shall restore the said places to the said Christians as soon as possible; those who have bought these places from Us, or acquired them by gift, should apply to the *vicarius*, if they have any claim from Our Benevolence, in order that thought may be taken for them also, by Our Clemency. All these things are to be delivered to the corporation of the Christians through your intervention, immediately and without delay.

Since, furthermore, the said Christians are known to have had not only those places at which they have been accustomed to assemble but also other places belonging to the legal right of their corporation (that is, of the churches, not of individual persons), you shall command, under the law which We have expressed above, that all these shall be restored, absolutely without any doubt or dispute, to the said Christians, that is, to their corporations and assemblies: preserving always the aforesaid condition, namely that those who return the said places without compensation may, as we have said, hope for indemnification from Our Benevolence.

In all these things you shall be bound to exercise your most effective intervention for the above-mentioned corporation of Christians, that Our command may be fulfilled as speedily as possible, and that in this matter thought may also be taken for the public tranquillity by Our Clemency. So shall it result that, as has been expressed above, the divine favour towards Us, which in so many matters We have experienced, shall for all time steadfastly and prosperously attend Our successes together with the happiness of the State.

It shall moreover be fitting, in order that the form of this Our Benevolence's ordinance may be able to come to the knowledge of all, for you by your own edict both to publish everywhere what has been written, and to bring it to the attention of all people, in order that this Our Benevolence's ordinance cannot escape notice (Lactantius, *The Deaths of the Persecutors* 48.2–12).

Full legality and the return of churches and burial places were probably the most any Christian had hoped for. Compensation for buyers who had bought confiscated church property from the treasury helped to prevent future disputes. But Constantine also made large gifts: in Rome, he gave the Lateran Palace to the church, and it was the residence of the bishops of Rome for the next thousand years. Elsewhere, there were cash subsidies for church costs, as a letter to the bishop of Carthage shows:

Constantine Augustus to Caecilian, bishop of Carthage.
Inasmuch as it has been my pleasure that through all the provinces, namely Africa, Numidia and Mauretania, something should be provided for expenses to certain persons of the ministers of the legitimate and most holy Catholic religion, I have sent a letter to Ursus, the most illustrious Treasurer-General of Africa, and I have indicated to him that he should be careful to pay to Your Constancy 3,000 *folles*. When you procure receipt of the aforesaid sum of money, you are to direct that it should be distributed among the above-mentioned persons according to the brief sent you by Hosius. But if you should then observe that anything is lacking for the fulfilment of this my policy in regard to them all, you ought unhesitatingly to demand from Heraclides, the procurator of Our estates, whatever you should consider to be necessary; for I ordered him, when he was

present, that if Your Gravity should ask for any money from him, he should be careful to pay it without any uncertainty...

May the Divinity of the Great God guard you for many years (Eusebius, *Ecclesiastical History* 10.6).

Hosius, bishop of Cordoba, had accompanied Constantine on his march to Rome, and was his chief informant about the churches. A *follis* was a bag counted and sealed at the mint, containing 3,125 two-denarius pieces. It is hard to quantify the value of the gift, in an inflationary period. We are, however, talking about 9,375,000 low-grade silver coins – a considerable sum – and Caecilian can ask for more.

Licinius in 313 had marched against Maximinus and defeated his army. Maximinus escaped and tried to regroup, but committed suicide when his situation became hopeless (Lactantius, *The Deaths of the Persecutors* 45.2 – 49.7). A later civil war was to pit Constantine against Licinius and leave the empire under Constantine's sole rule from 324. But before then, Constantine brought in decisive changes to christianize the Roman empire. Clergy were freed from the costly obligation better-off Romans had to serve on town councils (Eusebius, *Ecclesiastical History* 10.7 [313]),[8] gladiator shows were outlawed (*Theodosian Code* 15.12.1 [325]), and Sunday was made a public holiday (*Justinian Code* 3.12.2 [321]).

Some aspects of public life were slower than others in adjusting to the Christian takeover. Coins minted for Constantine until 317 in the west and 324 in the east have SOLI INVICTO COMITI ('For the Unconquered Sun, his Companion') stamped on the reverse (cf. Carson 1990: no. 624), and in 321 Constantine confirmed that it was still correct to ask soothsayers what it meant when part of the imperial palace was struck by lightning (*Theodosian Code* 16.10.1). But his commitment to Christianity was clear. It was the religion which delivered divine support to his campaign against Maxentius, as the inscription on the Arch of Constantine, dedicated at Rome in 315, shows: 'To the Emperor Caesar Flavius Constantinus, who, by the prompting of the Deity and by the greatness of his mind, with his forces avenged the State in a just war against the tyrant and all his party.'

But there was more to his conversion than gratitude for his victory.

---

[8] By 320, measures had to be taken to stop rich men getting ordained to avoid town-council membership: *Theodosian Code* 16.2.3.

In his *Speech to the Assembly of the Saints* 22, given (probably to a gathering of bishops) between 317 and 325, he outlines his motivations:

> We strive to the best of Our ability to fill with good hope those who are uninitiated in such doctrines, summoning God as Our helper in the undertaking. For it is no ordinary task to turn the minds of Our subjects to piety, if they happen to be virtuous, and to reform them, if they are evil and unbelieving, making them useful instead of useless. So, rejoicing in these undertakings, and believing it the task of a good man to praise the Saviour, I reject everything which the inferior state of fortune irrationally imposed by the mischance of ignorance, deeming repentance the greatest salvation. I should have wished that this revelation had been vouchsafed me long ago, since blessed is the man who from his earliest days has been steadfast and has rejoiced in the knowledge of things divine and the beauty of virtue.

This describes conversion to Christianity, refers to Jesus, affirms repentance and rejects the convert's former life. It is such a clear personal statement that it ought to lay to rest the doubts sometimes still expressed about the sincerity of Constantine's Christianity.

With Constantine's conversion this book ends. Really this moment was only a punctuation mark in the longer story of the conversion of the whole Roman world to Christianity. In 313 the churches had good numbers in the cities, and Christians were well represented in the civil service – thanks partly to a usually unmolested presence there dating from the mid-first century, and partly to Diocletian's having recruited so many new staff from a sector of society to which Christianity had proven attractive from the beginning. These advantages helped to offset the fact that the Roman political class was almost entirely polytheist when Constantine was converted.

Constantine, in his reign, was to make big changes. He intervened in theological deliberation – not only by being there, but more importantly by providing publicly funded travel for clergy to and from meetings such as the Councils of Arles (314) and Nicaea (325). Large-scale face-to-face meetings of this kind had never been practical before: creeds, councils and controversies (to borrow the title of J. Stevenson's sourcebook) were, in resource terms, a by-product of the Christian empire. Constantine's other important initiative was to build Constantinople: New Rome, and a permanent eastern capital for the empire, but equally importantly a city without polytheist temples. It was a strong statement of intent. MacMullen in *Christianity and Paganism in the Fourth to Eighth Centuries* (1997) shows how polytheism lived on, and stayed popular in some places. But in the Roman world as a whole, the change Constantine's conversion brought was never effectively reversed. The Emperor Julian (361–363) tried to bring polytheism back, but did not live long enough to make much progress.

Advised by Hosius of Cordoba, Constantine decided early on to restrict gifts and legal privileges to Catholic Christians. From the time of the New Testament, Christians had been at work pruning the bush: now government joined in. Diversity expressed itself in new ways in the fourth century. There were new divisions (Catholics versus Donatists, Catholics versus Arians, and so on), while older fringe Christianities (except Manichaeism) shrank, or lived on only in books, as theories for anti-heretical writers to attack. In a sense, therefore, Constantine's commitment was made to a Christian church which was reasonably united, and was identifiably the organization which Jesus had set up. A vigorous, highly adaptive movement since its inception, the church had won the argument against illegality, and made Christianity into the official religion of the Roman empire.

Primary-source finding list

This is a partial list of primary texts, intended to help with finding items for further reference. I assume no help is needed with Bible and Apocryphal/Deuterocanonical references. Sometimes, for instance for inscriptions referred to in Eisen 2000, it will be necessary to go to the (secondary) book referred to. Enough is given in the text and notes (I hope) to make this easy.

Many books in Greek are conventionally referred to by Latin titles. I have used English titles for (nearly) all ancient books, to make it clearer what they are about. The comparison of titles below should help with reference.

I have not always listed editions or translations, but column 4 will help in some cases in which a translation is available in a standard collection. Absence of a reference in column 4 does not necessarily mean that an English translation will be hard to find. Editions of papyri (column 1 references as 'P.Whatever...') are listed at http://scriptorium.lib.duke.edu/papyrus/texts/clist.html. Loeb editions are published by Heinemann, London, and Harvard University Press, Cambridge, MA. Books referred to by author and date in column 4 are listed in the bibliography.

Author, *anonymous work* or other reference	**English title**	**Latin title**	**Easy place to find it in English**
Acts of Andrew			Schneemelcher & Wilson 1991–2
Martyrdom of Apaioule and Pteleme			Reymond & Barns 1973

Author, *anonymous work* or other reference	English title	Latin title	Easy place to find it in English
Aristides	*Apologia*		Loeb John Damascene
Arnobius	*Against the Gentiles*	*Adversus nationes*	
Athanasius	*Life of Antony*	*Vita Antonii*	
	On the Councils of Ariminum and Seleuceia	*De synodis Arimini in Italia et Seleuciae in Isauria*	
Epistle of Barnabas			Loeb *Apostolic Fathers* I
Basil of Caesarea	*Letters*	*Epistulae*	
Martyrdom of Carpus, Papylus and Agathonice			
Clement of Alexandria	*Exhortation to Study*	*Protrepticus*	
	Tutor	*Paedagogus*	
	Miscellanies	*Stromateis*	
Clement of Rome	*1 Clement* or Clement, *1 Corinthians*		Loeb *Apostolic Fathers* I
2 Clement			
CIL	*Corpus of Latin Inscriptions*	*Corpus Inscriptionum Latinarum*	
Martyrdom of Conon			
Constantine	*Speech to the Assembly of the Saints*	*Oratio ad sanctos*	

Author, *anonymous work* or other reference	English title	Latin title	Easy place to find it in English
Cyprian	*On the Lapsed*	*De lapsis*	
	Letters	*Epistulae*	Clarke 1984–9
	Unity of the *Catholic Church*	*De ecclesiae* *catholicae unitate*	
Cyril of Jerusalem	*Catechisms*		
Dialogue of the *Saviour*			J. M. Robinson 1988
Didache			Loeb *Apostolic* *Fathers* I
Dio Cassius			Loeb *Dio's Roman* *History*
Epistle to Diognetus			Loeb *Apostolic* *Fathers* II
Ecclesiastes Rabbah			
Ephraem of Edessa	*56 Hymns against* *the Heresies*	*Hymni 56 contra* *haereses*	
Epiphanius	*Medicine-Box*	*Panarion*	
Eunapius	*Lives of the* *Philosophers*	*Vitae* *philosophorum*	Loeb Philostratus
Eusebius	*Chronicle*	*Chronicon*	
	Life of *Constantine*	*Vita Constantini*	Cameron & Hall
	Ecclesiastical *History*	*Historia* *Ecclesiastica*	Loeb Eusebius
	Martyrs of Palestine		
	Word-List	*Onomasticon*	

Author, *anonymous work* or other reference	English title	Latin title	Easy place to find it in English
	Against Philostratus on Apollonius of Tyana or *Against Hierocles*	*Contra Hieroclem*	
The Fathers according to Rabbi Nathan			Neusner 1986
Gelasius	*Letters*	*Epistulae*	
Hermas	*The Shepherd*	*Pastor*	Loeb *Apostolic Fathers* II
Hippolytus	*Refutation of all Heresies*	*Refutatio* or *Philosophumena*	
Ignatius	*Ephesians*		Loeb *Apostolic Fathers* I
	Magnesians		Loeb *Apostolic Fathers* I
	Philadelphians		Loeb *Apostolic Fathers* I
	Romans		Loeb *Apostolic Fathers* I
	Smyrnaeans		Loeb *Apostolic Fathers* I
Irenaeus	*Against Heresies*	*Contra haereses*	
Apocryphon of James			J. M. Robinson *1988*
Protevangelium of James			Schneemelcher & Wilson 1991–2
Jerome	*Chronicon*		
	Letters	*Epistulae*	

Author, anonymous work or other reference	English title	Latin title	Easy place to find it in English
Acts of John			Scheemelcher & Wilson 1991–2
Apocryphon of John			J. M. Robinson 1988
Josephus	*Jewish Antiquities*	*Antiquitates Iudaicae*	Loeb Josephus *Jewish Antiquities*
	Jewish War	*Bellum Iudaicum*	Loeb Josephus *Jewish War*
Justin	*First Apologia*		
	Second Apologia		
	Dialogue with Trypho	*Dialogus*	
Martyrdom of Justin			Stevenson 1987
Justinian Code		*Codex Iustiniani*	
Lactantius	*The Deaths of the Persecutors*	*De mortibus persecutorum*	
Lucian	*The Passing of Peregrinus*		Loeb Lucian
Mani	*Cologne Mani Codex*		
Marcus Aurelius	*Meditations*		Loeb Marcus Aurelius
Martyrdom of Marinus and Jacobus			
Acts of Mark			Schneemelcher & Wilson 1991–2
Minucius Felix	*Octavius*	*Octavius*	Loeb Tertullian

Author, *anonymous work* or other reference	English title	Latin title	Easy place to find it in English
Martyrdom of Montanus and Lucius			
Optatus of Milevis	*On the Donatist Schism* or *Against Parmenian*	*Adversus Parmenianum*	
Origen	*Against Celsus*	*Contra Celsum*	
	Commentary on John	*Commentarium in evangelium Ioannis*	
	Commentary on Matthew	*Commentarium in evangelium Matthaei*	
	Principles	*De principiis*	
Origin of the World			J. M. Robinson 1988
P.Egerton 2			
P.Giessen 40			
P.Oxy. 1.654 and 655			
P.Rylands 457			
Paul and Thecla	also called *Acts of Paul* or *Acts of Paul and Thecla* or *Acts of Thecla*		Schneemelcher & Wilson 1991–2
Martyrdom of Perpetua		*Passio Perpetuae*	
Gospel of Peter			J. M. Robinson 1988
Acts of Peter			Schneemelcher & Wilson 1991–2
Gospel of Philip			J. M. Robinson 1988

Author, *anonymous work* or other reference	English title	Latin title	Easy place to find it in English
Philo	*On the Contemplative Life*	*De vita contemplativa*	Loeb Philo
	Embassy to Gaius	*Legatio ad Gaium*	Loeb Philo
	The Worse Attacks the Better	*Quod deterius*	Loeb Philo
Philostratus	*Life of Apollonius of Tyana*		Loeb Philostratus
Martyrdom of Pionius			Robert 1994 (Greek and French)
Pliny	*Letters*	*Epistulae*	Loeb Pliny
Plotinus	*Enneads*		Loeb Plotinus
Polycarp	*Philippians*		Loeb *Apostolic Fathers* I
Martyrdom of Polycarp			Loeb *Apostolic Fathers* II
Porphyry	*Against the Christians*	*Contra Christianos*	
	Philosophy from Oracles	*De philosophia ex oraculis*	
Q			Kloppenborg 1988
Martyrdom of the Scillitans		*Acta Scillitanorum*	Stevenson 1987
Scriptores Historiae Augustae		otherwise referred to as *Historia Augusta*	Loeb *Scriptores Historiae Augustae*
Suetonius	*Claudius*		Loeb Suetonius
	Domitian		Loeb Suetonius

Author, anonymous work or other reference	English title	Latin title	Easy place to find it in English
	Nero		Loeb Suetonius
Tacitus	Annals	Annales	Loeb Tacitus
	Histories	Historiae	Loeb Tacitus
Babylonian Talmud			Steinsaltz 1989
Tatian	Address to the Greeks	Exhortatio ad Graecos	
Tertullian	Apologeticum	Apologeticum	Loeb Tertullian
	On Baptism	De baptismo	
	On Fasting	De ieiunio	
	On the Flesh of Christ	De carne Christi	
	To the Gentiles	Ad nationes	
	Against Marcion	Adversus Marcionem	
	To Scapula	Ad Scapulam	
	On Sexual Morality	De pudicitia	
	Ruling out of Court of the Heretics	De praescriptione haereticorum	
	The Testimony of the Soul	De testimonio animae	
	Against the Valentinians	Adversus Valentinianos	
Theodosian Code		Codex Theodosianus	Pharr 1969
Gospel of Thomas			J. M. Robinson 1988

Author, *anonymous work* or other reference	English title	Latin title	Easy place to find it in English
Acts of Thomas			Schneemelcher & Wilson 1991–2
Tosefta			Neusner 1990
Acts of Xanthippe			Schneemelcher & Wilson 1991–2

Bibliography

This is a list of secondary works referred to in this book. Editions of most primary sources are not given. Some source-collections (such as Stevenson's *New Eusebius*) are listed. Chapters in edited books are listed under the name of the chapter author: the editors' names are given, but the edited books are not listed separately.

d'Ancona, M., see Thiede & d'Ancona (1996)

Bainbridge, W. S., see Stark & Bainbridge (1985)

Barnes, T. D. (1968), 'Legislation against the Christians', *Journal of Roman Studies* 58: 32–50

Barns, J. W. B., see Reymond & Barns (1973)

Barrett, D. P., see Comfort & Barrett (1999)

Bauckham, R. J. (1990), *Jude and the Relatives of Jesus in the Early Church*, Edinburgh: T. and T. Clark

Bauer, F. C. (1873, 1875), *Paul*, 2 vols., London: Williams and Norgate

Bauer, W. (1971), *Orthodoxy and Heresy in Earliest Christianity*, Philadelphia, PA: Fortress. Translation of *Rechtgläubigkeit und Ketzerei im ältesten Christentum*, Tübingen: Mohr, 1934

Beck, E. (ed.) (1957), *Hymnen contra Haereses*, Paris and Louvain, L. Durbecq = *Corpus Scriptorum Christianorum Orientalium* 169

Berding, K. (1999), 'Polycarp of Smyrna's view of the authorship of 1 and 2 Timothy', *Vigiliae Christianae* 53: 349–360

Berry, P. (1995), *The Christian Inscription at Pompeii*, Lewiston, Queenston and Lampeter: Edwin Mellon

Blackman, E. C. (1948), *Marcion and his Influence*, London: SPCK

de Boer, M. C. (1998), 'The Nazoreans: living at the boundary of Judaism and Christianity', in G. N. Stanton & G. G. Stroumsa (eds.), *Tolerance and Intolerance in Early Judaism and Christianity*, Cambridge: Cambridge University Press: 239–262

Bowersock, G. W. (1995), *Martyrdom and Rome*, Cambridge: Cambridge University Press

Boyce, M. (ed.) (1984), *Textual Sources for the Study of Zoroastrianism*, Manchester: Manchester University Press

van den Broek, R. (1996), *Studies in Gnosticism and Alexandrian Christianity*, Leiden: Brill

Brooten, B. (1977), 'Junia ... outstanding among the apostles', in L. Swidler & A. Swidler (eds.), *Women Priests: A Catholic Commentary on the Vatican Declaration*, New York: Paulist: 141–144

———— (1982), *Women Leaders in the Ancient Synagogue*, Chico: Scholars

Brown, P. (1988), *The Body and Society: Men, Women and Sexual Renunciation in Early Christianity*, New York: Columbia University Press

Bruns, C. G. (1909), *Fontes iuris Romani anteiustiniani*, 7th ed., Tübingen: Mohr

Buell, D. K. (1999), *Making Christians: Clement of Alexandria and the Rhetoric of Legitimacy*, Princeton, NJ: Princeton University Press

Cameron, A. (1991), *Christianity and the Rhetoric of Empire*, Berkeley and Los Angeles, CA: University of California Press

Cameron, A., & Hall, S. G. (1999), *Eusebius: Life of Constantine*, Oxford: Oxford University Press

Campbell, R. A. (1994), *The Elders: Seniority within Earliest Christianity*, Edinburgh: T. and T. Clark

Cardman, F. (1999), 'Women, ministry and church order in early Christianity', in R. S. Kraemer & M. R. d'Angelo (eds.), *Women and Christian Origins*, Oxford: Oxford University Press: 300–329

Carson, R. A. G. (1990), *Coins of the Roman Empire*, London and New York: Routledge

Chadwick, H. (1966), *Early Christian Thought and the Classical Tradition*, Oxford: Clarendon

Clarke, G. W. (ed.) (1984–9), *The Letters of St Cyprian of Carthage*, 4 vols., New York: Newman

Comfort, P. W., & Barrett, D. P. (eds.) (1999), *The Complete Text of the Earliest Christian Manuscripts*, Grand Rapids: Baker

Cooper, K. (1996), *The Virgin and the Bride: Idealized Womanhood in Late Antiquity*, Cambridge, MA: Harvard University Press

Corcoran, S. (1996), *The Empire of the Tetrarchs: Imperial Pronouncements and Government* AD *284–324*, Oxford: Oxford University Press

Crossan, J. D. (1988), *The Cross that Spoke: The Origins of the Passion Narrative*, San Francisco, CA: Harper and Row

———— (1998), *The Birth of Christianity: Discovering What Happened in the Years Immediately After the Execution of Jesus*, San Francisco, CA: HarperSanFrancisco

Crouzel, H. (1989), *Origen*, Edinburgh: T. and T. Clark. Translation of *Origène*, Paris: Lethellieux, 1985

Davies, S. L. (1980), *The Revolt of the Widows: The Social World of the Apocryphal Acts*, Carbondale, IL: Edwardsville, IL: London and Amsterdam: Southern Illinois University Press

Dechow, J. F. (1988), 'Origen and early Christian pluralism: the context of his eschatology', in C. Kannengiesser & W. L. Petersen (eds.), *Origen of Alexandria: His World and his Legacy*, Notre Dame, IN: Notre Dame University Press: 337–356

Diehl, E. (ed.) (1925–67), *Inscriptiones Latinae Christianae Veteres*, 4 vols., Berlin: Weidmann

Dodgeon, M. H., & Lieu, S. N.C. (1991), *The Roman Frontier and the Persian Wars* AD *226–363* London: Routledge

Douglas, M. (1978), *Cultural Bias*, London: Royal Anthropological Institute of Great Britain and Ireland. Occasional Paper no. 35

———— (ed.) (1982), *Essays in the Sociology of Perception*, London: Routledge and Kegan Paul

Eck, W. (1999), 'The Bar Kokhba Revolt: the Roman point of view', *Journal of Roman Studies* 89: 76–89

Eisen, U. E. (2000), *Women Officeholders in Early Christianity*, Collegeville, MN: Liturgical. Translation of *Amtsträgerinnen im frühen Christentum: epigraphische und literarische Studien*, Göttingen: Vandenhoeck und Ruprecht, 1996

Ellis, E. E. (1999), *The Making of the New Testament Documents*, Leiden: Brill

Frend, W. H. C. (1965), *Martyrdom and Persecution in the Early Church*, Oxford: Oxford University Press

———— (1967), 'The Gospel of Thomas: is rehabilitation possible?', *Journal of Theological Studies* new series 18: 13–26

———— (1974), 'Open questions concerning the Christians and the Roman Empire in the age of the Severi', *Journal of Theological Studies* new series 25: 333–351

———— (1984), *The Rise of Christianity*, London: Darton, Longman and Todd

———— (1987), 'Prelude to the Great Persecution: the propaganda war', *Journal of Ecclesiastical History* 38: 1–18

———— (1996), *The Archaeology of Early Christianity: A History*, London: Geoffrey Chapman

Friedländer, M. (1898), *Der vorchristliche jüdische Gnosticismus*, Göttingen: Vandenhoeck und Ruprecht.

Goehring, J. E., see Pearson & Goehring (eds.) (1986)

Goodman, M. (1997), *The Roman World 44 BC–AD 180*, London and New York: Routledge

Grant, R. M. (1988), *Greek Apologists of the Second Century*, Philadelphia, PA: Westminster

Haggmark, A., see Hultgren & Haggmark (1996)

Hahneman, G. M. (1992), *The Muratorian Fragment and the Development of the Canon*, Oxford: Clarendon

Hall, S. G., see Cameron & Hall (1999)

Harnack, A. von (1905), *The Expansion of Christianity in the First Three Centuries*, New York: Putman. Translation of *Die Mission und Ausbreitung des Christentums in der ersten drei Jahrhunderten*, Leipzig: J. C. Hinrichs, 1902

———— (1911), *The Date of Acts and the Synoptic Gospels*, London: Williams and Norgate. Translation of *Neue Untersuchungen zur Apostelgeschichte*, Leipzig:J. C. Hinrichs, 1911

Harris, W. V. (1994), 'Child exposure in the Roman Empire', *Journal of Roman Studies* 84: 1–22

Heine, S. (1987), *Women and Early Christianity: Are the Feminist Scholars Right?*, London: SCM. Translation of *Frauen der frühen Christenheit*, Göttingen: Vandenhoeck und Ruprecht, 1986

Hill, C. E. (2000), 'Cerinthus: Gnostic or Chiliast? A new solution to an old problem', *Journal of Early Christian Studies* 8: 135–172

Hopkins, K. (1965), 'The age of Roman girls at marriage', *Population Studies* 18: 309–327

———— (1998), 'Christian number and its implications', *Journal of Early Christian Studies* 6: 185–226

———— (1999), *A World Full of Gods: Pagans, Jews and Christians in the Roman Empire*, London: Weidenfeld and Nicolson

Horbury, W. (1998), *Jews and Christians in Contact and Controversy*, Edinburgh: T. and T. Clark

Hultgren, A. J., & Haggmark, S. A. (eds.) (1996), *The Earliest Chris-*

tian Heretics: Readings from their Opponents, Minneapolis, MN: Fortress

James, M. R. (1924), *The Apocryphal New Testament*, Oxford: Claredon

Jeffers, J. S. (1991), *Conflict at Rome: Social Order and Hierarchy in Early Christianity*, Minneapolis, MN: Fortress

Jensen, A. (1996), *God's Self-Confident Daughters: Early Christianity and the Liberation of Women*, Louisville, KY: Westminster/John Knox. Translation of *Gottes selbstbewüsste Töchter: Frauenemanzipazion im frühen Christentum?*, Freiburg: Herder,1992

Johnson, L. T. (1986), *The Writings of the New Testament: An Interpretation*, Philadelphia, PA: Fortress

Kearsley, R. A. (1992), 'The epitaph of Aberkios', *New Documents Illustrating Early Christianity* 6: 177–181

Kenny, A. (1968), *A Stylometric Study of the New Testament*, Oxford: Clarendon

Kent, J. H. (1966), *Corinth: Results 8 part 3: Inscriptions 1926–1950*, Princeton, NJ: American School of Classical Studies at Athens

Kimelman, R. (1981), '*Birkat Ha-Minim* and the lack of evidence for an anti-Christian Jewish prayer in late antiquity', in E. P. Sanders, A. I. Baumgarten & A. Mendelson (eds.), *Jewish and Christian Self-Definition* II: *Aspects of Judaism in the Graeco-Roman Period*, London: SCM: 226–244

Klawiter, F. C. (1980), 'The role of martyrdom and persecution in developing the priestly authority of women in early Christianity: a case study of Montanism', *Church History* 49: 251–261

Kloppenborg, J. S. (1988), *Q Parallels: Synopsis, Critical Notes and Concordance*, Sonoma, CA: Polebridge

Koester, H. (1990), *Ancient Christian Gospels: Their History and Development*, London: SCM; Philadelphia, PA: Trinity Press International

Kraemer, R. S. (1994), *Her Share of the Blessings: Women's Religions among Pagans, Jews and Christians in the Greco-Roman World*, New York: Oxford University Press

Kümmel, W. G. (1975), *Introduction to the New Testament*, London: Abingdon

Lampe, P. (1987), *Die stadtrömischen Christen in den ersten beiden Jahrhunderten: Untersuchung zur Sozialgeschichte*, Tübingen: Mohr. *Wissenschaftliche Untersuchungen zum Neuen Testament* 2. Reihe 18

Lane Fox, R. J. (1986), *Pagans and Christians*, Harmondsworth: Penguin.

di Lella, A. A., see Skehan & di Lella (1986)

Lieu, S. N. C. (1985), *Manichaeism in the Later Roman Empire and Medieval China: A Historical Survey*, Manchester: Manchester University Press

————, see Dodgeon & Lieu (1991)

———— (1992), *Manichaeism in the Later Roman Empire and Medieval China*, Tübingen: Mohr

Logan, A. H. B. (1996), *Gnostic Truth and Christian Heresy: A Study in the History of Gnosticism*, Edinburgh: T. and T. Clark

———— (1999), 'Magi and visionaries in Gnosticism', in J. W. Drijvers & J. W. Watt (eds.), *Portraits of Spiritual Authority: Religious Power in Early Christianity, Byzantium and the Christian Orient*, Leiden: Brill: 27–44

Löhr, W. A. (1966), *Basilides und seine Schule*, Tübingen: Mohr. *Wissenschaftliche Untersuchungen zum Neuen Testament* 83

Lüdemann, G. (1996), *Heretics: The Other Side of Early Christianity*, London: SCM. Translation of *Ketzer. Die andere Seite des frühen Christentums*, Stuttgart: Radius Verlag, 1995

Maccoby, H. (1991), *Paul and Hellenism*, London: SCM

McGuire, A. (1999), 'Women, gender and gnosis in Gnostic texts and traditions', in R. S. Kraemer & M. R. d'Angelo (eds.), *Women and Christian Origins*, New York and Oxford: Oxford University Press: 257–299.

McKechnie, P. (1996), "'Women's religion" and second-century Christianity', *Journal of Ecclesiastical History* 47: 409–431; reprinted in E. Ferguson (ed.), *Recent Studies in Early Christianity* I: *Christianity and Society*, New York and London: Garland, 1999: 31–53

———— (1999), 'Christian grave-inscriptions from the *familia Caesaris*', *Journal of Ecclesiastical History* 50: 427–441

MacMullen, R. (1997), *Christianity and Paganism in the Fourth to Eighth Centuries*, New Haven, CT: Yale University Press

Marcovich, M. (ed.) (1986), *Hippolytus: Refutatio omnium haeresium*, Berlin: De Gruyter

Meeks, W. A. (1983), *The First Urban Christians: The Social World of the Apostle Paul*, New Haven, CT: Yale University Press

———— (1993), *The Origins of Christian Morality* (New Haven, Yale University Press, 1993)

Meggitt, J. J. (1998), *Paul, Poverty and Survival*, Edinburgh: T. and T. Clark

Meyer, M. (1992), *The Gospel of Thomas: The Hidden Sayings of Jesus*, San Francisco, CA: HarperSanFrancisco

Millar, F. (1977), *The Emperor in the Roman World*, London: Duckworth

Miller, P. C. (1994), *Dreams in Late Antiquity: Studies in the Imagination of a Culture*, Princeton, NJ: Princeton University Press

Neander, A. (1878), *Lectures on the History of Christian Dogmas*, London: George Bell. Translated by J. E. Ryland from J. L. Jacobi's 1856 ed.

Neill, S., & Wright, N. T. (1988), *The Interpretation of the New Testament 1861–1986*, Oxford: Oxford University Press

Neller, K. V. (1989–90), 'Diversity in the *Gospel of Thomas*: clues for a new direction?', *The Second Century* 7: 1–18

Neusner, J. (ed.) (1986), *The Fathers according to Rabbi Nathan: An Analytical Translation and Explanation*, Atlanta, GA: Scholars

——— (ed.) (1992), *The Tosefta*, Atlanta, GA: Scholars

Osborn, E. (1997), *Tertullian, First Theologian of the West*, Cambridge: Cambridge University Press

Pagels, E. (1982), *The Gnostic Gospels*, 2nd ed., Harmondsworth: Penguin

Patterson, S. J. (1993a), *The Gospel of Thomas and Jesus*, Sonoma, CA: Polebridge

——— (1993b), 'Wisdom in Q and Thomas', in L. G. Perdue, B. B. Scott & W. J. Wiseman (eds.), *In Search of Wisdom: Essays in Memory of John G. Gammie*, Louisville, KY: 187–221

Pearson, B. A. (1990), *Gnosticism, Judaism and Egyptian Christianity*, Minneapolis, MN: Fortress

Pearson, B. A., & Goehring, J. E. (eds.) (1986), *The Roots of Egyptian Christianity*, Philadelphia, PA: Fortress

Pharr, C. (1969), *The Theodosian Code and Novels*, New York: Greenwood

Pomeroy, S. B. (1983), 'Infanticide in Hellenistic Greece', in A. Cameron & A. Kuhrt (eds.), *Images of Women in Antiquity*, London: Croom Helm: 207–219

Potter, D. S. (1990), *Prophecy and History in the Crisis of the Roman Empire: A Historical Commentary on the Thirteenth Sibylline Oracle*, Oxford: Oxford University Press

Price. S. (1999), 'Latin Christian apologetics: Minucius Felix, Tertullian and Cyprian', in M. Edwards, M. Goodman & S. Price (eds.),

Apologetics in the Roman Empire, Oxford: Oxford University Press: 105–129

Quesnell, Q. (1975), 'The Mar Saba Clementine: a question of evidence', *Catholic Biblical Quarterly* 37: 48–67

Reymond, E. A. E., & Barns, J. W. B. (1973), *Four Martyrdoms from the Pierpont Morgan Codices*, Oxford: Clarendon

Rives, J. B. (1999), 'The decree of Decius and the religion of empire', *Journal of Roman Studies* 89: 135–154

Robeck, C. M., Jr (1992), *Prophecy in Carthage: Perpetua, Tertullian and Cyprian*, Cleveland, OH: Pilgrim

Robert, L. (1994), *Le Martyre de Pionios prêtre de Smyrne*, Washington DC: Dumbarton Oaks Research Library and Collection

Roberts, C. H. (1979), *Manuscript, Society and Belief in Early Christian Egypt*, London: British Academy and Oxford University Press

Robinson, J. A. T. (1976), *Redating the New Testament*, Philadelphia, PA: Westminster

Robinson, J. M. (1988), *The Nag Hammadi Library in English*, San Francisco, CA: Harper and Row

Roukema, R. (1999), *Gnosis and Faith in Early Christianity*, Harrisburg, PA: Trinity Press International. Translation of *Gnosis en geloof in het vroege christendom. Een inleiding tot de gnostiek*, Zoetermeer: Uitgeverij Meinema, 1998

Runia, D. T. (1993), *Philo in Early Christian Literature: A Survey*, Assen: Van Gorcum; Minneapolis, MN: Fortress

Safrai, S. (1987), *The Literature of the Sages* I: *Oral Tora, Halakha, Mishna, Tosefta, Talmud, External Tractates*, Assen and Maastricht: Van Gorcum; Philadelphia, PA: Fortress

Sanders, J. T. (1993), *Schismatics, Sectarians, Dissidents, Deviants: The First One Hundred Years of Jewish–Christian Relations*, London: SCM

Sawicki, M. (2000), *Crossing Galilee: Architectures of Contact in the Occupied Land of Jesus*, Harrisburg, PA: Trinity Press International

Schechter S. (1898), 'Genizah specimens', *Jewish Quarterly Review* 10: 654–659

Schneemelcher, W., & Wilson, R. McL. (1991–2), *New Testament Apocrypha*, 2 vols.: Louisville, KY: Westminster/John Knox

Schottroff, L. (1995), *Lydia's Impatient Sisters: A Feminist Social History of Early Christianity*, Louisville, KY: Westminster/John Knox. Translation of *Lydias ungeduldige Schwestern*, Gutersloh: Chr. Kaiser, 1994

Schürer, E. (1979), *The History of the Jewish People in the Age of Jesus*

Christ, 2 vols., 2nd ed., ed. G. Vermes, F. Millar & M. Black, Edinburgh: T. and T. Clark

Schüssler Fiorenza, E. (1976), 'Women apostles: the testament of Scripture', in A. M. Gardiner (ed.), *Women and Catholic Priesthood: An Expanded Vision*, New York: Paulist. Proceedings of the Detroit Ordination Conference

————— (1983), *In Memory of Her: A Feminist Theological Reconstruction of Christian Origins*, London: SCM

Scott, A. (1995), 'Churches or books? Sethian social organization', *Journal of Early Christian Studies* 3: 109–122

Shaw, B. D. (1987), 'The age of Roman girls at marriage: some reconsiderations', *Journal of Roman Studies* 77: 30–46

Sherwin-White, A. N. (1966), *The Letters of Pliny: A Historical and Social Commentary*, Oxford: Clarendon

Simmons, M. B. (1995), *Arnobius of Sicca*, Oxford: Clarendon

Skehan, P. W., & di Lella, A. A. (1986), *The Wisdom of Ben Sira: A New Translation with Notes*, New York: Doubleday. Anchor Bible 39

Smallwood, E. M. (1962), 'Atticus, Legate of Judaea under Trajan', *Journal of Roman Studies* 52: 131–133

Snodgrass, K. M. (1989–90), 'The *Gospel of Thomas*: a secondary Gospel', *The Second Century* 7: 39–56

Sordi, M. (1986), *The Christians and the Roman Empire*, London and Sydney: Croom Helm

Staniforth, M. (1987), *Ancient Christian Writings*, Harmondsworth: Penguin

Stark, R. (1966), *The Rise of Christianity: A Sociologist Reconsiders History*, Princeton, NJ: Princeton University Press

————— (1998) '*E contrario*', *Journal of Early Christian Studies* 6: 259–267

Stark, R., & Bainbridge, W. S. (1985), *The Future of Religion: Secularization, Revival and Cult Formation*, Berkeley and Los Angeles, CA: University of California Press

Stegemann, E. W., & Stegemann, W. (1999), *The Jesus Movement: A Social History of its First Century*, Minneapolis, MN: Fortress. Translation of *Urchristliche Sozialgeschichte: die Anfänge im Judentum und die Christusgemeinden in der mediterranen Welt*, Stuttgart: Kohlhammer, 1995

Steinsaltz, A. (ed.) (1989), *The Talmud: The Steinsaltz Edition*, New York: Random House

Stevenson, J. (ed.) (1987), *A New Eusebius: Documents Illustrating the*

History of the Church to AD *337* (new ed., revised by W. H. C. Frend), London: SPCK

———— (ed.) (1988), *Creeds, Councils and Controversies: Documents Illustrating the History of the Church* AD *337–461* (new ed., revised by W. H. C. Frend), London: SPCK

Swain, S. (1999), 'Defending Hellenism: Philostratus, *In Honour of Apollonius*', in M. Edwards, M. Goodman & S. Price (eds.), *Apologetics in the Roman Empire*, Oxford: Oxford University Press: 157–196

Syme, R. (1968), *Ammianus and the Historia Augusta*, Oxford: Clarendon

Testini, P. (1958), *Archeologia cristiana: nozione generali dalle origini alla fine del sec. VI*, Rome: Desclee

Theissen, G. (1982), *The Social Setting of Pauline Christianity*, Edinburgh: T. and T. Clark

———— (1999), *The Religion of the Earliest Churches: Creating a Symbolic World*, Minneapolis, MN: Fortress. Translation of *Eine Theorie der urchristlichen Religion*, Gutersloh: Chr. Kaiser, 1999

Thiede, C. P., & d'Ancona, M. (1996), *The Jesus Papyrus*, London: Weidenfeld and Nicolson

Tobin, J. (1997), *Herodes Attikos and the City of Athens: Patronage and Conflict under the Antonines*, Amsterdam: Gieben

Trevett, C. (1989), 'Apocalypse, Ignatius, Montanism: seeking the seeds', *Vigiliae Christianae* 67: 313–338

———— (1996), *Montanism: Gender, Authority and the New Prophecy*, Cambridge: Cambridge University Press

Valantasis, R. (1999), 'Is the *Gospel of Thomas* ascetical? Revisiting an old problem with a new theory', *Journal of Early Christian Studies* 7: 55–81

Vermes, G. (1995), *The Dead Sea Scrolls in English*, 4th ed., London: Penguin

Ward, B. (1975), *The Sayings of the Desert Fathers*, London: Mowbrays

Weaver, P. R. C. (1972), *Familia Caesaris: A Social Study of the Emperor's Freedmen and Slaves*, Cambridge: Cambridge University Press

Welburn, A. (1998), *Mani, the Angel and the Column of Glory: An Anthology of Manichaean Texts*, Edinburgh: Floris

Wiles, M. (1967), *The Making of Christian Doctrine: A Study in the Principles of Early Doctrinal Development*, Cambridge: Cambridge University Press

Wilken, R. L. (1971), *The Myth of Christian Beginnings*, New York: Doubleday

Williams, M. A. (1985), *The Immovable Race: A Gnostic Designation and the Theme of Stability in Late Antiquity*, Leiden: Brill

———— (1996), *Rethinking 'Gnosticism'*, Princeton, NJ: Princeton University Press

Williams, R. (ed.) (1989), *The Making of Orthodoxy*, Cambridge: Cambridge University Press

Wilson, R. McL., see Schneemelcher & Wilson (1991–2)

Wong, D. W. F. (1977), 'Natural and divine order in *I Clement*', *Vigiliae Christianae* 31: 81–87

Wright, N. T. (1988), *The Epistles of Paul to the Colossians and to Philemon: An Introduction and Commentary*, Leicester: IVP

————, see Neill & Wright (1988)

———— (1992, 1996), *Christian Origins and the Question of God*. I: *The New Testament and the People of God*; II: *Jesus and the Victory of God*, London: SPCK

Young, F. (1999), 'Greek apologists of the second century', in M. Edwards, M. Goodman & S. Price (eds.), *Apologetics in the Roman Empire*, Oxford: Oxford University Press: 81–104

Index